SOME ANSWERED QUESTIONS

Dining room in the House of ʻAbduʼlláh Páshá, the residence of ʻAbduʼl-Bahá in ʻAkká from 1896 to 1910 during the time when the talks in Some Answered Questions *were given. © Baháʼí World Centre.*

SOME ANSWERED QUESTIONS

'Abdu'l-Bahá

———————

Collected and translated from the Persian
by Laura Clifford Barney

Newly Revised by a Committee
at the Bahá'í World Centre

———————

BAHÁ'Í WORLD CENTRE

HAIFA

CONTENTS

PART 2

Some Christian Subjects

PART 3

On the Powers and Conditions of the Manifestations of God

PART 4

On the Origin, Powers, and Conditions of Man

Contents

PART 5

Miscellaneous Subjects

FOREWORD

THE SPREAD OF the Faith of Bahá'u'lláh to the West, in the closing decade of the nineteenth century, soon gave rise to a reciprocal eastward movement: Within a few short years the first groups of Western pilgrims arrived in the prison city of 'Akká, where the earthly life and ministry of the Author of the Faith had come to a close and where 'Abdu'l-Bahá, the Centre of His Covenant, continued to reside. One of the most outstanding figures among those early pilgrims was Laura Clifford Barney, the daughter of a socially prominent family of scholars and artists from Washington, D.C. She was introduced to the new Faith by May Bolles Maxwell in Paris around 1900 and soon thereafter made the first of what would be many successive visits to 'Akká.

These were the most perilous and dramatic years of 'Abdu'l-Bahá's ministry, when He was confined within the walls of the prison city by the Ottoman authorities, subjected to continual surveillance, and confronted with the constant threat of further exile or of execution. Under such circumstances of stricture and suspicion, it was dangerous to receive visitors of any kind, let alone host prominent Western guests. Yet 'Abdu'l-Bahá was determined to nurture the seeds of faith so recently germinated. Thus, in the heart of this dark period, during the years 1904–1906, Miss Barney was able to make several extended visits, sometimes for weeks or months at a time, during which she was privileged to join Him on numerous occasions and to pose questions on a wide range of subjects. Many of the conversations took place at the lunch table. Arrangements were made for one of 'Abdu'l-Bahá's sons-in-law, or for one of His three secretaries of that time, to take down in Persian the text of His replies. From the resulting collection of notes a selection was made; 'Abdu'l-Bahá then corrected these notes twice in His own hand, sometimes substantially revising them in the process as well as carefully reviewing the final wording.

At the completion of the selection and revision process, three different first editions of *Some Answered Questions* were released by major publishing houses in 1908: the original Persian text by E. J. Brill in Holland; Miss Barney's English translation by Kegan Paul, Trench, Trübner & Co. in London; and a French translation by Hippolyte Dreyfus (whom Miss Barney later married) by Ernest Leroux in Paris.

A brief perusal of the Table of Contents conveys a glimpse of the breadth of the subject matter covered. Part 1 includes a set of introductory talks on the influence exerted throughout human history by the Founders of some of the world religions, as well as several chapters elucidating certain prophecies of the Bible. Part 2 offers fresh interpretations of essential elements of Christian doctrine, such as baptism, the Trinity, the Eucharist, and the resurrection of Christ. Part 3 concerns the powers and conditions of the Manifestations of God—Their unique station in the world, the source of Their knowledge and influence, and the cyclical nature of Their appearance on the stage of history. Part 4 addresses the origins, powers, and conditions of man, including the implications of human evolution on earth, the immortality of the soul, the nature of the mind, and the connection between the soul and the body. Part 5 concludes with miscellaneous topics, from practical subjects such as labour relations and the punishment of criminals to more abstruse topics such as reincarnation and the Sufi notion of the unity of existence.

Broad and wide-ranging as the topics treated in *Some Answered Questions* may be, the book was not intended to be an exhaustive exposition of a self-contained system of thought, as attested by the volume's title. A number of fundamental teachings of the Faith are, therefore, not explicitly mentioned. Moreover, in the course of the months and years that the talks were given, the same topic would sometimes be addressed from different perspectives in separate conversations, with the result that the concepts required to fully understand a given subject may be spread across different chapters, or the contents of a subsequent chapter may form the basis for the understanding of an earlier one. Finally, it should also be noted that, although 'Abdu'l-Bahá reviewed and corrected the text, He did not attempt in the process to alter the basic form of the replies or to reorganize and consolidate the material. To develop a fuller picture of 'Abdu'l-Bahá's exposition of a given subject, then, the attentive reader should consider any chapter within the context of the entire book, and the book within the larger context of the entire body of the Bahá'í Teachings.

A notable case in point is the treatment of the subject of the evolution of species, which is taken up explicitly in Part 4, and which must be understood in light of several Bahá'í teachings, especially the principle of the harmony of science and religion. Religious belief should not contradict science and reason. A certain reading of some of the passages found in Chapters 46–51 may lead some believers to personal conclusions that contradict modern science. Yet the Universal House of Justice has explained that Bahá'ís strive to reconcile their understanding of the statements of 'Abdu'l-Bahá with established scientific perspectives, and therefore it is not necessary to conclude that these passages describe conceptions rejected by science, for example, a kind of "parallel" evolution that proposes a separate line of biological evolution for the human species parallel to the animal kingdom since the beginning of life on earth.

A careful review of 'Abdu'l-Bahá's statements in this volume and in other sources suggests that His concern is not with the mechanisms of evolution but with the philosophical, social, and spiritual implications of the new theory. His use of the term "species", for example, evokes the concept of eternal or permanent archetypes, which is not how the term is defined in contemporary biology. He takes into account a reality beyond the material realm. While 'Abdu'l-Bahá acknowledges elsewhere the physical attributes that human beings share in common with the animal and that are derived from the animal kingdom,[1] in these talks He emphasizes another capacity, a capacity for rational consciousness, that distinguishes man from the animal and that is not found in the animal kingdom or in nature itself. This unique capacity, an expression of the human spirit, is not a product of the evolutionary process, but exists potentially in creation. As 'Abdu'l-Bahá explains, ". . . since man was produced ten or a hundred thousand years ago from the same earthly elements, with the same measures and quantities, the same manner of composition and combination, and the same interactions with other beings—it follows that man was exactly the same then as exists now". "And if a thousand million years hence," He goes on to say, "the component elements of man are brought together, measured out in the same proportion, combined in the same manner, and subjected to the same interaction with other beings, exactly the same man will come into existence."[2] His essential argument, then, is not directed towards scientific findings but towards the materialist assertions that are built upon them. For Bahá'ís, the science of evolution is accepted, but the conclusion that humanity is merely an accidental branch of the animal kingdom—with all its attendant social implications—is not.

Over the years since the original publication of *Some Answered Questions*, it has become increasingly clear that the translation would benefit from a careful and thorough revision. Miss Barney, as she herself stated, was a student of the Persian language and, however able, could not have entirely mastered its intricacies; and she could not of course have taken advantage of the brilliant illumination that was later to be cast upon the Sacred Texts of the Faith by the authoritative translations of Shoghi Effendi. Moreover, only a few necessary corrections had been made to the English translation during the course of its many reprintings, leaving it largely unchanged from the text of the first edition.

The centenary of 'Abdu'l-Bahá's journeys to the West, then, presents a fitting occasion both to honour Laura Clifford Barney's imperishable contribution as the primary catalyst and first translator of this volume, and to present an improved translation of these "priceless explanations".[3] The main objective of this retranslation has been to better represent the substance and the style of the original, in particular by capturing more clearly the subtleties of 'Abdu'l-Bahá's explanations, approximating more closely a style that is at once conversational and elevated, and by rendering more consistently the philosophical terms used throughout the text. While not bound by the original translation, this version nevertheless strives to retain many of its elegant expressions and felicitous turns of phrase.

Since its release, *Some Answered Questions* has been an authoritative repository of 'Abdu'l-Bahá's profound insight and an indispensable component of every Bahá'í library. Shoghi Effendi observed that the book expounds the basic beliefs of the Cause in a simple and clear language and regarded its content as essential for grasping the significance and implications of the Bahá'í Revelation. In *Some Answered Questions*, he wrote, one "will find the clue to all the perplexing questions that agitate the mind of man in his search after true knowledge. The more this Book is read with care and patience, the greater are its revelations, and the more complete the understanding of its inner truth and significance."[4] It is hoped that the new translation will assist future generations to access this inexhaustible mine "of knowledge regarding basic spiritual, ethical, and social problems".[5]

AUTHOR'S PREFACE TO THE FIRST EDITION

"I HAVE GIVEN TO you my tired moments," were the words of 'Abdu'l-Bahá as He rose from table after answering one of my questions.

As it was on this day, so it continued; between the hours of work, His fatigue would find relief in renewed activity; occasionally He was able to speak at length; but often, even though the subject might require more time, He would be called away after a few moments; again, days and even weeks would pass, in which He had no opportunity of instructing me. But I could well be patient, for I had always before me the greater lesson—the lesson of His personal life.

During my several visits to 'Akká, these answers were written down in Persian while 'Abdu'l-Bahá spoke, not with a view to publication, but simply that I might have them for future study. At first they had to be adapted to the verbal translation of the interpreter; and later, when I had acquired a slight knowledge of Persian, to my limited vocabulary. This accounts for repetition of figures and phrases, for no one has a more extensive command of felicitous expressions than 'Abdu'l-Bahá. In these lessons He is the teacher adapting Himself to His pupil, and not the orator or poet.

This book presents only certain aspects of the Bahá'í Faith, which is universal in its message and has for each questioner the answer suited to his special development and needs.

In my case the teachings were made simple, to correspond to my rudimentary knowledge, and are therefore in no way complete and exhaustive, as the Table of Contents may suggest—the Table of Contents having been added merely to indicate the subjects treated of. But I believe that what has been so valuable to me may be of use to others, since all men, notwithstanding their differences, are united in their search for reality; and I have therefore asked 'Abdu'l-Bahá's permission to publish these talks.

Originally they were not given in any special order, but have now been roughly classified for the convenience of the reader. The Persian text has been closely followed, at times even to the detriment of the English, a few alterations being made in the translation merely where the literal rendering seemed too involved and obscure; and the interpolated words, required to make the meaning clearer, have not been indicated in any way in order to avoid the too frequent interruption of the thought by technical or explanatory signs. Also many of the Persian and Arabic names have been written in their simplest form without strictly adhering to a scientific system which would be confusing to the average reader.

LAURA CLIFFORD BARNEY

PART I

*On the Influence of the
Prophets in the Evolution
of Humanity*

I

NATURE IS GOVERNED BY
A UNIVERSAL LAW

N ATURE IS THAT condition or reality which outwardly 1
is the source of the life and death, or, in other words,
of the composition and decomposition, of all things.

This nature is subject to a sound organization, to invio- 2
lable laws, to a perfect order, and to a consummate design,
from which it never departs. To such an extent is this true
that were you to gaze with the eye of insight and discern-
ment, you would observe that all things—from the smallest
invisible atom to the largest globes in the world of existence, such as the sun or the other great stars and luminous
bodies—are most perfectly organized, be it with regard to
their order, their composition, their outward form, or their
motion, and that all are subject to one universal law from
which they never depart.

When you consider nature itself, however, you see that 3
it has neither awareness nor will. For instance, the nature of
fire is to burn; it burns without consciousness or will. The
nature of water is to flow; it flows without consciousness or
will. The nature of the sun is to shed light; it shines without
consciousness or will. The nature of vapour is to rise; it rises
without consciousness or will. It is therefore evident that

the natural movements of all created things are compelled, and that nothing moves of its own will save animals and, in particular, man.

4   Man is able to resist and oppose nature inasmuch as he discovers the natures of things and, by virtue of this discovery, has mastery over nature itself. Indeed, all the crafts that man has devised proceed from this discovery. For example, he has invented the telegraph, which connects the East and the West. It is therefore evident that man rules over nature.

5   Now, can such organization, order, and laws as you observe in existence be attributed merely to the effect of nature, notwithstanding that nature itself has neither consciousness nor understanding? It is therefore evident that this nature, which has neither consciousness nor understanding, is in the grasp of the omnipotent Lord, Who is the Ruler of the world of nature and Who causes it to manifest whatsoever He desires.

6   Some say that human existence is among those things that have appeared in the world of being and that are due to the exigencies of nature. Were this true, man would be the branch and nature the root. But is it possible that there could exist a will, a consciousness, and certain perfections in the branch which are absent in the root?

7   Hence it is clear that nature, in its very essence, is in the grasp of God's might, and that it is that Eternal and Almighty One Who subjects nature to ideal laws and organizing principles, and Who rules over it.

2

PROOFS AND ARGUMENTS FOR
THE EXISTENCE OF GOD

AMONG THE PROOFS and arguments for the existence 1
of God is the fact that man has not created himself,
but rather that his creator and fashioner is another than he.
And it is certain and indisputable that the creator of man
is not like man himself, because a powerless being cannot
create another being, and an active creator must possess all
perfections to produce his handiwork.

Is it possible for the handiwork to be perfect and the 2
craftsman imperfect? Is it possible for a painting to be a
masterpiece and the painter to be deficient in his craft, notwithstanding that he is its creator? No: The painting cannot be like the painter, for otherwise it would have painted
itself. And no matter how perfect the painting may be, in
comparison with the painter it is utterly deficient.

Thus the contingent world is the source of deficiencies 3
and God is the source of perfection. The very deficiencies
of the contingent world testify to God's perfections. For
example, when you consider man, you observe that he is
weak, and this very weakness of the creature betokens the
power of One Who is Eternal and Almighty; for were it
not for power, weakness could not be imagined. Thus the

weakness of the creature is evidence of the power of God: Without power there could be no weakness. This weakness makes it evident that there is a power in the world.

4   Again, in the contingent world there is poverty; hence there must be wealth for there to be poverty in the world. In the contingent world there is ignorance; hence there must be knowledge for there to be ignorance. If there were no knowledge, neither could there be ignorance; for ignorance is the non-existence of knowledge, and if there were no existence, non-existence could not be.

5   It is certain that the entire contingent world is subject to an order and a law which it can never disobey. Even man is forced to submit to death, sleep, and other conditions—that is, in certain matters he is compelled, and this very compulsion implies the existence of One Who is All-Compelling. So long as the contingent world is characterized by dependency, and so long as this dependency is one of its essential requirements, there must be One Who in His own Essence is independent of all things. In the same way, the very existence of a sick person shows that there must be one who is healthy; for without the latter the existence of the former could not be established.

6   It is therefore evident that there is an Eternal and Almighty One Who is the sum of all perfections, for otherwise He would be even as the creatures. Likewise, throughout the world of existence the smallest created thing attests to the existence of a creator. For instance, this piece of bread attests that it has a maker.

Gracious God! The change in the outward form of the   7
smallest thing proves the existence of a creator: Then how
could this vast, boundless universe have created itself and
come to exist solely through the mutual interaction of the
elements? How patently false is such a notion!

These are theoretical arguments adduced for weak souls,   8
but if the eye of inner vision be opened, a hundred thousand
clear proofs will be seen. Thus, when man feels the indwell-
ing spirit, he is in no need of arguments for its existence;
but for those who are deprived of the grace of the spirit, it
is necessary to set forth external arguments.

3

THE NEED FOR AN EDUCATOR

1 WHEN WE CONSIDER existence, we observe that the mineral, the vegetable, the animal, and the human realms, each and all, are in need of an educator.

2 If the land is deprived of a cultivator, it becomes a thicket of thriving weeds, but if a farmer is found to cultivate it, the resulting harvest provides sustenance for living things. It is therefore evident that the land is in need of the farmer's cultivation. Consider the trees: If they remain uncultivated, they bear no fruit, and without fruit they are of no use. But when committed to a gardener's care, the barren tree becomes fruitful, and, through cultivation, crossing, and grafting, the tree with bitter fruit yields sweet fruit. These are rational arguments, which are what the people of the world require in this day.

3 Consider likewise the animals: If an animal is trained, it becomes domesticated, whereas man, if he is left without education, becomes like an animal. Indeed, if man is abandoned to the rule of nature, he sinks even lower than the animal, whereas if he is educated he becomes even as an angel. For most animals do not devour their own kind, but men in the Sudan, in the middle of Africa, rend and eat each other.

Now observe that it is education that brings East and ⁴ West under man's dominion, produces all these marvellous crafts, promotes these mighty arts and sciences, and gives rise to these new discoveries and undertakings. Were it not for an educator, the means of comfort, civilization, and human virtues could in no wise have been acquired. If a man is left alone in a wilderness where he sees none of his own kind, he will undoubtedly become a mere animal. It is therefore clear that an educator is needed.

But education is of three kinds: material, human, and ⁵ spiritual. Material education aims at the growth and development of the body, and consists in securing its sustenance and obtaining the means of its ease and comfort. This education is common to both man and animal.

Human education, however, consists in civilization and ⁶ progress, that is, sound governance, social order, human welfare, commerce and industry, arts and sciences, momentous discoveries, and great undertakings, which are the central features distinguishing man from the animal.

As to divine education, it is the education of the King- ⁷ dom and consists in acquiring divine perfections. This is indeed true education, for by its virtue man becomes the focal centre of divine blessings and the embodiment of the verse "Let Us make man in Our image, after Our likeness."¹ This is the ultimate goal of the world of humanity.

Now, we need an educator who can be at the same ⁸ time a material, a human, and a spiritual educator, that his authority may have effect at every degree of existence. And should anyone say, "I am endowed with perfect reason and comprehension, and have no need for such an educator", he would be denying the obvious. It is as though a child were to say, "I have no need of education, but will act and seek the perfections of existence according to my own thinking and intelligence", or as though a blind man were to claim, "I have no need of sight, for there are many blind people who get by."

9   It is therefore clear and evident that man stands in need of an educator. This educator must undeniably be perfect in every way and distinguished above all men. For if he were like others he could never be their educator, particularly since he must at once be their material, human, and spiritual educator. That is, he must organize and administer their material affairs and establish a social order, that they may aid and assist each other in securing the means of livelihood and that their material affairs may be ordered and arranged in every respect.

10   He must likewise lay the foundations of human education—that is, he must so educate human minds and thoughts that they may become capable of substantive progress; that science and knowledge may expand; that the realities of things, the mysteries of the universe, and the properties of all that exists may be revealed; that learning, discoveries, and major undertakings may day by day increase; and that matters of the intellect may be deduced from and conveyed through the sensible.

11   He must also impart spiritual education, so that minds may apprehend the metaphysical world, breathe the sanctified breaths of the Holy Spirit, and enter into relationship

with the Concourse on high, and that human realities may become the manifestations of divine blessings, that perchance all the names and attributes of God may be reflected in the mirror of the human reality and the meaning of the blessed verse "Let us make man in our image, after our likeness" may be realized.

It is clear, however, that mere human power is incapable of fulfilling this great office, and that the results of human thought alone cannot secure such bounties. How can a single person, with no aid or assistance, lay the foundations of such a lofty edifice? A divine and spiritual power is therefore needed to enable him to carry out this mission. Behold! One sanctified Soul revives the world of humanity, transforms the face of the globe, develops the minds, quickens the souls, inaugurates a new life, establishes new foundations, orders the world, gathers the nations and religions under the shadow of one banner, delivers man from the realm of baseness and deficiency, and exhorts and encourages him to develop his innate and acquired perfections. Certainly nothing short of a divine power could accomplish this feat! One must examine this matter fairly, as this indeed is an occasion for fairness.

A Cause which all the governments and peoples of the earth, notwithstanding all their powers and their armies, are unable to promote and promulgate, one holy Soul promulgates without aid or assistance! Can this be accomplished through the agency of mere human power? No, by God! For example, Christ, alone and single-handed, raised the banner of peace and amity—a feat that the combined forces of all

12

13

the mighty governments of the world are unable to accomplish. Consider how numerous are the divers governments and peoples—such as Italy, France, Germany, Russia, England, and the like—who have been gathered together under the same canopy! The point is that the advent of Christ brought about fellowship among these differing peoples. Indeed, some among the peoples who believed in Christ were so closely united as to offer up their life and substance for one another. Such was the case until the days of Constantine, through whom the Cause of Christ was exalted. After a time, however, and as a result of differing motives, divisions broke out again among them. Our meaning is that Christ united these nations, but after a long while the governments caused the resurgence of discord.

14   The main point is that Christ accomplished what all the kings of the earth were powerless to achieve. He united differing nations and changed ancient customs. Consider what great differences existed between Romans, Greeks, Syrians, Egyptians, Phoenicians, and Israelites, as well as other peoples of Europe. Christ abolished these differences and became the cause of concord among these peoples. Although after a long while the governments disrupted this unity, Christ had indeed accomplished His task.

15   Our meaning is that the universal Educator must be at once a material, a human, and a spiritual educator, and, soaring above the world of nature, must be possessed of another power, so that He may assume the station of a divine teacher. Were He not to wield such a celestial power, He would not be able to educate, for He would be imperfect Himself.

How then could He foster perfection? If He were ignorant, how could He make others wise? If He were unjust, how could He make others just? If He were earthly, how could He make others heavenly?

Now, we must consider fairly whether these divine 16 Manifestations that have appeared had all these attributes or not. If they were devoid of these attributes and perfections, then they were not true educators.

Therefore it is through rational arguments that we must 17 prove to rational minds the prophethood of Moses, of Christ, and of the other divine Manifestations. And the proofs and arguments which we provide here are based on rational and not on traditional arguments.

It has thus been established by rational arguments that 18 the world of existence stands in utmost need of an educator, and that its education must be achieved through a celestial power. There is no doubt that this celestial power is divine revelation, and that the world must be educated through this power which transcends human power.

4
ABRAHAM

1   A MONG THOSE WHO possessed this divine power
and were assisted by it was Abraham. The proof is this:
Abraham was born in Mesopotamia of a family that was
ignorant of the oneness of God; He opposed His own people and government, and even His own kin; He rejected all
their gods; and, alone and single-handed, He withstood a
powerful nation. Such opposition and resistance were not
simple or trivial. It is as though one were in this day to deny
Christ among Christian nations who firmly cling to the
Bible, or as though one were—God forbid!—to blaspheme
Christ in the papal court, oppose all His followers, and to
act thus in the most vehement manner.

2   These people believed not in one God but in many
gods, to whom they ascribed miracles, and hence they all
rose up against Abraham. No one supported Him except
His nephew Lot and one or two other individuals of no
consequence. At last the intensity of His enemies' opposition obliged Him, utterly wronged, to forsake His native
land. In reality He was banished that He might be reduced
to naught and that no trace of Him might remain. Abraham
then came to these regions, that is, to the Holy Land.

3   My point is that His enemies imagined that this exile

would lead to His destruction and ruin. And indeed, if a man is banished from his native land, deprived of his rights, and oppressed from every side, he is bound—even if he be a king—to be reduced to naught. But Abraham stood fast and showed forth extraordinary constancy, and God changed His exile into abiding honour, till at last He established the oneness of God, for at that time the generality of mankind were idol worshippers.

This exile became the cause of the progress of Abra- 4 ham's descendants. This exile resulted in their being given the Holy Land. This exile resulted in the diffusion of Abraham's teachings. This exile resulted in the appearance of a Jacob from the seed of Abraham, and of a Joseph who became ruler in Egypt. This exile resulted in the appearance of a Moses from that same seed. This exile resulted in the appearance of a being such as Christ from that lineage. This exile resulted in a Hagar being found, of whom Ishmael was begotten, and from whom Muḥammad in turn descended. This exile resulted in the appearance of the Báb from the lineage of Abraham. This exile resulted in the appearance of the Prophets of Israel from the progeny of Abraham— and so will it continue forevermore. This exile resulted in the whole of Europe and most of Asia entering under the shadow of the God of Israel. Behold what a power it was that enabled an emigrant to establish such a family, to found such a nation, and to promulgate such teachings. Now, can anyone claim that all this was purely fortuitous? We must be fair: Was this Man an Educator or not?

It behoves us to ponder awhile that if the emigration of 5

Abraham from Ur to Aleppo in Syria produced such results, what will be the effect of the exile of Bahá'u'lláh from Ṭihrán to Baghdád, and from thence to Constantinople, to Rumelia, and to the Holy Land!

6   Behold then what an accomplished Educator Abraham was!

5

MOSES

MOSES WAS FOR a long time a shepherd in the wilderness. To outward seeming He was a man Who had been reared in the bosom of tyranny, had become reputed among men as a murderer, had taken up the shepherd's staff, and was fiercely hated and reviled by Pharaoh's government and people. It was such a man Who freed a great people from the fetters of captivity and persuaded them to leave Egypt and settle in the Holy Land.

That people had sunk to the depths of degradation and were lifted up to the heights of glory. They were captives and were set free. They were the most ignorant of peoples and became the most learned. By virtue of that which He established, they so progressed as to be singled out among all nations, and their fame spread to every land, to such a degree that when the inhabitants of neighbouring lands wanted to praise someone they would say, "Surely he must be an Israelite!" Moses established laws and ordinances that conferred new life upon the people of Israel and led them to attain the highest degree of civilization at that time.

Such was their progress that the philosophers of Greece would come to seek knowledge from the learned men of Israel. Among them was Socrates, who came to Syria and acquired from the children of Israel the teachings of the oneness of God and the immortality of the spirit. He then returned to Greece and promulgated these teachings, whereupon the people of that land rose up in opposition to him, accused him of impiety, arraigned him before the court, and condemned him to death by poison.

4   Now, how could a man who was a stammerer, who had been brought up in the house of Pharaoh, who was known among men as a murderer, and who out of fear had long been a fugitive and a shepherd, establish in the world so mighty a Cause that the wisest philosophers of the earth would be incapable of producing a thousandth part thereof? This is clearly an extraordinary feat.

5   A man with a stammering tongue can hardly sustain an ordinary conversation, let alone accomplish what He did! No: Were He not assisted by a divine power, He would never have been able to carry out such a mighty task. These are arguments that none can deny. The materialistic thinkers, the Greek philosophers, and the great men of Rome who became renowned in the world were each versed in but one branch of learning. Thus Galen and Hippocrates were celebrated for their skill in medicine, Aristotle in logic and speculative reasoning, and Plato in ethics and divine philosophy. How can a mere shepherd lay the foundation for all these branches of learning? There is no doubt that He was assisted by an extraordinary power.

6   Observe how the people are subjected to tests and trials. Moses struck down an Egyptian to prevent an act of oppression, became known among men as a murderer—especially

since the victim belonged to the ruling nation—and was obliged to flee, and it was after all this that He was raised up as a Prophet. Behold how, in spite of His disrepute, He was aided through an extraordinary power to establish such great institutions and mighty undertakings!

6

CHRIST

1   A FTERWARDS CHRIST APPEARED, saying, "I am born of the Holy Spirit." If it is easy today, among Christians, to acknowledge the truth of this claim, at the time it was very difficult. Thus, according to the text of the Gospel, the Pharisees said, "Is this not the son of Joseph of Nazareth, whom we know? How then can he say, 'I have come down from heaven'?"[2]

2   Briefly, this Man, Who appeared lowly in the eyes of all, arose nonetheless with such power as to abrogate a fifteen-hundred-year-old Dispensation, notwithstanding that the least deviation from its laws would expose the offender to grave danger and bring about his death and annihilation. Moreover, in the time of Christ the general morals and manners of the Israelites had become entirely confused and corrupted, and Israel had fallen into a state of utmost degradation, misery, and bondage. At one time they fell captive to the Chaldeans and the Persians; at another they were under the yoke of the Assyrian Empire. One day they became the subjects and vassals of the Greeks; another they were subjugated and humiliated by the Romans.

3   This young Man, Christ, through an extraordinary power abrogated the ancient Mosaic Law and undertook

to reform the morals of the people. He once again laid the foundation of eternal honour for the Israelites—nay, He undertook to rehabilitate the fortunes of the entire human race—and spread abroad teachings that were not reserved for Israel alone but formed the basis for the universal happiness of human society.

The first to arise to destroy Him were the Israelites— 4 His own people and kindred. And to outward seeming they indeed overcame Him and reduced Him to utter abasement, till at last they crowned Him with the crown of thorns and crucified Him. But this Man, while outwardly immersed in deepest affliction, proclaimed: "This Sun will rise, this Light will shine resplendent, My grace will encompass the world, and all Mine enemies will be confounded." And even as He spoke, so it came to pass, for all the kings of the earth were unable to resist Him. Nay, all their standards were cast down, while the standard of that Wronged One was raised to the loftiest heights.

Is this at all possible in accordance with the rules of 5 human reason? No, by God! Then it is clear and evident that this glorious Being was a true Educator of the world of humanity and that He was aided and assisted by a divine power.

7

MUḤAMMAD

¹ NOW AS TO Muḥammad, the people of Europe and America have heard certain tales about the Prophet, to which they have given credence even though the providers of these accounts, many of whom belonged to the ranks of the Christian clergy, were either ignorant or ill-intentioned. Likewise, a number of ignorant Muslims relayed unfounded tales concerning Muḥammad, which in their minds redounded to His glory. Thus some benighted Muslims made His polygamy the object of their highest praise and held it to be a sign of His wondrous powers, since these ignorant souls considered the multiplicity of wives to be a miraculous thing. The accounts of European historians rely for the most part upon the sayings of such ignorant people.

² For example, a foolish individual once told a Christian priest that the proof of true greatness lies in surpassing bravery and bloodshed, and that in a single day one of the followers of Muḥammad had beheaded a hundred men on the battlefield! This led the priest to surmise that the proof of Muḥammad's religion consisted in killing, which is nothing but vain imagination. On the contrary, Muḥammad's military expeditions were always defensive in nature. The clear proof is this: For thirteen years both He and His companions

endured in Mecca the most intense persecutions and were the constant target of the darts of hatred. Some of His companions were killed and their possessions pillaged; others forsook their native country and fled to foreign lands. Muḥammad Himself was subjected to the severest persecutions and was obliged, when His enemies resolved to kill Him, to flee Mecca in the middle of the night and emigrate to Medina. Yet even then His enemies did not relent, but pursued the Muslims all the way to Medina and to Abyssinia.

These Arab tribes were most barbarous and rapacious,   3 and in comparison with them the wild and fierce natives of America were the Platos of the age, for they did not bury their children alive as these Arabs did their daughters, claiming this to be an act of honour and taking pride therein. Thus many of the men would threaten their wives, saying, "If a daughter is born to you, I will kill you." Even to the present day the Arabs dread having daughters.

Moreover, one man could take a thousand wives, and   4 most husbands had more than ten wives in their household. When these tribes waged war against each other, the victors would take captive the women and children of the vanquished, regard them as slaves, and engage in buying and selling them.

If a man died and left behind ten wives, the sons of these   5 women would rush at each other's mothers, and as soon as one of them had thrown his mantle over the head of one of his stepmothers and claimed her as his lawful property, that unfortunate woman would become the captive and slave of her stepson and the latter could do with her as he pleased.

He could kill her; or shut her up in a pit; or beat, curse, and torment her day after day until at last she perished. In all this he was, in accordance with the laws and customs of the Arabs, free to do as he pleased. The rancour and jealousy, the hatred and enmity that must have existed between the wives of a man and their respective children are perfectly clear and require no elaboration. Consider then what the life and condition of those wronged women must have been!

6   Moreover, these Arab tribes subsisted upon mutual pillage and robbery, so that they were perpetually engaged in strife and warfare, killing one another, plundering each other's property, and seizing the women and children and selling them to strangers. How often would the sons and daughters of a prince spend the day in luxury and ease and find themselves at nightfall reduced to utter abasement, wretchedness, and bondage. Yesterday they were princes, today they are captives; yesterday they were honoured ladies, today they are slaves.

7   It was among such tribes that Muḥammad was sent forth. For thirteen years He suffered at their hands every conceivable tribulation, till at last He fled the city and emigrated to Medina. And yet, far from desisting, these people joined forces, raised an army, and attacked with the aim of exterminating every man, woman, and child among His followers. It was under such circumstances and against such people that Muḥammad was forced to take up arms. This is the plain truth—we are not prompted by fanatical attachment, nor do we blindly seek to defend, but we examine and relate matters with fairness. You should likewise consider in

fairness the following: If Christ Himself had been placed in similar circumstances and among such lawless and barbarous tribes; if for thirteen years He and His disciples had patiently endured every manner of cruelty at their hands; if they were forced through this oppression to forsake their homeland and take to the wilderness; and if these lawless tribes still persisted in pursuing them with the aim of slaughtering the men, pillaging their property, and seizing their women and children—how would Christ have dealt with them? If this oppression had been directed towards Him alone, He would have forgiven them, and such an act of forgiveness would have been most acceptable and praiseworthy; but had He seen that cruel and bloodthirsty murderers were intent upon killing, pillaging, and tormenting a number of defenceless souls and taking captive the women and children, it is certain that He would have defended the oppressed and stayed the hand of the oppressors.

What objection, then, can be directed against Muḥam- 8 mad? Is it this, that He did not, with His followers and their women and children, place himself at the mercy of these lawless tribes? Moreover, to free these tribes from their bloodthirstiness was the greatest gift, and to curb and restrain them was pure bounty. It is like a man who holds in his hand a cup of poison and who is about to drink it. A loving friend would certainly shatter the cup and restrain the drinker. If Christ had been placed in similar circumstances, He would have undoubtedly delivered, through an all-conquering power, those men, women, and children from the claws of such ravenous wolves.

9   Muḥammad never fought against the Christians; on the contrary, He treated them with consideration and accorded them complete freedom. In Najrán there lived a community of Christians, and they were under His care and protection. Muḥammad said: "Should anyone infringe upon their rights, I myself will be his enemy and will charge him before God." In the edicts He promulgated, it is clearly stated that the lives, property, and honour of Jews and Christians are under the protection of God; that a Muslim husband may not prevent his Christian wife from going to church, nor oblige her to wear a veil; that if she died he must entrust her remains to the care of a priest; and that if the Christians desired to build a church the Muslims must support them. Furthermore, in time of war between Islam and her enemies, the Christians were to be exempt from fighting, unless they desired of their own accord to join and assist the Muslims in battle, in view of the protection they enjoyed. In compensation for this exemption, they were to pay each year a small amount. In short, there are seven lengthy edicts on these subjects, copies of some of which are to this day extant in Jerusalem.[3] This is the very truth and not merely my own assertion: The edict of the second Caliph[4] is still in the custody of the Orthodox Patriarch of Jerusalem, and the matter is beyond doubt. Nevertheless, after a time, rancour and envy arose between Muslims and Christians as transgressions were committed by both sides.

10   Beyond this truth, whatever Muslims, Christians, or others may say is pure fabrication and proceeds from fanaticism, ignorance, or intense hostility. For example, the Muslims

claim that the moon was cleft asunder by Muḥammad and fell upon the mountain of Mecca. They imagine the moon to be a small body which Muḥammad divided in twain, casting one part on one mountain and the other part on another! These tales are prompted by sheer fanaticism. Likewise, the accounts that the Christian clergy provide and the charges that they level are always exaggerated and often baseless.

Briefly, Muḥammad appeared in the desert of Ḥijáz in the Arabian Peninsula, which was a treeless and barren wilderness: sandy, desolate in the extreme, and in some places, such as Mecca and Medina, exceedingly hot. Its inhabitants were nomads, had the morals and manners of desert-dwellers, and were entirely bereft of knowledge and learning. Even Muḥammad Himself was illiterate, and the Qur'án was originally written upon the blade-bones of sheep or on palm leaves. Infer then from this the conditions prevailing among the people to whom Muḥammad was sent! 11

His first reproach to them was this: "Why do you reject the Torah and the Gospel, and wherefore do you refuse to believe in Christ and in Moses?" This statement came indeed hard upon them, for they asked: "What then is to be said of our fathers and forefathers, who did not believe in the Torah and the Gospel?" He answered, "They had gone astray, and it is incumbent upon you to renounce those who do not believe in the Torah and the Gospel, though they be your own forefathers." 12

It was in such a land and amidst such barbarous tribes that an illiterate Man brought forth a Book in which the 13 attributes and perfections of God, the prophethood of His Messengers, the precepts of His religion, and certain fields of knowledge and questions of human learning have been expounded in a most perfect and eloquent manner.

14   For example, as you know, before the observations of the renowned astronomer of later times,[5] that is, from the first centuries down to the fifteenth century of the Christian era, all the mathematicians of the world were unanimous in upholding the centrality of the earth and the movement of the sun. This modern astronomer was the source of the new theory that postulated the movement of the earth and the fixity of the sun. Until his time, all the mathematicians and philosophers of the world held to the Ptolemaic system, and whosoever uttered a word against it was considered ignorant. It is true that Pythagoras, and Plato during the latter part of his life, conceived that the sun's annual movement around the zodiac did not proceed from the sun itself but from the earth's movement around it, but this theory was entirely forgotten and the Ptolemaic theory was universally accepted by all mathematicians. But in the Qur'án a number of verses were revealed which contradicted the Ptolemaic system. One of them, "The sun moves in a fixed place of its own",[6] alludes to the fixity of the sun and its movement around an axis. Likewise, in another verse, "And each swims in its own heaven",[7] the movement of the sun, the moon, the earth, and the other celestial bodies is specified. When the Qur'án was spread abroad, all the mathematicians scoffed and attributed this view to ignorance. Even the Muslim divines, finding these verses contrary to the

Ptolemaic system, were obliged to interpret them figuratively, for the latter was accepted as incontrovertible fact and yet was explicitly contradicted by the Qur'án.

It was not before the fifteenth century of the Christian era, nearly nine hundred years after Muḥammad, that new observations were made by a famous mathematician,[8] that the telescope was invented, that important discoveries were made, that the rotation of the earth and the fixity of the sun were proven, and that the latter's movement about an axis was likewise discovered. Then it became evident that the explicit text of the Qur'án was in full agreement with reality and that the Ptolemaic system was sheer imagination.

In short, multitudes of Eastern peoples were reared for thirteen centuries under the shadow of the Muḥammadan Faith. During the Middle Ages, while Europe had sunk to the lowest depths of barbarity, the Arabs excelled all other nations of the earth in sciences and crafts, mathematics, civilization, governance, and other arts. The Educator and Prime Mover of the tribes of the Arabian Peninsula, and the Founder of the civilization of human perfections among those contending clans, was an illiterate Man, Muḥammad. Was this illustrious Man a universal Educator or not? Let us be fair.

8

THE BÁB

¹ AS FOR THE Báb⁹—may my soul be His sacrifice!—it was at a young age, that is, in the twenty-fifth year of His blessed life, that He arose to proclaim His Cause. Among the Shí'ihs it is universally acknowledged that He never studied in any school, nor acquired learning from any teacher. To this the people of Shíráz, each and all, bear witness. Nevertheless, He suddenly appeared before the people, endowed with consummate knowledge, and though but a merchant, confounded all the divines of Persia. Alone, He undertook a task that can scarcely be conceived, for the Persians are known throughout the world for their religious fanaticism. This illustrious Being arose with such power as to shake the foundations of the religious laws, customs, manners, morals, and habits of Persia, and instituted a new law, faith, and religion. Though the eminent men of the State, the majority of the people, and the leaders of religion arose one and all to destroy and annihilate Him, He single-handedly withstood them and set all of Persia in motion. How numerous the divines, the leaders, and the inhabitants of that land who with perfect joy and gladness offered up their lives in His path and hastened to the field of martyrdom!

The government, the nation, the clergy, and prominent 2
leaders sought to extinguish His light, but to no avail. At
last His moon rose, His star shone forth, His foundation was
secured, and His horizon was flooded with light. He trained
a large multitude through divine education and exerted a
marvellous influence upon the thoughts, customs, morals,
and manners of the Persians. He proclaimed the glad-tidings
of the manifestation of the Sun of Bahá to all His followers
and readied them for faith and certitude.

The manifestation of such marvellous signs and mighty 3
undertakings, the influence exerted upon the thoughts and
minds of the people, the laying of the foundations of progress, and the establishment of the prerequisites of success
and prosperity by a young merchant constitute the greatest
proof that He was a universal Educator—a fact that no fair-
minded person would ever hesitate to acknowledge.

9

BAHÁ'U'LLÁH

1   BAHÁ'U'LLÁH[10] APPEARED AT a time when Persia was plunged in the darkest ignorance and consumed by the blindest fanaticism. You have no doubt read at length the accounts that European histories provide of the morals, manners, and thoughts of the Persians during the last few centuries, and these require no repetition. Suffice it to say that Persia had sunk to such abysmal depths that foreign travellers would all deplore that a country which had in former times occupied the pinnacle of greatness and civilization had by then fallen into such abasement, desolation, and ruin, and that its people had been reduced to utter wretchedness.

2   It was at such a time that Bahá'u'lláh appeared. His father was a court minister, not a divine, and it is well known throughout Persia that He never studied in a school or associated with the learned and the divines. He passed the early part of His life in the utmost comfort and happiness, and His companions and associates were Persians of rank rather than learned men.

3   As soon as the Báb revealed His Cause, Bahá'u'lláh proclaimed: "This great Man is the Lord of the righteous, and

it is incumbent upon all to bear allegiance unto Him." He arose to promote the Cause of the Báb, adducing decisive proofs and conclusive arguments of His truth. Although the divines of the nation had obliged the Persian government to exert the most vehement opposition; although they had all issued decrees ordering the massacre, pillage, persecution, and annihilation of the Báb's followers; and although throughout the land the people had undertaken to kill, burn, and plunder them, and even harass their women and children—despite all this, Bahá'u'lláh was engaged, with the utmost constancy and composure, in exalting the word of the Báb. Nor did He seek for a moment to conceal Himself, but associated openly and visibly with His enemies, occupied Himself with adducing proofs and arguments, and became renowned for exalting the Word of God. Time and again He suffered intense adversities, and at every moment His life was in grave danger.

He was put in chains and thrown into a subterranean 4 dungeon. His extensive hereditary possessions were entirely plundered, He was four times exiled from land to land, and in the end He came to abide in the Most Great Prison.[11]

Notwithstanding all this, the call of God was ceaselessly 5 raised and the fame of His Cause was noised abroad. Such were the knowledge, learning, and perfections He evinced that everyone in Persia was astonished. All the learned people—friend and foe alike—who attained His presence in Ṭihrán, Baghdád, Constantinople, Adrianople, and 'Akká received a complete and convincing answer to their every question. All readily acknowledged that in every perfection He was peerless and unique throughout the world.

6   It often happened in Baghdád that Muslim, Jewish, and Christian divines and European men of learning would be gathered in His blessed presence. They would each ask a different question and, despite their varying beliefs, would each receive so complete and convincing a reply as to be fully satisfied. Even the Persian divines residing in Karbilá and Najaf[12] chose a learned man by the name of Mullá Ḥasan 'Amú and dispatched him as their representative. He came into His blessed presence and asked a number of questions on their behalf, to which Bahá'u'lláh responded. He then said, "The divines fully recognize the extent of your knowledge and attainments, and it is acknowledged by all that you are without peer or equal in every field of learning. It is moreover evident that you have never studied or acquired this learning. But the divines say that they are not satisfied with this and cannot acknowledge the truth of your claim on the basis of your knowledge and attainments alone. They therefore ask you to produce a miracle in order to satisfy and assure their hearts."

7   Bahá'u'lláh replied, "Although they have no right to ask this, since it is for God to test His creatures and not for them to test God, yet their request is in this case accepted and allowed. But the Cause of God is not a theatrical stage where every hour a new performance may be offered and every day a new demand presented. For otherwise the Cause of God would become the plaything of children.

"Let the divines, therefore, assemble and choose unani- 8
mously one miracle, and let them stipulate in writing that
once it has been performed they will no longer entertain
any doubt, but will all acknowledge and confess the truth of
this Cause. Let them seal that paper and bring it to Me. They
must fix this as the criterion of truth: If it be performed,
they should have no remaining doubt; and if not, We shall
stand convicted of imposture."

That learned man arose and replied, "There is no more 9
to be said." He kissed Bahá'u'lláh's knee, even though he
was not a believer, and departed. Then he gathered the
divines and conveyed Bahá'u'lláh's message. They consulted
together and said, "This man is a magician; perchance he
will perform some enchantment, and then we will have no
recourse", and so they dared not respond.

Mullá Ḥasan 'Amú, however, reported this fact in many 10
gatherings. He left Karbilá for Kirmánsháh and Ṭihrán,
where he provided all with a detailed account of this episode
and spoke of the fear and inaction of the divines.

Our point is that all the adversaries of Bahá'u'lláh in the 11
East acknowledged His greatness, distinction, knowledge,
and learning, and that in spite of their enmity they referred
to Him as "the renowned Bahá'u'lláh".

In brief, this most great Luminary appeared suddenly 12
above the horizon of Persia, and all the people of that land,
whether ministers, divines, or the general populace, rose
against Him with the fiercest animosity, claiming that He
was bent upon annihilating and extinguishing their religion,

laws, nation, and empire, even as had been said of Christ. Yet Bahá'u'lláh, alone and single-handed, withstood them all without faltering in the slightest.

13   At last they said, "So long as this man is in Persia there will be no peace or tranquillity. He should be banished, that Persia might again find rest." They subjected Bahá'u'lláh, therefore, to severe hardships so that He would be forced to seek permission to leave Persia, and they imagined that the lamp of the Cause would be thereby extinguished. But this persecution produced the contrary effect: The Cause grew in stature and its flame waxed brighter. It had until then spread only within Persia; this caused it to spread to other regions. Later they said, "Iraq is too close to Persia; we must dispatch Him to distant lands." Thus the Persian government persisted until Bahá'u'lláh was exiled from Iraq to Constantinople. But again they saw that He did not falter in the least. They said, "Constantinople is a crossroads for divers peoples and nations, and there are many Persians there." Hence they took further steps and had Him exiled to Adrianople. But that flame gathered still more intensity and the Cause grew even greater in stature. Finally the Persians said, "None of these locations was a place of humiliation: He must be sent to a place where He will be disgraced and subjected to trials and persecutions, and where His kindred and followers will suffer the direst afflictions." Thus they chose the prison city of 'Akká, which was reserved for rebels, murderers, thieves, and highway robbers, and in this wise they made Him associate with such people. But the power of God was made manifest, for this prison became the means

of the promotion of His Faith and the glorification of His Word. The greatness of Bahá'u'lláh became apparent in that He succeeded, from within such a prison and under such humiliating circumstances, in wholly transforming the condition of Persia, in overcoming His enemies, and in proving to all the resistless power of His Cause. His sacred teachings spread to all regions and His Cause was firmly established.

In every province of Persia His enemies arose with the utmost hatred, seizing and killing, beating and burning, uprooting a thousand households, and resorting to every violent means to extinguish His Cause. Notwithstanding all this, He promoted His Cause and promulgated His teachings from within this prison of murderers, thieves, and highwaymen, awakening many of His most virulent enemies and making them firm believers. Such was the influence of His actions that the Persian government itself arose from its slumber and regretted what had been wrought at the hands of the wicked divines. 14

When Bahá'u'lláh arrived at this prison in the Holy Land, discerning souls were awakened to the fact that the prophecies which God had voiced through the tongue of His Prophets two or three thousand years before had been realized and that His promises had been fulfilled, for He had revealed unto certain Prophets and announced unto the Holy Land that the Lord of Hosts would be manifested therein. All these promises were fulfilled, and, but for the opposition of His enemies and His banishment and exile, it can scarcely be imagined how Bahá'u'lláh could have left Persia and pitched His tent in this sacred land. His enemies 15 intended that this imprisonment should completely destroy and annihilate His Cause, but His incarceration became instead the greatest confirmation and the means of its promotion. The call of God reached the East and the West, and the rays of the Sun of Truth illumined every land. Praise be to God! Though He was a prisoner, His tent was raised on Mount Carmel, and He moved about with the utmost majesty. And whoever entered His presence, be it friend or stranger, would exclaim, "This is not a captive but a king!"

16 Immediately upon His arrival in prison, He addressed an epistle to Napoleon which He sent through the French ambassador, the substance of which was: "Ask what crime We have committed to be confined in this prison."[13] Napoleon made no reply. Then a second epistle was issued, which is contained in the Súriy-i-Haykal, and which in substance says: "O Napoleon! Since thou hast failed to heed and answer My call, thou shalt lose Thy dominion and be reduced to naught."[14] This epistle was dispatched to Napoleon by post, through the care of César Catafago[15] and with the full knowledge of His companions in exile. The text of this address quickly reached all of Persia, for the Kitáb-i-Haykal was sent at that time to every corner of that land and this address was included therein. This took place in the year 1869, and as this Súriy-i-Haykal had been circulated throughout Persia and India, all the believers had it in their hands and were awaiting the outcome of this address. Not long after, in 1870, the fire of war was ignited between Germany and France, and although no one at the time anticipated the triumph of Germany, Napoleon was resoundingly

defeated, surrendered to his enemies, and saw his glory changed into deepest abasement.

Tablets were likewise dispatched to other kings, among them an epistle to His Majesty Náṣiri'd-Dín Sháh. In that epistle Bahá'u'lláh said: "Summon Me to thy presence and gather all the divines, and ask for proof and testimony, that truth might be distinguished from error."[16] His Majesty sent Bahá'u'lláh's epistle to the divines and assigned them this task, but they dared not undertake it. He then asked seven of the most renowned divines to respond to this epistle. After a while they returned it, saying, "This man is an opponent of the Faith and an enemy of the King." His Majesty the Sháh of Persia was sorely vexed and said, "This is a matter of proof and testimony, of truth and error. What has it to do with enmity towards the government? How pitiful that we have shown forth such respect to these divines, and yet they cannot even reply to this address."

Briefly, all that was recorded in the Tablets to the kings has come to pass. One need only compare their contents with the events that have transpired since the year 1870 to see that every prediction has been fulfilled, save for a few that remain to be manifested in the future.

Moreover, foreign peoples and non-believers attributed wondrous works to Bahá'u'lláh. Some believed He was a saint, and some even wrote accounts to this effect, such as Siyyid Dávúdí, a Sunní divine of Baghdád, who composed a short treatise in which he related in some connection certain extraordinary feats of Bahá'u'lláh. To this day there are people throughout the East who do not believe in

17

18

19

Bahá'u'lláh as a Manifestation of God, but who regard Him as a saint and attribute miracles to Him.

20   To summarize, not a single soul, whether friend or foe, who attained Bahá'u'lláh's presence failed to acknowledge and attest to His greatness. Although he might not become a believer, he would invariably bear witness to His greatness. No sooner would someone appear before Him than the encounter would produce such an impression as to prevent him, in most cases, from uttering a word. How often would a bitter enemy resolve in his heart to say such-and-such or to argue so-and-so when he had attained His presence, only to find himself amazed, bewildered, and reduced to utter silence!

21   Bahá'u'lláh never studied Arabic, had a teacher or tutor, or entered a school. Nevertheless His eloquence and fluency in spoken Arabic, as well as in His Arabic Tablets, would astonish the most articulate and accomplished among the Arab men of letters, and all acknowledged that in this His attainments were without peer or equal.

22   If we carefully examine the text of the Torah, we see that none of the Manifestations of God ever said to those who denied Them, "Whatever miracle you desire, I am ready to perform, and I will submit to whatever test you propose." Yet in His epistle to the Sháh Bahá'u'lláh clearly stated: "Gather together the divines and summon Me to thy presence, that the proof and testimony might be established."

23   For fifty years Bahá'u'lláh withstood His enemies like a mountain: They all sought to annihilate Him; they all assailed Him; they plotted a thousand times to crucify and

destroy Him; and throughout those fifty years He was in the greatest peril.

As to Persia, which to this day remains in such an abject 24 and ruinous state, every man of wisdom, whether from within or without her borders, who knows her true state of affairs recognizes that her progress, her prosperity, and her civilization depend entirely upon the promulgation of the teachings and the dissemination of the principles of this glorious Being.

In His blessed lifetime Christ educated, in reality, only 25 eleven souls, the greatest of whom, Peter, nonetheless denied Him thrice when put to the test. Notwithstanding this, behold how the Cause of Christ subsequently pervaded the whole earth! In this day Bahá'u'lláh has educated thousands of souls who, under the threat of the sword, have raised to the highest heaven the cry of "O Thou the Glory of Glories!"[17] and whose faces have shone as brightly as gold in the crucible of trials. Infer then from this what shall transpire in the future!

Now, we must be fair and acknowledge what an Educa- 26 tor of mankind this illustrious Being was, what marvellous signs He has manifested, and what power and might have been realized in the world of existence through Him.

10

RATIONAL PROOFS AND
TRADITIONAL ARGUMENTS FROM
THE SACRED SCRIPTURES

1 TODAY AT TABLE let us speak a little of proofs. Had you come to this blessed spot in the days of the manifestation of that most resplendent Light,[18] entered the court of His presence, and beheld His luminous countenance, you would have recognized that His utterance and His beauty were in want of no further proof. How numerous the souls who, upon attaining His presence, became at once confirmed believers, dispensing with any further proof! Even those who were steeped in the deepest hatred and denial would, upon meeting Bahá'u'lláh, testify to His greatness, saying, "This is indeed a distinguished man, but how regrettable that he makes such a claim! For whatever else he might say would be acceptable."

2 Now, since that Luminary of truth has set, all stand in need of proofs, and so we have been occupied with providing rational proofs. Let us mention another, and this undeniable proof should alone suffice any fair-minded soul: It is that this illustrious Being advanced His Cause from within the Most Great Prison, whence His light shone forth, His fame encircled the globe, and the word of His glory reached

both East and West. To this day such a thing has never come to pass, if the matter be examined with fairness. But there are certain souls who, even if they were to hear every proof in the world, would not judge fairly! Governments and peoples with all their might failed to resist Him, while He, alone and single-handed, wronged and imprisoned, accomplished whatsoever He had purposed.

I will not mention the miracles of Bahá'u'lláh, for the hearer might say that these are merely traditions which may or may not be true. Such, too, is the case with the Gospel, where the accounts of the miracles of Christ come down to us from the Apostles and not from other observers, and are denied by the Jews. Were I nonetheless to mention the supernatural feats of Bahá'u'lláh, they are numerous and unequivocally acknowledged in the East, even by some of the non-believers. But these accounts cannot be a decisive proof and testimony for all, since the hearer might say that they are not factually true, as the followers of other denominations also recount miracles from their leaders. For instance, Hindus recount certain miracles of Brahma. How can we know that those are false and that these are true? If these are reported accounts, so too are those; if these are widely attested, then the same holds true of those. Thus such accounts do not constitute a sufficient proof. Of course, a miracle may be a proof for the eyewitness, but even then he might not be sure whether what he beheld was a true miracle or mere sorcery. Indeed, extraordinary feats have also been attributed to certain magicians.

In brief, our meaning is that many marvellous things

appeared from Bahá'u'lláh, but we do not recount them, for not only do they not constitute a proof and testimony for all mankind, but they are not even a decisive proof for those who witnessed them and who may ascribe them to magic.

5   Moreover, most of the miracles attributed to the Prophets have an inner meaning. For instance, it is recorded in the Gospel that upon the martyrdom of Christ darkness fell, the earth shook, the veil of the Temple was rent in twain, and the dead arose from their graves. If this had outwardly come to pass, it would have been a stupendous thing. Such an event would have undoubtedly been recorded in the chronicles of the time and would have seized with dismay the hearts of men. At the very least the soldiers would have removed Christ from the cross or would have fled. But as these events have not been recorded in any history, it is evident that they are not to be understood literally but according to their inner meaning. Our purpose is not to deny, but merely to say that these accounts do not constitute a decisive proof, and that they have an inner meaning—nothing more.

6   Accordingly, today at table we will refer to explanations of traditional arguments drawn from the Sacred Scriptures, for all that we have spoken of thus far have been rational arguments.

7   Since this is the station of searching after truth and seeking the knowledge of the real—that station wherein the sore athirst longs for the water of life and the struggling fish reaches the sea, wherein the ailing soul seeks the true physician and partakes of divine healing, wherein the lost caravan finds the path of truth and the aimless and wandering ship

attains the shore of salvation—the seeker must therefore be endowed with certain attributes. First, he must be fair-minded and detached from all save God. His heart must be entirely directed towards the Supreme Horizon and freed from the bondage of vain and selfish desires, for these are obstacles on the path. Furthermore, he must endure every tribulation, embody the utmost purity and sanctity, and renounce the love or hatred of all the peoples of the world, lest his love for one thing hinder him from investigating another, or his hatred for something prevent him from discerning its truth. This is the station of search, and the seeker must be endowed with these qualities and attributes—that is, until he attains this station it will be impossible for him to gain the knowledge of the Sun of Truth.[19]

Let us return to our theme. All the peoples of the world are awaiting two Manifestations, Who must be contemporaneous. This is what they all have been promised. In the Torah, the Jews are promised the Lord of Hosts and the Messiah. In the Gospel, the return of Christ and Elijah is foretold. In the religion of Muḥammad, there is the promise of the Mahdi and the Messiah. The same holds true of the Zoroastrians and others, but to belabour this matter would prolong our discourse. Our meaning is that all have been promised the advent of two successive Manifestations. It has been prophesied that, through these twin Manifestations, the earth will become another earth; all existence will be renewed; the contingent world will be clothed with the robe of a new life; justice and righteousness will encompass the globe; hatred and enmity will disappear; whatever is the cause of division among peoples, races, and nations will be obliterated; and that which ensures unity, harmony, and concord will be promoted. The heedless will arise from their slumber; the blind will see; the deaf will hear; the dumb will speak; the sick will be healed; the dead will be quickened; and war will give way to peace. Enmity will be transmuted into love; the root causes of contention and strife will be eliminated; mankind will attain true felicity; this world will mirror forth the heavenly Kingdom; and the earth below will become the throne of the realm above. All nations will become one nation; all religions will become one religion; all mankind will become one family and one kindred; all the regions of the earth will become as one; racial, national, personal, linguistic, and political prejudices will be effaced and extinguished; and all will attain everlasting life under the shadow of the Lord of Hosts.

9 Now, one must prove the advent of these twin Manifestations by reference to the Sacred Scriptures and by inference from the sayings of the Prophets. For our intention now is to provide arguments drawn from the Sacred Scriptures, since rational arguments establishing the truth of these two Manifestations were presented at table a few days ago.[20]

10 The Book of Daniel fixes the period between the rebuilding of Jerusalem and the martyrdom of Christ at seventy weeks,[21] for it is through the martyrdom of Christ that the sacrifice is ended and the altar destroyed. This prophecy thus refers to the advent of Christ.

11 These seventy weeks begin with the restoration and rebuilding of Jerusalem, concerning which four edicts were

46

issued by three kings. The first was by Cyrus in 536 B.C., and this is recorded in the first chapter of the Book of Ezra. The second edict regarding the rebuilding of Jerusalem was issued by Darius of Persia in 519 B.C., and this is recorded in the sixth chapter of Ezra. The third was issued by Artaxerxes in the seventh year of his reign, that is, in 457 B.C., and this is recorded in the seventh chapter of Ezra. The fourth edict was issued by Artaxerxes in 444 B.C., and this is recorded in the second chapter of Nehemiah.

What Daniel intended is the third edict, which was issued in 457 B.C. Seventy weeks makes 490 days. Each day, according to the text of the Bible, is one year, for in the Torah it is said: "The day of the Lord is one year."[22] Therefore, 490 days is 490 years. The third edict of Artaxerxes was issued 457 years before the birth of Christ, and Christ was thirty-three years old at the time of His martyrdom and ascension. Thirty-three added to 457 is 490, which is the time announced by Daniel for the advent of Christ.

But in Daniel 9:25 this is expressed in another manner, that is, as seven weeks and sixty-two weeks, which outwardly differs from the first statement. Many have been at a loss to reconcile these two statements. How can reference be made to seventy weeks in one place and to sixty-two weeks and seven weeks in another? These two statements do not accord.

In reality Daniel is referring to two different dates. One begins with the edict Artaxerxes issued to Ezra to rebuild Jerusalem, and corresponds to the seventy weeks which came to an end with the ascension of Christ, when sacrifice and oblation were ended through His martyrdom. The second begins after the completion of the rebuilding of Jerusalem, which is sixty-two weeks until the ascension of Christ. The rebuilding of Jerusalem took seven weeks, which is equivalent to forty-nine years. Seven weeks added to sixty-two weeks makes sixty-nine weeks, and in the last week the ascension of Christ took place. This completes the seventy weeks, and no contradiction remains.

15   Now that the advent of Christ has been proven through the prophecies of Daniel, let us establish the advent of Bahá'u'lláh and of the Báb. So far we have only provided rational arguments; let us now turn to traditional ones.

16   In Daniel 8:13 it is said: "Then I heard one saint speaking, and another saint said unto that certain saint which spake, How long shall be the vision concerning the daily sacrifice, and the transgression of desolation, to give both the sanctuary and the host to be trodden under foot? And he said unto me, Unto two thousand and three hundred days; then shall the sanctuary be cleansed", until it says: "at the time of the end shall be the vision". That is to say, how long shall this misfortune, this ruin, this abasement and degradation endure? Or, when will the morn of Revelation dawn? Then he said, "two thousand and three hundred days; then shall the sanctuary be cleansed". Briefly, the point is that he fixes a period of 2,300 years, for according to the text of the Torah each day is one year. Therefore, from the date of the edict of Artaxerxes to rebuild Jerusalem until the day of the birth of Christ there are 456 years, and from the birth of Christ until the day of the advent of the Báb there are 1,844 years,

and if 456 years are added to this number it makes 2,300 years. That is to say, the fulfilment of the vision of Daniel took place in A.D. 1844, and this is the year of the advent of the Báb. Examine the text of the Book of Daniel and observe how clearly he fixes the year of His advent! There could indeed be no clearer prophecy for a Manifestation than this.

In Matthew 24:3 Christ clearly says that what Daniel meant by this prophecy was the date of the advent, and this is the verse: "As He sat upon the mount of Olives, the disciples came unto Him privately, saying, Tell us, when shall these things be? and what shall be the sign of Thy coming, and of the end of the world?" Among the words He uttered in reply were the following: "When ye therefore shall see the abomination of desolation, spoken of by Daniel the prophet, stand in the holy place, (whoso readeth, let him understand)." Thus He referred them to the eighth chapter of the Book of Daniel, implying that whoever reads it should grasp when that time shall be. Consider how clearly the advent of the Báb has been specified in the Torah and the Gospel!

Let us now establish the date of the advent of Bahá'u'lláh from the Torah. This date is calculated in lunar years from the revelation of the mission and the emigration of Muḥammad. For in the religion of Muḥammad the lunar calendar is used, and all the ordinances regarding religious observances have been expressed in terms of that calendar.

In Daniel 12:6 it is said: "And one said to the man clothed in linen, which was upon the waters of the river, How long

49

shall it be to the end of these wonders? And I heard the man clothed in linen, which was upon the waters of the river, when he held up his right hand and his left hand unto heaven, and sware by Him that liveth for ever that it shall be for a time, times, and an half; and when He shall have accomplished to scatter the power of the holy people, all these things shall be finished."

20 As I have already explained the meaning of "day", no further explanation is needed, but let me briefly say that each day of the Father is equivalent to one year, and each year consists of twelve months. Thus three and a half years makes forty-two months, and forty-two months is 1,260 days, and each day in the Bible is equivalent to one year. And it is in the very year 1260 from the emigration of Muḥammad, according to the Muslim calendar, that the Báb, the Herald of Bahá'u'lláh, revealed His mission.

21 Afterwards, in verses 11 and 12, it is said: "And from the time that the daily sacrifice shall be taken away, and the abomination that maketh desolate be set up, there shall be a thousand two hundred and ninety days. Blessed is he that waiteth, and cometh to the thousand three hundred and five and thirty days."

22 The commencement of this lunar reckoning is from the day of the proclamation of the prophethood of Muḥammad in the land of Ḥijáz; and that was three years after the revelation of His mission, because in the beginning the prophethood of Muḥammad was concealed, and no one knew of it save Khadíjih and Ibn-i-Nawfal,[23] until it was publicly announced three years later. And it was in the year 1290

from the proclamation of the mission of Muḥammad that Bahá'u'lláh announced His Revelation.[24]

II

COMMENTARY ON THE ELEVENTH CHAPTER
OF THE REVELATION OF JOHN

1   IN REVELATION 11:1–2 it is said: "And there was given me a reed like unto a rod: and the angel stood, saying, Rise, and measure the temple of God, and the altar, and them that worship therein. But the court which is without the temple leave out, and measure it not; for it is given unto the Gentiles: and the holy city shall they tread under foot forty and two months."

2   By this reed is meant the Perfect Man, and the reason for His being likened to a reed is that when the latter is entirely freed and emptied of its pith, it becomes capable of producing wondrous melodies. Moreover, these songs and airs proceed not from the reed itself but from the player who blows into it. In the same way, the sanctified heart of that blessed Being is free and empty of all save God, is averse to and exempt from attachment to every selfish inclination, and is intimately acquainted with the breath of the Divine Spirit. That which He utters proceeds not from Himself but from the ideal Player and from divine revelation. Hence He is likened to a reed, and that reed is like a rod; that is, it is the succour of the weak and the support of every mortal soul.

It is the rod of the True Shepherd by which He guards His flock and leads it about in the pastures of the Kingdom.

Then it is said that the angel addressed him, saying, "Rise, and measure the temple of God, and the altar, and them that worship therein"; that is, weigh and gauge. To gauge is to determine the quantity of a thing. Thus the angel said: Weigh the Holy of Holies, and the altar, and them that are worshipping therein—that is, investigate their true condition; discover their rank and station, their attainments, their perfections, their conduct, and their attributes; and acquaint thyself with the mysteries of those holy souls who abide in the station of purity and sanctity in the Holy of Holies. 3

"But the court which is without the temple leave out, and measure it not; for it is given unto the Gentiles." When, in the beginning of the seventh century of the Christian era, Jerusalem was conquered, the Holy of Holies—that is, the edifice that Solomon had erected—was outwardly preserved, but its outer court was seized and given over to the Gentiles. 4

"And the holy city shall they tread under foot forty and two months"; that is, the Gentiles will seize and subdue Jerusalem for forty-two months, or 1,260 days, or—each day being equivalent to a year—1,260 years, which is the duration of the Qur'anic Dispensation. For according to the text of the Bible each day is a year, as it is said in Ezekiel 4:6: "thou shalt bear the iniquity of the house of Judah forty days: I have appointed thee each day for a year". 5

This is a prophecy concerning the duration of the 6

Dispensation of Islam, when Jerusalem was trodden underfoot, meaning that it was dishonoured, while the Holy of Holies remained preserved, guarded, and honoured. This state of affairs continued until the year 1260. This 1,260 years is a prophecy concerning the advent of the Báb, the "Gate" leading to Bahá'u'lláh, which took place in the year A.H. 1260. As the period of 1,260 years has been completed, the Holy City of Jerusalem is now beginning to prosper and flourish again. Anyone who saw Jerusalem sixty years ago, and who sees it again today, will recognize how it has come to prosper and flourish and how it has regained its honour.

7   This is the outward sense of these verses of the Revelation of John, but they also have an inward interpretation and a symbolic meaning, which is as follows. The religion of God consists of two parts: One is the very foundation and belongs to the spiritual realm; that is, it pertains to spiritual virtues and divine qualities. This part suffers neither change nor alteration: It is the Holy of Holies, which constitutes the essence of the religion of Adam, Noah, Abraham, Moses, Christ, Muḥammad, the Báb, and Bahá'u'lláh, and which will endure throughout all the prophetic Dispensations. It will never be abrogated, for it consists in spiritual rather than material truth. It is faith, knowledge, certitude, justice, piety, high-mindedness, trustworthiness, love of God, and charity. It is mercy to the poor, assistance to the oppressed, generosity to the needy, and upliftment of the fallen. It is purity, detachment, humility, forbearance, patience, and constancy. These are divine qualities. These commandments will never be abrogated, but will remain in force and effect

for all eternity. These human virtues are renewed in every Dispensation; for at the close of each Dispensation the spirit of the law of God, which consists in the human virtues, vanishes in substance and persists only in form.

Thus, at the end of the Mosaic Dispensation, which coincided with the advent of Christ, the true religion of God vanished from among the Jews, leaving behind a form without a spirit. The Holy of Holies was no more, but the outer court of the Temple—which signifies the outward form of the religion—fell into the hands of the Gentiles. In the same way, the very heart of the religion of Christ, which consists in the greatest human virtues, is no more, but its outward form has remained in the hands of the priests and monks. Likewise, the foundation of the religion of Muḥammad is no more, but its outward form remains in the hands of the Muslim divines. 8

Those foundations of the religion of God, however, which are spiritual and consist in human virtues, are never subject to abrogation but are eternal and everlasting, and are renewed in every prophetic Dispensation. 9

The second part of the religion of God, which pertains to the material world and which concerns such things as fasting; prayer; worship; marriage; divorce; manumission; legal rulings; transactions; and penalties and punishments for murder, assault, theft, and injury, is changed and altered in every prophetic Dispensation and may be abrogated—for policies, transactions, punishments, and other laws are bound to change according to the exigencies of the time. 10

Briefly, what is meant by the term "Holy of Holies" is 11

that spiritual law which can never be changed or abrogated, and what is meant by the "Holy City" is the material law which may indeed be abrogated; and this material law—the Holy City—was to be trodden underfoot for 1,260 years.

12   "And I will give power unto my two witnesses, and they shall prophesy a thousand two hundred and three-score days, clothed in sackcloth."[25] By these two witnesses are intended Muḥammad the Messenger of God and 'Alí the son of Abú Ṭálib. In the Qur'án it is said that God addressed Muḥammad, saying, "We made Thee a witness, a herald, and a warner";[26] that is, We have established Thee as one Who bears witness, Who imparts the glad-tidings of that which is to come, and Who warns of the wrath of God. A "witness" means one by whose affirmation matters are ascertained. The commandments of these two witnesses were to be followed for 1,260 days, each day corresponding to a year. Now, Muḥammad was the root and 'Alí the branch, like Moses and Joshua. It is said they were "clothed in sackcloth", meaning that they appeared to wear not a new raiment but an old one. In other words, they would initially appear to be of no consequence in the eyes of other peoples and their Cause would not seem new. For the spiritual principles of the religion of Muḥammad correspond to those of Christ in the Gospel, and His material commandments correspond for the most part to those of the Torah. This is the symbolism of the old raiment.

13   "These are the two olive trees, and the two candlesticks standing before the God of the earth."[27] These two Souls have been likened to olive trees, since all the lamps of that

time were lit at night with olive oil. In other words, these are two Souls from whom the oil of divine wisdom—which is the cause of the illumination of the world—will appear, and through whom the lights of God will shine bright and resplendent. Thus have they also been likened to candlesticks. The candlestick is the locus of the light and the place from whence it emanates. In the same way, the light of guidance would shine resplendent from these luminous Countenances.

They are "standing before God"—that is, they have 14 arisen in His service and are educating His creatures. For instance, they so educated the barbarous, desert-dwelling tribes of the Arabian Peninsula as to cause them to attain the loftiest heights of human civilization at the time and to spread their fame and renown throughout the world.

"And if any man will hurt them, fire proceedeth out 15 of their mouth, and devoureth their enemies."[28] This means that no soul would be able to withstand their might. That is, should anyone seek to subvert their teachings or their law, he would be overcome and defeated by virtue of that law which proceeds, whether in brief or in full, from their mouth. In other words, they would issue a command that would destroy any enemy that would attempt to harm or oppose them. And so it came to pass, for their opponents were all vanquished, dispersed, and destroyed, and these two witnesses were outwardly assisted by the power of God.

"These have power to shut heaven, that it rain not in the 16 days of their prophecy."[29] This means that they would rule supreme in that age. In other words, the law and teachings of Muḥammad, and the exposition and commentaries of 'Alí, are a heavenly grace. Should they wish to bestow this grace, it is in their power to do so, and should they wish otherwise, no rain will fall, and by "rain" is meant here the outpouring grace.

17   "And have power over waters to turn them to blood".[30] This means that the prophethood of Muḥammad was similar to that of Moses, and the power of 'Alí like that of Joshua. That is, it was in their power, had they so desired, to turn the waters of the Nile into blood for the Egyptians and the deniers—or, in other words, to turn, in consequence of their ignorance and pride, that which was the source of their life into the cause of their death. Thus the sovereignty, wealth, and power of Pharaoh and of his people, which were the source of that nation's life, became, as a result of their opposition, denial, and pride, the very cause of their death, ruin, destruction, degradation, and wretchedness. Hence these two witnesses have power to destroy nations.

18   "And to smite the earth with all plagues, as often as they will".[31] This means that they would also be endowed with outward power and ascendancy, that they might school the workers of iniquity and the embodiments of oppression and tyranny. For God had granted these two witnesses both outward might and inward power, and so it is that they reformed and educated the wicked, bloodthirsty, and iniquitous Arabs of the desert who were like ravening wolves and beasts.

19   "And when they shall have finished their testimony"[32]— that is, when they have accomplished that which they were

bidden, and have delivered the divine message, and promoted the religion of God, and spread abroad His heavenly teachings, so that the signs of spiritual life might be manifested in the souls of men, the light of human virtues might shine forth, and these desert tribes might achieve substantive progress.

"The beast that ascendeth out of the bottomless pit shall 20 make war against them, and shall overcome them, and kill them."[33] By this beast is meant the Umayyads, who assailed these witnesses from the pit of error. And indeed it came to pass that the Umayyads assailed the religion of Muḥammad and the truth of 'Alí, which consist in the love of God.

"The beast made war against these two witnesses."[34] By 21 this is intended a spiritual war, meaning that the beast would act in complete opposition to the teachings, conduct, and character of these two witnesses, to such an extent that the virtues and perfections that had been diffused among the peoples and nations by virtue of their power would entirely vanish, and animal qualities and carnal desires would predominate. Therefore, this beast would wage war against them and would gain ascendancy, meaning that the darkness of the error propagated by this beast would prevail throughout the world and slay those two witnesses—that is, it would extinguish their spiritual life amidst the people, obliterate their divine laws and teachings, and trample underfoot the religion of God, leaving behind naught but a dead and soulless body.

"And their dead bodies shall lie in the street of the great 22 city, which spiritually is called Sodom and Egypt, where also our Lord was crucified."[35] By "their bodies" is meant the religion of God and by "the street", exposure to public view. "Sodom and Egypt, where also our Lord was crucified" refers to the land of Syria and especially to Jerusalem, for the Umayyads had their seat of power in this land and it was here that the religion of God and the divine teachings first disappeared, leaving behind a soulless body. "Their bodies" refers to the religion of God, which remained as a dead and soulless body.

23   "And they of the people and kindreds and tongues and nations shall see their dead bodies three days and an half, and shall not suffer their dead bodies to be put in graves."[36] As was already explained, in the terminology of the Sacred Scriptures three days and a half signifies three years and a half, and three years and a half represents forty-two months, and forty-two months—1,260 days. Since according to the explicit text of the Bible each day is equivalent to a year, this means that for 1,260 years, which is the duration of the Qur'anic Dispensation, the nations, tribes, and peoples would behold their bodies; that is, they would keep the religion of God before their eyes but would not act in accordance with it. Yet they would not suffer these bodies—the religion of God—to be laid to rest in the grave. That is, they would hold fast to its outward form and not let it entirely vanish from their midst nor allow the body to be wholly destroyed and annihilated. Rather, they would forsake its reality while outwardly preserving its name and remembrance.

24   That which is intended here are such kindreds, peoples, and nations as were gathered beneath the shadow of the

Qur'án. These are they who would not allow the Cause and religion of God to be destroyed and annihilated outwardly as well. Thus, some manner of prayer and fasting was practised among them, but the very foundations of the religion of God, which are goodly character, upright conduct, and the knowledge of the divine mysteries, had disappeared; the light of human virtues, which proceeds from the love and knowledge of God, had been extinguished; the darkness of oppression and tyranny, of carnal desires and satanic attributes, prevailed; and the body of the religion of God, like unto a corpse, was exposed to public view.

For 1,260 days, each day being a year—that is, for the duration of the Islamic Dispensation—all that these two Persons had established as the foundations of the religion of God was forfeited by their followers. To such an extent were the traces of human virtues—which are the bestowals of God and which constituted the spirit of this religion— erased that truthfulness, justice, love, concord, purity, sanctity, detachment, and all the heavenly attributes vanished from their midst, and what remained of the religion was mere prayer and fasting. This condition lasted for 1,260 years, which corresponds to the Dispensation of the Qur'án. It was as though these two Persons had died and their bodies were left without a soul.

"And they that dwell upon the earth shall rejoice over them, and make merry, and shall send gifts one to another; because these two prophets tormented them that dwelt on the earth."[37] By "them that dwelt on the earth" is meant other peoples and nations, such as those of Europe and of distant Asian lands, who, seeing that the character of Islam had entirely changed; that the religion of God had been forsaken; that virtue, decency, and honour had vanished; and that characters had been subverted, rejoiced that the morals of the Muslims had been corrupted and that they stood therefore to be vanquished by other nations. And this indeed came to pass in a most conspicuous manner. Witness how this people who once wielded supreme power have been abased and subjugated!

27   The other nations "shall send gifts to one another", meaning that they would help each other, for "these two prophets tormented them that dwelt upon the earth"; that is, they subdued and subjugated the other peoples and nations of the earth.

28   "And after three days and an half the Spirit of life from God entered into them, and they stood upon their feet; and great fear fell upon them which saw them."[38] Three days and a half, as we explained earlier, is 1,260 years. These two Persons whose bodies were lying soulless—that is, the teachings and the religion that Muḥammad had established and that 'Alí had promoted, whose reality had vanished, and of which only an empty form had remained—were again endowed with spirit. That is, the spirituality of the religion of God that had become materiality, the virtues that had become vices, the love of God that had become hatred, the light that had become darkness, the divine qualities that had become satanic attributes, the justice that had become tyranny, the mercy that had become malice, the sincerity that had become hypocrisy, the guidance that had become error, the purity

that had become carnality—all these divine teachings, heavenly virtues and perfections, and spiritual bounties—were, after three and a half days (which by the terminology of the Sacred Scriptures is 1,260 years) renewed by the advent of the Báb and by the allegiance of Quddús.

Thus did the breezes of sanctity waft, the light of truth shine, the life-giving springtime arrive, and the morn of guidance dawn. These two dead bodies were once again quickened to life, and these two great Personages—one the Founder and the other the promoter—arose and were as two candlesticks, for they illumined the whole world with the light of truth.   29

"And they heard a great voice from heaven saying unto them, Come up hither. And they ascended up to heaven in a cloud",[39] meaning that from the invisible heaven they heard the voice of God, saying: You have accomplished all that was called for with regard to educating the people and conveying the glad-tidings of that which is to come. You have delivered My message to the people, raised the call of Truth, and fulfilled your every obligation. Now, even as Christ, you must lay down your lives in the path of the Beloved and suffer a martyr's death. And so that Sun of Reality and that Moon of Guidance[40] both set, Christ-like, beneath the horizon of the supreme sacrifice and ascended to the realm of Heaven.   30

"And their enemies beheld them."[41] That is, many of their enemies realized after their martyrdom the sublimity of their station and the excellence of their virtues, and testified to their greatness and their perfections.   31

32 "And the same hour was there a great earthquake, and the tenth part of the city fell, and in the earthquake were slain of men seven thousand."[42] This earthquake occurred in S͟híráz after the martyrdom of the Báb. The city was plunged into turmoil, and many people were killed. Great agitation ensued, moreover, from diseases, cholera, scarcity, famine, starvation, and other afflictions—an agitation the like of which had never before been witnessed.

33 "And the remnant were affrighted, and gave glory to the God of heaven."[43] When the earthquake took place in Fárs, the survivors were wailing and lamenting day and night, and were occupied with praising and imploring God. So great was their fear and agitation that at night they could find no rest or composure.

34 "The second woe is past; and, behold, the third woe cometh quickly."[44] The first woe was the advent of the Apostle of God, Muḥammad the son of 'Abdu'lláh, peace be upon Him. The second woe was that of the Báb, upon Him be glory and praise. The third woe is the great Day of the advent of the Lord of Hosts and the revelation of the promised Beauty. The explanation of this matter is provided in the thirtieth chapter of Ezekiel, where it is said: "The word of the Lord came again unto me, saying, Son of man, prophesy and say, Thus saith the Lord God; Howl ye, Woe worth the day! For the day is near, even the day of the Lord is near."[45] It is therefore evident then that the day of woe is the day of the Lord; for in that day woe is upon the heedless, the sinners, and the ignorant. That is why it is said, "The second woe is past; and, behold, the third woe cometh quickly."

This third woe is the day of the manifestation of Bahá'u'lláh, the Day of God, and it is near to the day of the appearance of the Báb.

"And the seventh angel sounded; and there were great [35] voices in heaven, saying, The kingdoms of this world are become the kingdoms of our Lord, and of His Christ; and He shall reign for ever and ever."[46] That angel refers to human souls who have been endowed with heavenly attributes and invested with an angelic nature and disposition. Voices will be lifted up and the appearance of the divine Manifestation will be proclaimed and noised abroad. It will be announced that this day is the day of the advent of the Lord of Hosts, and this Dispensation the merciful Dispensation of the Divine Providence. It has been promised and recorded in all the Sacred Books and Scriptures that in this Day of God His divine and spiritual sovereignty will be established, the world will be renewed, a fresh spirit will be breathed into the body of creation, the divine springtime will be ushered in, the clouds of mercy will rain down, the Sun of Truth will shine forth, the life-giving breezes will blow: The world of humanity will be arrayed in a new garment; the face of the earth will become even as the highest paradise; humanity will be educated; war, dissension, strife, and contention will vanish; truthfulness, uprightness, peace, and godliness will prevail; love, concord, and union will encompass the world; and God will rule forevermore—that is, a spiritual and everlasting sovereignty will be established. Such is the Day of God. For all the days which have come and gone were the days of Abraham, Moses, Christ, or of the other Prophets, but this day is the Day of God, inasmuch as the Sun of Truth will shine forth therein with the utmost intensity and radiance.

36 "And the four and twenty elders, which sat before God on their seats, fell upon their faces, and worshipped God, saying, We give Thee thanks, O Lord God Almighty, which art, and wast, and art to come; because Thou hast taken to Thee Thy great power, and hast reigned."[47] In every Dispensation there have been twelve chosen ones: In the time of Joseph there were twelve brothers; in the time of Moses there were twelve heads or chiefs of the tribes; in the time of Christ there were twelve Apostles; and in the time of Muḥammad there were twelve Imáms. But in this glorious Revelation there are twenty-four such souls, double the number of all the others, for so does its greatness require.[48] These holy souls are in the presence of God seated upon their thrones, meaning that they reign eternally.

37 These twenty-four glorious souls, though they are established upon the throne of everlasting sovereignty, nonetheless bow down in adoration to, and are humble and submissive before, that universal Manifestation of God, saying, "We give Thee thanks, O Lord God Almighty, which art, and wast, and art to come; because Thou hast taken to Thee Thy great power, and hast reigned." That is, Thou wilt promulgate all Thy teachings, gather all the people of the earth under Thy shadow, and bring all men together under a single tabernacle. And although sovereignty has always belonged to God, and He has ever been and will forever continue to be the supreme Sovereign, the reference in this

instance is to the sovereignty of the Manifestation of His own Self, Who will promulgate such laws and teachings as are the very spirit of the world of humanity and the cause of everlasting life. That universal Manifestation will subdue the world through a spiritual power, not through war and strife. He will array the world with peace and harmony, not with swords and spears. He will establish this divine sovereignty through genuine love, not through military might. He will promote these divine teachings through kindness and amity, not through violence and arms. Even though these nations and peoples are, in view of the divergence of their conditions, the disparity of their customs and characters, and the diversity of their religions and races, even as the wolf and the lamb, the leopard and the kid, and the sucking child and the asp, He will so educate them that they will embrace, consort with, and confide in each other. Racial antipathy, religious animosity, and national rivalries will be entirely effaced, and all will attain perfect fellowship and complete harmony under the shade of the Blessed Tree.

"And the nations were angry," for Thy teachings ran counter to the selfish desires of the other nations, "and Thy wrath is come,"[49] meaning that all suffered grievous loss for failing to follow Thy counsels, admonitions, and teachings; were deprived of grace everlasting; and were veiled from the light of the Sun of Truth. 38

"And the time of the dead, that they should be judged"[50] means that the time has come that the dead—that is, those who are deprived of the spirit of the love of God and bereft of that life which is holy and everlasting—should be judged 39 with equity, meaning that each should be raised up according to their worthiness and capacity, and that the truth should be fully divulged as to what depths of degradation they occupy in this world of existence and how they should, in reality, be accounted among the dead.

40 "That Thou shouldest give reward unto Thy servants the prophets, and to the saints, and them that fear Thy name, small and great";[51] that is, that Thou wilt single out the righteous for Thy boundless grace, cause them to shine even as heavenly stars above the horizon of ancient glory, and aid them to show forth such conduct and character as to illumine the world of humanity and to become the means of guidance and the source of everlasting life in the divine Kingdom.

41 "And shouldest destroy them which destroy the earth".[52] That is, Thou wilt entirely deprive the heedless; for the blindness of the blind will be exposed and the sight of them that see will become evident; the ignorance and folly of the exponents of error will be recognized and the knowledge and wisdom of the rightly guided will be manifested; and thus the destroyers will be destroyed.

42 "And the temple of God was opened in heaven."[53] This means that the divine Jerusalem has appeared and the Holy of Holies has become manifest. Among the people of true knowledge, the Holy of Holies refers to the essence of the religion of God and His true teachings, which have remained unchanged throughout all the prophetic Dispensations, as was explained previously, while Jerusalem encompasses the reality of the religion of God, which is the Holy

of Holies, as well as all the laws, mutual relationships, rites, and material ordinances, which constitute the city. That is why it is called the heavenly Jerusalem. Briefly, in the course of the Dispensation of the Sun of Truth, the lights of God will shine forth with the utmost splendour, and thus the essence of the divine teachings will be realized in the world of being, the darkness of ignorance and folly will be dispelled, the world will become another world, spiritual illumination will encompass all, and hence the Holy of Holies will appear.

"And the temple of God was opened in heaven."[54] This 43 means also that through the dissemination of these divine teachings, the disclosure of these heavenly mysteries, and the dawning of the Sun of Truth, the portals of progress and advancement will be flung open on all sides and the signs of celestial blessings and bestowals will be made manifest.

"And there was seen in His temple the ark of His Testament."[55] This means that the Book of His Covenant will 44 appear in His Jerusalem, the Tablet of the Testament will be recorded, and the meaning of the Covenant and Testament will become evident. The call of God will resound throughout East and West, and the earth will be filled with the renown of the Cause of God. The violators of the Covenant will be humbled and abased, and the faithful will attain honour and glory, for they hold fast to the Book of the Covenant and are firm and unwavering in the path of the Testament.

"And there were lightnings, and voices, and thunderings, and an earthquake, and great hail",[56] meaning that after 45 the appearance of the Book of the Covenant there will be a great tempest, the lightning of divine anger and wrath will flash, the thunder of the violation of the Covenant will break, the tremor of doubt will shake the earth, the hail of torments will rain upon the violators of the Covenant, and those who claim to believe will be subjected to tests and trials.

COMMENTARY ON THE ELEVENTH
CHAPTER OF ISAIAH

I N ISAIAH 11:1–9 it is said: "And there shall come forth ¹
a rod out of the stem of Jesse, and a Branch shall grow
out of his roots: And the spirit of the Lord shall rest upon
him, the spirit of wisdom and understanding, the spirit of
counsel and might, the spirit of knowledge and of the fear
of the Lord; And shall make him of quick understanding in
the fear of the Lord: and he shall not judge after the sight
of his eyes, neither reprove after the hearing of his ears: But
with righteousness shall he judge the poor, and reprove with
equity for the meek of the earth: and he shall smite the
earth with the rod of his mouth, and with the breath of his
lips shall he slay the wicked. And righteousness shall be the
girdle of his loins, and faithfulness the girdle of his reins.
The wolf also shall dwell with the lamb, and the leopard
shall lie down with the kid; and the calf and the young lion
and the fatling together; and a little child shall lead them.
And the cow and the bear shall feed; their young ones shall
lie down together: and the lion shall eat straw like the ox.
And the sucking child shall play on the hole of the asp, and
the weaned child shall put his hand on the cockatrice' den.
They shall not hurt nor destroy in all my holy mountain: for

the earth shall be full of the knowledge of the Lord, as the waters cover the sea."

2   This "rod out of the stem of Jesse" might seem to apply to Christ, for Joseph was a descendant of Jesse, the father of David. However, since Christ had come into being through the Divine Spirit, He called Himself the Son of God. Had this not been the case, this passage could have indeed applied to Him. Moreover, the events that are said to occur in the days of that rod, if they be interpreted figuratively, came to pass only in part, and if they be taken literally, failed absolutely and entirely to take place in the days of Christ.

3   For instance, we might say that the leopard and the kid, the lion and the calf, the sucking child and the asp, represent the various nations, the hostile peoples and contending kindreds of the earth who in their opposition and enmity were even as the wolf and the lamb, and who through the breezes of the messianic Spirit came to be endowed with the spirit of unity and fellowship, were quickened to life, and associated intimately one with another. But the condition referred to in the statement "They shall not hurt nor destroy in all My holy mountain: for the earth shall be full of the knowledge of the Lord, as the waters cover the sea" did not materialize in the Dispensation of Christ. For to this day there are various hostile and contending nations in the world: Few acknowledge the God of Israel, and most are deprived of the knowledge of God. Likewise, universal peace was not established with the advent of Christ; that is, peace and well-being were not realized among the hostile and contending nations, disputes and conflicts were

not resolved, and harmony and sincerity were not attained. Thus, even to this day intense enmity, hatred, and conflict prevail among the Christian peoples themselves.

But these verses apply word for word to Bahá'u'lláh. 4 Moreover, in this wondrous Dispensation the earth will become another earth and the world of humanity will be arrayed with perfect composure and adornment. Strife, contention, and bloodshed will give way to peace, sincerity, and harmony. Among the nations, peoples, kindreds, and governments, love and amity will prevail and cooperation and close connection will be firmly established. Ultimately, war will be entirely banned, and when the laws of the Most Holy Book are enacted, arguments and disputes will, with perfect justice, be settled before a universal tribunal of governments and peoples, and any difficulties which may arise will be resolved. The five continents of the world will become as one, its divers nations will become one nation, the earth will become one homeland, and the human race will become one people. Countries will be so intimately connected, and peoples and nations so commingled and united, that the human race will become as one family and one kindred. The light of heavenly love will shine and the gloomy darkness of hatred and enmity will be dispelled as far as possible. Universal peace will raise its pavilion in the midmost heart of creation and the blessed Tree of Life will so grow and flourish as to stretch its sheltering shade over the East and the West. Strong and weak, rich and poor, contending kindreds and hostile nations—which are like the wolf and the lamb, the leopard and kid, the lion and the calf—will treat one another with the utmost love, unity, justice, and equity. The earth will be filled with knowledge and learning, with the realities and mysteries of creation, and with the knowledge of God.

5   Now, in this glorious age, which is the century of Bahá'u'lláh, consider how far knowledge and learning have progressed, how fully the mysteries of creation have been unveiled, and how many great undertakings have been embarked upon and are multiplying day by day! Soon will material knowledge and learning, as well as spiritual knowledge, make such progress and display such wonders as to dazzle every eye and to disclose the full meaning of the verse of Isaiah: "for the earth shall be full of the knowledge of the Lord".

6   Consider likewise that in the short span of time since the advent of Bahá'u'lláh, people of all nations, kindreds, and races have entered beneath the shadow of this Cause. Christians, Jews, Zoroastrians, Hindus, Buddhists, and Persians all consort together with perfect love and fellowship, as if for a thousand years they had belonged to the same kindred and family—indeed, as if they were father and son, mother and daughter, sister and brother. This is one of the meanings of the fellowship between the wolf and the lamb, the leopard and the kid, and the lion and the calf.

7   One of the great events which is to occur in the Day of the manifestation of that Incomparable Branch is the hoisting of the Standard of God among all nations. By this is meant that all nations and kindreds will be gathered together under the shadow of this Divine Banner, which is

no other than the Lordly Branch itself, and will become a single nation. Religious and sectarian antagonism, the hostility of races and peoples, and differences among nations will be eliminated. All men will adhere to one religion, will have one common faith, will be blended into one race and become a single people. All will dwell in one common fatherland, which is the planet itself.[57] Universal peace and concord will be established among all nations. That Incomparable Branch will gather together all Israel; that is, in His Dispensation Israel will be gathered in the Holy Land, and the Jewish people who are now scattered in the East and the West, the North and the South, will be assembled together.

Now, observe that these events did not take place in the Christian Dispensation, for the nations did not enlist under that single banner—that divine Branch—but in this Dispensation of the Lord of Hosts all nations and peoples will enter beneath His shadow. Likewise Israel, which had been scattered throughout the world, was not gathered together in the Holy Land in the course of the Christian Dispensation, but in the beginning of the Dispensation of Bahá'u'lláh this divine promise, which has been clearly stated in all the Books of the Prophets, has begun to materialize. Observe how from all corners of the world Jewish peoples are coming to the Holy Land, acquiring villages and lands to inhabit, and increasing day by day to such an extent that all Palestine is becoming their home.

8

13

COMMENTARY ON THE TWELFTH CHAPTER OF THE REVELATION OF JOHN

1   WE HAVE EXPLAINED before that what the Sacred Scriptures most often mean by the Holy City or divine Jerusalem is the religion of God, which has at times been likened to a bride, or called "Jerusalem", or depicted as the new heaven and the new earth. Thus in Revelation, chapter 21, it is said: "And I saw a new heaven and a new earth: for the first heaven and the first earth were passed away; and there was no more sea. And I John saw the holy city, new Jerusalem, coming down from God out of heaven, prepared as a bride adorned for her husband. And I heard a great voice out of heaven saying, Behold, the tabernacle of God is with men, and He will dwell with them, and they shall be His people, and God Himself shall be with them, and be their God."[58]

2   Consider how unmistakably "the first heaven" and "the first earth" refer to the outward aspects of the former religion. For it is said that "the first heaven and earth were passed away; and there was no more sea". That is, the earth is the arena of the last judgement, and in this arena there will be no more sea, meaning that the law and teachings of God will have spread throughout the earth, all mankind will have embraced

His Cause, and the earth will have been entirely peopled by the faithful. Thus there will be no more sea, for man dwells upon solid land and not in the sea—that is, in that Dispensation the sphere of influence of that religion will encompass every land that man has trodden, and it will be established upon solid ground whereon the feet do not falter.

Likewise, the religion of God is described as the Holy City or the New Jerusalem. Clearly, the New Jerusalem which descends from heaven is not a city of stone and lime, of brick and mortar, but is rather the religion of God which descends from heaven and is described as new. For it is obvious that the Jerusalem which is built of stone and mortar does not descend from heaven and is not renewed, but that what is renewed is the religion of God.

Furthermore, the religion of God is likened to an adorned bride who appears with the utmost grace, as it has been said in chapter 21 of the Revelation of John: "And I John saw the holy city, new Jerusalem, coming down from God out of heaven, prepared as a bride adorned for her husband."[59] And in chapter 12 it is said: "And there appeared a great wonder in heaven; a woman clothed with the sun, and the moon under her feet, and upon her head a crown of twelve stars." This woman is that bride, the religion of God, that descended upon Muḥammad. The sun with which she was clothed, and the moon which was under her feet, are the two governments which are under the shadow of that religion, the Persian and the Ottoman, for the emblem of Persia is the sun and that of the Ottoman Empire is the crescent moon. Thus the sun and the moon allude to two governments under the shadow of the religion of God. Afterwards it is said: "upon her head a crown of twelve stars". These twelve stars represent the twelve Imáms, who were the promoters of the religion of Muḥammad and the educators of the nation, and who shone as stars in the heaven of guidance.

5   Then it is said: "And she being with child cried, travailing in birth, and pained to be delivered",[60] meaning that this religion will suffer great difficulties and endure great toil and trouble until a perfect offspring is produced therefrom—that is, until the subsequent and promised Manifestation, Who is a perfect offspring, is reared in the bosom of this religion, which is even as its mother. By this offspring is meant the Báb, the Primal Point, Who was in truth born from the religion of Muḥammad. In other words, that sacred Reality which was the child and the result of the religion of God—its mother—and which was its Promised One, came into being in the heavenly kingdom of that religion, but was caught up unto God to elude the ascendancy of the dragon. After 1,260 days the dragon was destroyed and the offspring of the religion of God, the Promised One, was made manifest.

6   "And there appeared another wonder in heaven; and behold a great red dragon, having seven heads and ten horns, and seven crowns upon his heads. And his tail drew the third part of the stars of heaven, and did cast them to the earth."[61] This dragon represents the Umayyads, who seized the reins of the religion of Muḥammad; and the seven heads and seven crowns represent the seven dominions

and kingdoms over which they came to rule: the Roman dominion in Syria; the Persian, the Arabian, and the Egyptian dominions; the dominion of Africa—that is, Tunisia, Morocco, and Algeria; the dominion of Andalusia, which is now Spain; and the dominion of the Turkish tribes of Transoxania. The Umayyads gained power over all these dominions. The ten horns represent the names of the Umayyad rulers, for, barring repetition, they are ten sovereigns, or ten names of chiefs and rulers. The first is Abú Sufyán and the last is Marván. Some of their names have been repeated, including two Mu'áviyihs, three Yazíds, two Valíds, and two Marváns. If, however, these names are each counted only once, they number ten in total. These Umayyads—the first of whom was Abú Sufyán, the former chief of Mecca and founder of the dynasty, and the last of whom was Marván—destroyed a third of the holy and sanctified souls who descended from the pure lineage of Muḥammad and who were even as the stars of heaven.

"And the dragon stood before the woman which was ready to be delivered, for to devour her child as soon as it was born."[62] This woman is the religion of God, as was before explained. The dragon's standing near her signifies that it was keeping watch to devour her child as soon as it had been delivered. This child was the promised Manifestation, Who is the offspring of the religion of Muḥammad. The Umayyads were ever anxious to lay hold on the Promised One Who was to appear from the lineage of Muḥammad, that they might destroy and annihilate Him, for they greatly feared His advent. And so wherever they found a descendant of Muḥammad who was respected in the eyes of the people, they killed him.

8   "And she brought forth a man child, who was to rule all nations with a rod of iron."[63] This glorious son is the promised Manifestation, Who was born of the religion of God and reared in the bosom of the divine teachings. The iron rod is a symbol of might and power—it is not a sword—and means that He will shepherd all the nations of the earth by virtue of His divine might and power. And by this son is meant the Báb.

9   "And her child was caught up unto God, and to His throne."[64] This is a prophecy concerning the Báb, Who ascended to the Kingdom, the Throne of God, and the Seat of His sovereignty. Consider how closely this conforms to what indeed came to pass.

10   "And the woman fled into the wilderness";[65] that is, the religion of God betook itself to the desert, meaning the vast desert of Ḥijáz and the Arabian Peninsula.

11   "Where she hath a place prepared of God";[66] that is, the Arabian Peninsula became the home, the habitation, and the focal centre of the religion of God.

12   "That they should feed her there a thousand two hundred and threescore days".[67] According to the terminology of the Bible, these 1,260 days mean 1,260 years, as was before explained. Thus for 1,260 years the religion of God was fostered in the vast desert of Arabia, until the Promised One appeared. After these 1,260 years that religion ceased to be in effect, for the fruit of that tree had been manifested and its result had been produced.

Consider how closely the prophecies correspond one 13
to another! The Book of Revelation fixes the advent of the
Promised One after forty-two months. The Prophet Daniel specifies three times and a half, which is also forty-two
months or 1,260 days. Another passage of the Revelation of
John directly states 1,260 days, and it is explicitly indicated
in the Bible that each day signifies one year. Nothing could
be clearer than this agreement of the prophecies with each
other. The Báb appeared in the year A.H. 1260 according to
the calendar followed by all Muslims. There are no clearer
prophecies than this in the Bible for any Manifestation. If one
be fair, the agreement between the times indicated by these
glorious Souls is the most conclusive proof and can in no
wise be subject to any other interpretation. Blessed are the
fair-minded who search after truth.

When justice is lacking, however, the people challenge, 14
dispute, and deny the obvious. Their conduct is like that of
the Pharisees in the time of Christ, who would obstinately
deny the interpretations and utterances He and His Apostles
made, and who would wilfully obscure the truth before the
ignorant masses, saying, "These prophecies do not apply to
Jesus, but to the Promised One Who will erelong appear
according to the conditions mentioned in the Torah"—
among which being that He would be a king, sit upon the
throne of David, enforce the law of the Torah, inaugurate
the most great justice, and cause the wolf and the lamb to
gather at the same spring. And thus did they veil the people
from recognizing Christ.

14

MATERIAL AND SPIRITUAL CYCLES

1   I N THIS MATERIAL world, time has changing cycles and place is subject to varying conditions. Seasons follow one another and individuals progress, regress, and develop. At one point it is springtime and at another the autumn season; at one point it is summer and at another it is winter.

2   The vernal season has rain-laden clouds and musk-scented breezes, life-giving zephyrs, and perfectly mild weather. The rain falls; the sun shines; the reviving winds blow; the world is renewed; and the breath of life reveals itself in plant, animal, and man alike. Earthly beings pass from one condition to another. All things are clothed with a new vesture: The black earth is swathed in abundant grass, mountains and plains don an emerald-green robe, trees bear leaves and blossoms, gardens bring forth flowers and sweet herbs, the world becomes another world, and all creation is imbued with a new life. The earth, which was as a soul-less body, finds a new spirit and displays the utmost beauty, grace, and charm. Thus the springtide produces a new life and infuses a new spirit.

3   Then comes summertime, when the heat intensifies and growth and development manifest the fullness of their power. The life force reaches its plenitude in the vegetable

kingdom: Fruits and crops appear, the harvest time arrives, the seed becomes the sheaf, and provision is made for the winter months.

Then comes unrelenting autumn, when unwholesome 4 gales blow, barren winds waft, and the season of dearth and want arrives. All things wither; the pleasant air becomes hard and chill; the breezes of spring turn into the blasts of fall; trees, once green and verdant, become wasted and bare; flowers and herbs fade away in sorrow; and delicate gardens become darksome heaps of dust.

There follows the winter season, when cold winds blow 5 and tempests arise. It snows and storms, it hails and rains, it thunders and lightens, and lethargy and torpor take hold. Plants become as dead, and animals languish and waste away.

When this stage is reached, the life-giving springtide 6 returns once again and a new cycle is inaugurated. Spring-time, with its hosts of vitality and grace, and in the pleni-tude of its greatness and majesty, pitches its tent upon the mountains and plains. Once more the temples of created things are revived and the creation of contingent beings is renewed. Living bodies grow and develop, fields and plains become green and verdant, trees put forth blossoms, and last year's spring returns once again in the height of its majesty and glory. The very existence of things must ever depend upon, and be perpetuated through, these cycles and successions. Such are the cycles and revolutions of the material world.

The spiritual cycles associated with the Prophets of God 7 proceed in like manner. That is, the day of the advent of the

Holy Manifestations is the spiritual springtime. It is divine splendour and heavenly grace; it is the wafting of the breeze of life and the dawning of the Sun of Truth. Spirits are revived, hearts are refreshed, souls are refined, all existence is stirred into motion, and human realities are rejoiced and grow in attainments and perfections. Universal progress is achieved, the souls are gathered up, and the dead are quickened to life—for it is the day of resurrection, the season of commotion and ferment, the hour of joy and gladness, and the time of rapture and abandon.

8   That soul-stirring springtime then gives rise to the fruitful summer. The Word of God is proclaimed, His Law is promulgated, and all things reach a state of perfection. The heavenly table is spread, the breezes of holiness perfume the East and the West, the teachings of God conquer the whole earth, souls are educated, laudable results are produced, universal progress is made in the human realm, the divine bounties encompass all things, and the Sun of Truth shines above the horizon of the heavenly Kingdom in the height of its power and intensity.

9   When that Sun reaches its zenith it begins to decline, and that summer season of the spirit is followed by autumn. Growth and development are arrested; soft breezes turn into blighting winds; and the season of dearth and want dissipates the vitality and beauty of the gardens, the fields, and the bowers. That is, spiritual attractions vanish, divine qualities decay, the radiance of the hearts is dimmed, the spirituality of the souls is dulled, virtues become vices, and sanctity and purity are no more. Of the law of God naught remains but

a name, and of the divine teachings naught but an outward form. The foundations of the religion of God are destroyed and annihilated, mere customs and traditions take their place, divisions appear, and steadfastness is changed into perplexity. Spirits die away, hearts wither, and souls languish.

Winter arrives—that is, the chill of ignorance and un- 10 awareness envelops the world, and the darkness of wayward and selfish desires prevails. Apathy and defiance ensue, with indolence and folly, baseness and animal qualities, coldness and stone-like torpor, even as in the wintertime when the terrestrial globe is deprived of the influence of the rays of the sun and becomes waste and desolate. Once the realm of minds and thoughts reaches this stage, there remains naught but perpetual death and unending non-existence.

When, however, the winter season has run its course, the 11 spiritual springtime returns again and a new cycle reveals its splendour. The breezes of the spirit blow, the radiant morn breaks, the clouds of the Merciful rain down, the rays of the Sun of Truth shine forth, and the world of being is invested with a new life and arrayed in a wondrous robe. All the signs and bestowals of the former springtime, and perhaps even greater ones, reappear in this new season.

The spiritual cycles of the Sun of Truth, like the cycles 12 of the physical sun, are in a state of perpetual motion and renewal. The Sun of Truth can be likened to the material sun, which rises from many different points. One day it rises from the sign of Cancer and another from the sign of Libra; one day it casts its rays from the sign of Aquarius and another from that of Aries. Yet the sun is but one sun and one single reality. The possessors of true knowledge are lovers of the sun and are not attached to its dawning points. Those who are endued with insight are seekers of the truth itself, not of its exponents and manifestations. Thus they bow in adoration before the sun, from whatever sign and above whatever horizon it may appear, and seek the truth from any sanctified soul who might reveal it. Such people inevitably discover the truth and are not veiled from the light of the Sun of the divine firmament. Thus the lover of the rays and the seeker of the light will always turn towards the sun, whether it be shining from the sign of Aries, or bestowing its grace from the sign of Cancer, or casting its rays from the sign of Gemini.

13   But the foolish and the ignorant are enamoured with the zodiacal signs and enraptured with the dawning points, not with the sun itself. When it was in Cancer they turned towards it, but when it passed into Libra they continued, attached as they were to the former sign, to fix their gaze upon and hold fast unto that sign, and thus they deprived themselves of the rays of the sun when once it had moved. Thus the Sun of Truth at one time shed its rays from the sign of Abraham; later it dawned above the sign of Moses and illumined the horizon; and later still it shone forth with the utmost power, heat, and radiance from the sign of Christ. Those who were searching after truth worshipped it wherever they saw it, but those who were attached to Abraham, when once that Sun cast its rays upon Sinai and illumined the reality of Moses, were deprived thereof. And those who clung to Moses, when once the Sun of Truth

shed its heavenly splendour in the fullness of its radiance from the point of Christ, were likewise veiled, and so forth.

Therefore one must search after truth, become enraptured and enthralled with any sanctified soul in whom one finds it, and become wholly attracted to the outpouring grace of God. Like a moth, one must be a lover of the light, in whatever lamp it may shine; and like a nightingale, one must be enamoured of the rose, in whatever bower it may bloom. 14

Were the sun to rise from the west, it would still be the sun. Indeed, from whatever point the sun may rise, it is still the sun. One must not take its appearance to be confined to a single point and regard the other points as deprived. One must not be veiled by its rising in the east and consider the west as the place of its setting and decline. One must seek after the manifold grace of God, search out the divine effulgences, and become enraptured and enthralled with any reality in which they are clearly and plainly found. Consider that, if the Jews had not clung to the horizon of Moses but had fixed their gaze upon the Sun of Truth, they would have undoubtedly beheld that Sun shining in the fullness of its divine splendour in that true dawning point that was Christ. But a thousand times alas! They clung to the name of Moses and deprived themselves of that supernal grace and heavenly splendour. 15

15

TRUE FELICITY

1 THE HONOUR AND exaltation of every existing thing are contingent upon certain causes and conditions.

2 The excellence, adornment, and perfection of the earth consist in this, that through the outpourings of the vernal showers it should become green and verdant; that plants should spring forth; that flowers and herbs should grow; that blossom-filled trees should produce an abundant yield and bring forth fresh and succulent fruit; that gardens should be arrayed; that meadows should be adorned; that plains and mountains should don an emerald robe; and that fields and bowers, villages and cities should be decked forth. This is the felicity[68] of the mineral world.

3 The height of exaltation and perfection of the vegetable world consists in this, that a tree should stand tall beside a stream of fresh water, that a gentle breeze should blow and the sun bestow its warmth upon it, that a gardener should tend it, and that day by day it should grow and yield fruit. But its real felicity consists in progressing into the animal and human worlds and in replacing that which has been consumed in the bodies of animals and men.

4 The exaltation of the animal world is to possess perfect members, organs, and powers, and to have all its needs

supplied. This is the height of its glory, honour, and exaltation. So the supreme felicity of an animal resides in a green and verdant meadow, in a flowing stream of the sweetest water, and in a forest brimming with life. If these things are provided, no greater felicity can be imagined for the animal. For example, were a bird to build its nest in a green and verdant forest, in a pleasant height, upon a mighty tree, and atop a lofty branch, and were it to have at its disposal all the seed and water that it requires, then this would constitute its perfect felicity.

But true felicity for the animal consists in passing from the animal world into the human realm, like the microscopic beings that, through the air and the water, enter into the body of man, are assimilated, and replace that which has been consumed in his body. This is the greatest honour and felicity for the animal world, and no greater honour can be conceived for it.

Therefore, it is clear and evident that such material ease, comfort, and abundance are the height of felicity for minerals, plants, and animals. And indeed no wealth, prosperity, comfort, or ease in our material world can equal the wealth of a bird, for it has all the expanse of the fields and mountains for a dwelling place; all the seed and harvests for wealth and sustenance; and all the lands, villages, meadows, pastures, forests, and wilderness for possessions. Now which is the richer—this bird or the wealthiest of men? For no matter how many seeds that bird may gather up or give away, its wealth does not diminish.

Then it is clear that the honour and exaltation of man

cannot reside solely in material delights and earthly benefits. This material felicity is wholly secondary, while the exaltation of man resides primarily in such virtues and attainments as are the adornments of the human reality. These consist in divine blessings, heavenly bounties, heartfelt emotions, the love and knowledge of God, the education of the people, the perceptions of the mind, and the discoveries of science. They consist in justice and equity, truthfulness and benevolence, inner courage and innate humanity, safeguarding the rights of others and preserving the sanctity of covenants and agreements. They consist in rectitude of conduct under all circumstances, love of truth under all conditions, self-abnegation for the good of all people, kindness and compassion for all nations, obedience to the teachings of God, service to the heavenly Kingdom, guidance for all mankind, and education for all races and nations. This is the felicity of the human world! This is the exaltation of man in the contingent realm! This is eternal life and heavenly honour!

8 These gifts, however, do not manifest themselves in the reality of man save through a celestial and divine power and through the heavenly teachings, for they require a supernatural power. Traces of these perfections may well appear in the world of nature, but they are as fleeting and ephemeral as rays of sunlight upon the wall.

9 As the compassionate Lord has crowned the head of man with such a refulgent diadem, we must strive that its luminous gems may cast their light upon the whole world.

PART 2

Some Christian Subjects

16

INTELLIGIBLE REALITIES AND THEIR
EXPRESSION THROUGH SENSIBLE FORMS

THERE IS A point that is pivotal to grasping the essence 1
of the other questions that we have discussed or will be
discussing, namely, that human knowledge is of two kinds.

One is the knowledge acquired through the senses. That 2
which the eye, the ear, or the senses of smell, taste, or touch
can perceive is called "sensible". For example, the sun is
sensible, as it can be seen. Likewise, sounds are sensible, as
the ear can hear them; odours, as they can be inhaled and
perceived by the sense of smell; foods, as the palate can perceive their sweetness, sourness, bitterness, or saltiness; heat
and cold, as the sense of touch can perceive them. These are
called sensible realities.

The other kind of human knowledge is that of intel- 3
ligible things; that is, it consists of intelligible realities which
have no outward form or place and which are not sensible.
For example, the power of the mind is not sensible, nor are
any of the human attributes: These are intelligible realities.
Love, likewise, is an intelligible and not a sensible reality.
For the ear does not hear these realities, the eye does not
see them, the smell does not sense them, the taste does not
detect them, the touch does not perceive them. Even the

ether, the forces of which are said in natural philosophy to be heat, light, electricity, and magnetism, is an intelligible and not a sensible reality. Likewise, nature itself is an intelligible and not a sensible reality; the human spirit is an intelligible and not a sensible reality.

4   But when you undertake to express these intelligible realities, you have no recourse but to cast them in the mould of the sensible, for outwardly there is nothing beyond the sensible. Thus, when you wish to express the reality of the spirit and its conditions and degrees, you are obliged to describe them in terms of sensible things, since outwardly there exists nothing but the sensible. For example, grief and happiness are intelligible things, but when you wish to express these spiritual conditions you say, "My heart became heavy", or "My heart was uplifted", although one's heart is not literally made heavy or lifted up. Rather, it is a spiritual or intelligible condition, the expression of which requires the use of sensible terms. Another example is when you say, "So-and-so has greatly advanced", although he has remained in the same place, or "So-and-so has a high position", whereas, like everyone else, he continues to walk upon the earth. This elevation and advancement are spiritual conditions and intelligible realities, but to express them you must use sensible terms, since outwardly there is nothing beyond the sensible.

5   To cite another example, knowledge is figuratively described as light, and ignorance as darkness. But reflect: Is knowledge sensible light or ignorance sensible darkness? Certainly not. These are only intelligible conditions, but

when you wish to express them outwardly you call knowledge light and ignorance darkness and say, "My heart was dark and it became illumined." Now, the light of knowledge and the darkness of ignorance are intelligible realities, not sensible ones, but when we seek to express them outwardly, we are obliged to give them a sensible form.

Thus it is evident that the dove which descended upon Christ[69] was not a physical dove but a spiritual condition expressed, for the sake of comprehension, by a sensible figure. For example, in the Old Testament it is said that God appeared as a pillar of fire.[70] Now, that which is intended is not a sensible form but an intelligible reality that has been expressed in such a form.

6

Christ says, "The Father is in the Son, and the Son is in the Father."[71] Now, was Christ within God or was God within Christ? No, by God! This is an intelligible condition which has been expressed in a sensible figure.

7

We come to the explanation of the words of Bahá'u'lláh when He says: "O King! I was but a man like others, asleep upon My couch, when lo, the breezes of the All-Glorious were wafted over Me, and taught Me the knowledge of all that hath been. This thing is not from Me, but from One Who is Almighty and All-Knowing."[72] This is the station of divine revelation. It is not a sensible, but an intelligible reality. It is sanctified from and transcendent above past, present, and future. It is a comparison and an analogy—a metaphor and not a literal truth. It is not the condition that is commonly understood by the human mind when it is said that someone was asleep and then awoke, but signifies a passage

8

from one state to another. For example, sleeping is the state of repose, and wakefulness is the state of motion. Sleeping is the state of silence, and wakefulness is the state of utterance. Sleeping is the state of concealment, and wakefulness is that of manifestation.

9   For example, in Persian and Arabic it is said that the earth was asleep, spring came, and it awoke; or that the earth was dead, spring came, and it found life again. These expressions are comparisons, analogies, similes, and figurative interpretations in the realm of inner meaning.

10   Briefly, the Manifestations of God have ever been and will ever be luminous Realities, and no change or alteration ever takes place in Their essence. At most, before Their revelation They are still and silent, like one who is asleep, and after Their revelation They are eloquent and effulgent, like one who is awake.

17

THE BIRTH OF CHRIST

QUESTION: HOW WAS Christ born of the Holy Spirit? 1
Answer: In regard to this question, the divine and 2
the material philosophers disagree. The former believe that
Christ was born of the Holy Spirit, while the latter deem
such a thing to be impossible and untenable, and hold that
He must have necessarily had a human father.

In the Qur'án it is said: "And We sent Our Spirit to her, 3
and He took before her the form of a perfect man",[73] meaning that the Holy Spirit assumed a human form, as an image
appears in a mirror, and conversed with Mary.

The material philosophers believe that there must be 4
pairing, and assert that a living body cannot come into
being from a lifeless one or materialize without the union
of male and female. They believe that, beyond man, this is
impossible in animals, and that, beyond animals, it is impossible even in plants. For this pairing of male and female
exists in all the animals and plants. They even argue that the
Qur'án itself affirms this pairing of all things: "Glory be to
Him Who hath created all the pairs, of such things as earth
produceth, and out of men themselves, and of things beyond
their ken";[74] that is, man, animals, and plants are all found in

pairs. "And of everything have We created two kinds";[75] that is, We have created all things in pairs.

5 Briefly, they say that a man without a human father cannot be imagined. The divine philosophers, however, reply: "Such a thing is not impossible, although it has not been observed, and there is a difference between that which is impossible and that which has merely not been observed. For example, in the days before the telegraph, the instantaneous communication of East and West had not been observed but was not impossible; likewise, the photograph and the phonograph had not been observed but were not impossible."

6 The material philosophers insist upon their belief, and the divine philosophers reply: "Is this terrestrial globe eternal or was it originated?" The material philosophers answer that, according to well-established scientific findings, it is proven to be originated; that in the beginning it was a molten sphere and gradually became temperate; that a crust was formed around it; and that upon this crust plants came into being, then animals, and finally man.

7 The divine philosophers say: "It follows clearly from your statement that the human species upon the terrestrial globe was originated and is not eternal. Then surely the first man had neither father nor mother, for the existence of the human species has an origin in time. Now, which is more problematic: that man should come into being, albeit gradually, with neither father nor mother, or that he should come into being without a father? As you admit that the first man came into being with neither father nor mother, whether it

be gradually or in a short period of time, there can remain no doubt that a man without a human father is also possible and logically admissible. One cannot therefore simply reject this as impossible, and to do so would betray a lack of fairness. For example, if you say that this lamp was once lit with neither wick nor oil, and then say that it is impossible for it to be lit without the wick, this betrays a lack of fairness." Christ had a mother, but the first man, according to the material philosophers, had neither father nor mother.

18

THE GREATNESS OF CHRIST

1 QUESTION: WHAT IS the virtue and benefit of being without a father?

2 Answer: A great man is a great man, whether or not he is born of a human father. If being without a father were a virtue, Adam would excel and surpass all the Prophets and Messengers, for He had neither father nor mother. That which is conducive to greatness and glory are the splendours and outpourings of the divine perfections. The sun is born of matter and form, which can be likened to father and mother, and still it is absolute perfection; darkness has neither matter nor form, neither father nor mother, and yet it is sheer imperfection. The matter of Adam's physical life was dust, but the physical matter of Abraham was a pure seed; and it is certain that a pure and goodly seed is superior to earth and stone.

3 Furthermore, in John 1:12–13 it is said: "But as many as received Him, to them gave He power to become the sons of God, even to them that believe on His name: Which were born, not of blood, nor of the will of the flesh, nor of the will of man, but of God."[76] It follows clearly from this verse of John that even the existence of the Apostles proceeds from a spiritual reality rather than from a material power.

The honour and greatness of Christ reside not in His being without a father, but rather in His divine perfections, outpourings, and splendours. Were the greatness of Christ due to His lacking a father, Adam would be even greater, for He had neither father nor mother.

It is said in the Old Testament, "And the Lord God 4 formed man of the dust of the ground, and breathed into his nostrils the breath of life; and man became a living soul."[77] Observe that Adam is said to have come into being from the spirit of life. Moreover, John's utterance in regard to the Apostles proves that they also proceeded from the heavenly Father. Hence it is clear and evident that the holy reality— the true existence—of every great man proceeds from God and owes its being to the breath of the Holy Spirit.

Our meaning is that, if being without a father were the 5 greatest of human attainments, then Adam would surpass everyone, for He had neither father nor mother. Is it better for a man to be created from living matter or from dust? Certainly it is better to be created from living matter. But Christ was born from, and came into existence through, the Holy Spirit.

In brief, the honour and glory of those sanctified Souls, 6 the Manifestations of God, are due to Their heavenly perfections, outpourings, and splendours, and to nothing else.

19

TRUE BAPTISM

1 IN MATTHEW 3:13–15, it is said: "Then cometh Jesus from Galilee to Jordan unto John, to be baptized of him. But John forbad Him, saying, I have need to be baptized of Thee, and comest Thou to me? And Jesus answering said unto him, Suffer it to be so now: for thus it becometh us to fulfil all righteousness. Then he suffered Him."

2 Question: Given His innate perfection, what need did Christ have of baptism and what was the wisdom thereof?

3 Answer: The essence of baptism is purification by repentance. John admonished and exhorted the people, caused them to repent, and then baptized them. It is evident then that this purification is a symbol of repentance from all sin, as though one were saying: "O God! Just as my body has been cleansed and purified from material defilements, so cleanse and purify my spirit from the defilements of the world of nature, which are unworthy of Thy divine threshold." Repentance is the return from rebelliousness to obedience. It is after experiencing remoteness and deprivation from God that man repents and purifies himself. Thus, this purification is a symbol saying: "O God! Render my heart goodly and pure, and cleanse and sanctify it from all save Thy love."

As Christ desired that this custom instituted by John be 4
practised by all at that time, He Himself submitted to it,
that souls might be awakened and that the law which had
issued from the former religion might be fulfilled. For even
though this custom was instituted by John, it represented in
reality the purification of repentance which has been practised in all the divine religions.

It is not that Christ was in need of baptism, but He 5
submitted to it because at that time this action was praiseworthy and acceptable before God and presaged the glad-
tidings of the Kingdom. However, He later said that true
baptism was not with material water but with spirit and
with water, and, elsewhere, with spirit and with fire.[78] What
is meant here by "water" is not material water, for elsewhere it is explicitly stated that baptism must be with spirit
and with fire, and the latter makes it clear that the intention is not material fire and water, since baptism with fire
is impossible.

Therefore, by "spirit" is meant divine grace; by "water", 6
knowledge and life; and by "fire", the love of God. For
material water cleanses not the heart of man but his body.
Rather, the heavenly water and spirit, which are knowledge
and life, cleanse and purify the heart of man. In other words,
the heart that partakes of the outpouring grace of the Holy
Spirit and becomes sanctified is made goodly and pure. The
purpose is that the reality of man be purified and sanctified
from the defilements of the world of nature, which are vile
attributes such as anger, lust, worldliness, pride, dishonesty,
hypocrisy, deceit, self-love, and so on.

7 Man cannot free himself from the onslaught of vain and selfish desires save through the confirming grace of the Holy Spirit. That is why it is said that baptism must be with the spirit, with water, and with fire—that is, with the spirit of divine grace, the water of knowledge and life, and the fire of the love of God. It is with this spirit, this water, and this fire that man must be baptized, that he may partake of everlasting grace. For otherwise, of what avail is it to be baptized with material water? No, this baptism with water was a symbol of repentance and of seeking remission of sins.

8 But in the Dispensation of Bahá'u'lláh this symbol is no longer required, for its reality, which is to be baptized with the spirit and the love of God, has been established and realized.

20

BAPTISM AND THE CHANGING
LAW OF GOD

QUESTION: IS THE purification of baptism useful and
necessary or is it useless and unnecessary? If the former, why was it abrogated despite its necessity? And if the
latter, why did John practise it despite its being unnecessary?

Answer: The change and transformation of conditions,
and the succession and revolution of ages, are among the
essential requirements of the contingent world, and essential
requirements cannot be separated from the reality of things.
Thus it is impossible to separate heat from fire, or wetness
from water, or the rays from the sun, for these are essential requirements. And since change and transformation are
among the requirements of all contingent things, the commandments of God are also changed in accordance with
the changing times. For example, in the days of Moses, that
which was required by and consonant with the conditions
prevailing at that time was the Mosaic Law. However, in the
days of Christ, those conditions had so changed as to render
the Mosaic Law unsuited and ill-adapted to the needs of
mankind, and it was therefore abrogated. Thus Christ broke
the Sabbath and forbade divorce. After Him four disciples,
Peter and Paul among them, permitted the eating of such

animal foods as had been forbidden in the Torah, excepting the consumption of the meat of animals that had been strangled, of sacrifices made to idols, and of blood. They also forbade fornication.[79] Thus they maintained these four commandments. Later, Paul permitted the eating of strangled animals, of those sacrificed to idols, and of blood, but maintained the prohibition of fornication. Thus in Romans 14:14 he writes: "I know, and am persuaded by the Lord Jesus, that there is nothing unclean of itself: but to him that esteemeth any thing to be unclean, to him it is unclean." Moreover, in Titus 1:15 it is written: "Unto the pure all things are pure: but unto them that are defiled and unbelieving is nothing pure; but even their mind and conscience is defiled."

3   Now, this change, alteration, and abrogation was due to the fact that the age of Christ could not be compared to that of Moses. The conditions and requirements had entirely changed, and the former commandments were therefore abrogated.

4   The body of the world can be compared to that of a man, and the Prophets and Messengers of God to able physicians. A human being does not remain always in the same condition: Different ailments occur and each calls for a specific remedy. Thus an able physician does not treat all ailments in the same manner but varies the treatments and remedies in accordance with the requirements of these various ailments and conditions. One person may suffer severely from an ailment caused by an excess of heat: The able physician perforce administers cooling medicines.[80] When, at another time, this person's constitution changes and the heat

is supplanted by an excess of cold, the physician, of necessity, sets aside the cooling medicines and prescribes heating ones. This change and alteration is required by the condition of the patient and is an evident proof of the skill of the physician.

Consider, for example: Could the Law of the Torah be enforced in this day and age? No, by God! This would be entirely impossible, and it is for this reason that at the time of Christ the Law of the Torah was perforce abrogated by God. Consider, likewise, that in the days of John the Baptist the purification of baptism served to awaken and admonish the people and to cause them to repent of all sin and to await the advent of the Kingdom of Christ. But today in Asia, the Catholics and the Orthodox plunge infants into a mixture of water and olive oil, in such wise that some fall ill from this ordeal and tremble and struggle at the time of baptism. Elsewhere the priest sprinkles the baptismal water onto the forehead. But in neither case do these children experience any spiritual feelings. What good then can this do? Other peoples wonder and question why this infant is being plunged into the water, since it confers neither spiritual awareness nor faith nor awakening but is merely a custom that is being followed. In the time of John the Baptist, however, it was not so: John would first admonish the people, lead them to repent of sin, and exhort them to anticipate the advent of Christ. Then, whoever received the purification of baptism would repent of his sins with utmost meekness and humility, cleanse and purify his body likewise from outward defilements, and with perfect yearning await, night and day and from moment to moment, the advent of Christ and admittance into His Kingdom.

6   In brief, our meaning is that the change and transformation in the conditions and exigencies of the times is the cause of the abrogation of religious laws, for the time comes when those earlier commandments no longer suit the prevailing conditions. Consider how greatly the exigencies of the modern age differ from those of medieval times! Is it possible that the commandments of former centuries could be enforced in these latter times? It is clear and evident that this would be entirely impossible. Likewise, after the lapse of many centuries, that which is called for at the present time will no longer be suited to the needs of that future age, and change and transformation will be inevitable.

7   In Europe the laws are continually being changed and modified. How numerous the laws that once existed in European systems and canons and that have since been annulled! These changes are due to the transformation of thoughts, customs, and conditions, and without them the well-being of the human world would be disrupted.

8   For example, the Torah prescribes the sentence of death for whoever breaks the Sabbath. There are indeed ten such death sentences in the Torah. Could these commandments be carried out in our time? It is evident that it would be utterly impossible. Thus they have been changed and transformed, and this change and transformation in the laws constitutes in itself a sufficient proof of the consummate wisdom of God.

9   This subject requires deep consideration, and the reason is clear and evident. Well is it with them that reflect!

21

THE BREAD AND THE WINE

QUESTION: CHRIST SAID: "I am the living bread [1] which came down from heaven: if any man eat of this bread, he shall live for ever."[81] What is the meaning of this utterance?

Answer: By this bread is meant the heavenly sustenance [2] of divine perfections. In other words, whoso partakes of this sustenance—that is, whoso acquires the outpouring grace of God, draws illumination from His light, and obtains his portion of the perfections of Christ—will attain everlasting life. What is meant by blood, likewise, is the spirit of life, which consists in divine perfections, heavenly splendours, and eternal grace. For all the parts of the body acquire the substance of life from the circulation of the blood.

In John 6:26 it is said: "Ye seek Me, not because ye saw [3] the miracles, but because ye did eat of the loaves, and were filled." It is evident that the loaves of which the disciples ate, and with which they were filled, were the heavenly grace, for in verse 33 of the same chapter it is said: "For the bread of God is He which cometh down from heaven, and giveth life unto the world." It is evident that the body of Christ did not descend from heaven but came from the womb of Mary: What descended from the heaven of God was the spirit of Christ. The Jews, presuming that Christ was speaking of His body, objected, as is recorded in verse 42 of the same chapter: "And they said, Is not this Jesus, the son of Joseph, whose father and mother we know? how is it then that he saith, I came down from heaven?"

4   Consider how evident it is that what Christ intended by the heavenly bread was His spirit, His manifold grace, His perfections, and His teachings; for in verse 63 of the aforementioned chapter it is said: "It is the spirit that quickeneth; the flesh profiteth nothing."

5   It has therefore been made evident that the spirit of Christ was a celestial bounty which descended from heaven, and that whosoever receives the outpourings of this spirit—that is, embraces its heavenly teachings—will attain everlasting life. Thus it is said in verse 35: "And Jesus said unto them, I am the bread of life: he that cometh to Me shall never hunger; and he that believeth on Me shall never thirst."

6   Observe that He expresses "coming to Him" as eating, and "believing in Him" as drinking. It is therefore clearly established that the heavenly sustenance consists in the divine bounties, spiritual splendours, heavenly teachings, and all-embracing truths of Christ, and that to eat means to draw nigh unto Him and to drink means to believe in Him. For Christ had both an elemental and a heavenly body. The elemental body was crucified, but the heavenly one is alive, eternal, and the source of everlasting life. The elemental body was His human nature and the heavenly body His divine nature. Gracious God! Some imagine that the bread

of the Eucharist is the reality of Christ, and that the Divinity and the Holy Spirit have descended into it and are present therein, whereas when once the Eucharist is taken, in a few minutes it is wholly disintegrated and entirely transformed. How then can such an error be conceived? I beg the forgiveness of God for such a grave delusion!

The purport of these words is that, through the manifestation of Christ, the sacred teachings, which are everlasting grace, were spread abroad, the lights of guidance shone forth, and the spirit of life was conferred upon human realities. Whosoever was guided aright found life, and whosoever remained astray was overtaken by everlasting death. That bread which came down from heaven was the celestial body of Christ and His spiritual elements, of which the disciples ate and through which they attained everlasting life. 7

The disciples had taken many meals from the hand of Christ; why then did the last supper come to be distinguished? It is thus evident that by the heavenly bread is meant not this material bread but the divine sustenance of the spiritual body of Christ, that is, the divine grace and the heavenly perfections of which His disciples partook and with which they were filled. 8

Consider likewise that when Christ blessed the bread and gave it to His disciples, saying, "this is My body",[82] He was visibly and distinctly present with them in person and in body, and was not transformed into bread and wine. Had He become the bread and wine itself, He could not have remained distinctly present before them in body and in person. 9

10   It is therefore clear that the bread and wine were symbols, meaning: My grace and My perfections have been given you, and since you have partaken of this manifold grace, you have attained everlasting life and received your share and portion of the heavenly sustenance.

22

THE MIRACLES OF CHRIST

QUESTION: CERTAIN MIRACLES have been attributed
to Christ. Should these accounts be taken literally or
do they have other meanings? For it has been established
through sound investigation that the inherent nature of
each thing does not change, that all created things are subject to a universal law and organization from which they
cannot deviate, and that hence nothing can possibly violate
that universal law.

Answer: The Manifestations of God are sources of miraculous deeds and marvellous signs. Any difficult or impossible
matter is to Them possible and permitted. For They show
forth extraordinary feats through an extraordinary power,
and They influence the world of nature through a power
that transcends nature. From each one of Them, marvellous
things have appeared.

But in the Sacred Scriptures a special terminology is used,
and in the sight of the Manifestations of God these marvels
and miracles are of no importance, so much so that They
do not even wish them to be mentioned. For even if these
miracles were considered the greatest of proofs, they would
constitute a clear evidence only for those who were present
when they took place, not for those who were absent.

4   For example, were a non-believing seeker to be told of the miracles of Moses and Christ, he would deny them and say: "Miracles have also long been ascribed to certain idols by the testimony of a multitude and recorded in books. Thus the Brahmans have compiled an entire book regarding the miracles of Brahma." The seeker would then ask: "How can we know that the Jews and the Christians speak the truth and that the Brahmans lie? For both are traditions, both are widely attested, and both have been recorded in a book. Each can be viewed as plausible or implausible, as with every other account: If one is true, both must be true; if one is accepted, both must be accepted." Therefore, miracles cannot be a conclusive proof, for even if they are valid proofs for those who were present, they fail to convince those who were not.

5   However, in the day of God's Manifestation, they that are endued with insight will find all things pertaining to Him to be miraculous. For these things are distinguished above all else, and this distinction is in itself an absolute miracle. Consider how Christ, alone and single-handed, with no helper or protector, with no legions or armies, and with the utmost meekness, raised aloft the banner of God before all the peoples of the world; how He withstood them; and how at last He subdued them all, even though outwardly He was crucified. Now, this is an absolute miracle which can in no wise be denied. Indeed, the truth of Christ stands in no need of further proof.

6   These outward miracles are of no importance to the followers of truth. For example, if a blind man is made to see,

in the end he will again lose his sight, for he will die and be deprived of all his senses and faculties. Thus, causing the blind to see is of no lasting importance, since the faculty of sight is bound to be lost again in the end. And if a dead body be revived, what is gained thereby, since it must die again? What is important is to bestow true insight and everlasting life, that is, a spiritual and divine life; for this material life will not endure and its existence is tantamount to non-existence. Even as Christ said in reply to one of His disciples: "let the dead bury their dead"; for "That which is born of the flesh is flesh; and that which is born of the Spirit is spirit."[83]

Consider that Christ reckoned as dead those who were 7 nonetheless outwardly and physically alive; for true life is life eternal and true existence is spiritual existence. Thus if the Sacred Scriptures speak of raising the dead, the meaning is that they attained everlasting life; if they say that one who was blind was made to see, the meaning of this seeing is true insight; if they say that one who was deaf was made to hear, the meaning is that he acquired an inner ear and attained spiritual hearing. This is established by the very text of the Gospel where Christ says that they are like those of whom Isaiah once said, They have eyes and see not, they have ears and hear not; and I heal them.[84]

Our meaning is not that the Manifestations of God are 8 unable to perform miracles, for this indeed lies within Their power. But that which is of import and consequence in Their eyes is inner sight, spiritual hearing, and eternal life. Thus, wherever it is recorded in the Sacred Scriptures that such a one was blind and was made to see, the meaning is that he was inwardly blind and gained spiritual insight, or that he was ignorant and found knowledge, or was heedless and became aware, or was earthly and became heavenly.

9   As this inner sight, hearing, life, and healing are eternal, so are they truly important. Otherwise, what importance, worth, and value can mere animal life and powers possess? Even as an idle fancy, in a few days it will pass. For instance, if an unlit lamp is lighted, it will be extinguished again, but the light of the sun always shines resplendent, and this is what is important.

23

THE RESURRECTION OF CHRIST

Q UESTION: WHAT IS the meaning of Christ's resur- 1
rection after three days?

Answer: The resurrection of the Manifestations of God 2
is not of the body. All that pertains to Them—all Their
states and conditions, all that They do, found, teach, interpret, illustrate, and instruct—is of a mystical and spiritual
character and does not belong to the realm of materiality.

Such is the case of Christ's coming from heaven. It has 3
been explicitly stated in numerous passages of the Gospel
that the Son of man came down from heaven, or is in
heaven, or will go up to heaven. Thus in John 6:38 it is
said: "For I came down from heaven", and in John 6:42 it is
recorded: "And they said, Is not this Jesus, the son of Joseph,
whose father and mother we know? how is it then that he
saith, I came down from heaven?", and in John 3:13 it is
stated: "And no man hath ascended up to heaven, but He
that came down from heaven, even the Son of man which
is in heaven."

Consider how it is said that the Son of man is in heaven, 4
even though at that time Christ was dwelling upon the
earth. Consider likewise that it explicitly says that Christ
came from heaven, although He came from the womb of

Mary and His body was born of her. It is therefore clear that the assertion that the Son of man came down from heaven has a mystical rather than a literal meaning, and is a spiritual rather than a material event. The meaning is that though in appearance Christ was born of the womb of Mary, yet in reality He came from heaven, the seat of the Sun of Truth that shines in the divine realm of the supernal Kingdom. And since it is established that Christ came from the spiritual heaven of the divine Kingdom, His disappearance into the earth for three days must also have a mystical rather than a literal meaning. In the same manner, His resurrection from the bosom of the earth is a mystical matter and expresses a spiritual rather than a material condition. And His ascension to heaven, likewise, is spiritual and not material in nature.

5 Aside from this, it has been established by science that the material heaven is a limitless space, void and empty, wherein countless stars and planets move.

6 We explain, therefore, the meaning of Christ's resurrection in the following way: After the martyrdom of Christ, the Apostles were perplexed and dismayed. The reality of Christ, which consists in His teachings, His bounties, His perfections, and His spiritual power, was hidden and concealed for two or three days after His martyrdom, and had no outward appearance or manifestation—indeed, it was as though it were entirely lost. For those who truly believed were few in number, and even those few were perplexed and dismayed. The Cause of Christ was thus as a lifeless body. After three days the Apostles became firm and steadfast, arose to aid the Cause of Christ, resolved to promote the

divine teachings and practise their Lord's admonitions, and endeavoured to serve Him. Then did the reality of Christ become resplendent, His grace shine forth, His religion find new life, and His teachings and admonitions become manifest and visible. In other words, the Cause of Christ, which was like unto a lifeless body, was quickened to life and surrounded by the grace of the Holy Spirit.

Such is the meaning of the resurrection of Christ, and 7 this was a true resurrection. But as the clergy did not grasp the meaning of the Gospels and did not comprehend this mystery, it has been claimed that religion is opposed to science, for among other things the ascension of Christ in a physical body to the material heavens is contrary to the mathematical sciences. But when the truth of this matter is clarified and this symbol is explained, it is in no way contradicted by science but rather affirmed by both science and reason.

24

THE DESCENT OF THE HOLY SPIRIT
UPON THE APOSTLES

1 QUESTION: IT IS recorded in the Gospels that the Holy Spirit descended upon the Apostles. What was the manner and meaning of this descent?

2 Answer: The descent of the Holy Spirit is not like the entrance of air into the human body. It is a metaphor and an analogy rather than a literal image or account. That which is intended is like the descent of the sun into a mirror, that is, when its splendour is reflected therein.

3 After the death of Christ, the Apostles were troubled and diverged in their thoughts and opinions; later they became steadfast and united. At Pentecost they gathered together, detached themselves from the world, forsook their own desires, renounced all earthly comfort and happiness, sacrificed body and soul to their Beloved, left their homes, took leave of all their cares and belongings, and even forgot their own existence. Then was divine assistance vouchsafed and the power of the Holy Spirit manifested. The spirituality of Christ triumphed, and the love of God took hold. On that day, they received divine confirmations, and each departed in a different direction to teach the Cause of God and unloosed his tongue to set forth the proofs and testimonies.

Thus the descent of the Holy Spirit means that the 4 Apostles were attracted by the messianic Spirit, attained constancy and steadfastness, found a new life through the spirit of God's love, and saw Christ to be their ever-living helper and protector. They were mere drops and became the ocean; they were feeble gnats and became soaring eagles; they were all weakness and became endowed with strength. They were like mirrors that are turned towards the sun: It is certain that the rays and the effulgence of the sun will be reflected therein.

25

THE HOLY SPIRIT

1 QUESTION: WHAT IS meant by "the Holy Spirit"?

2 Answer: By "the Holy Spirit" is meant the outpouring grace of God and the effulgent rays that emanate from His Manifestation. Thus Christ was the focal centre of the rays of the Sun of Truth, and from this mighty centre—the reality of Christ—the grace of God shone upon the other mirrors which were the realities of the Apostles.

3 The descent of the Holy Spirit upon the Apostles means that that glorious and divine grace cast its light and splendour upon their realities. For otherwise egress and regress, descent and inherence are characteristics of bodies and not of spirits—that is, egress and inherence pertain only to sensible realities, not to intelligible subtleties; and intelligible realities, such as reason, love, knowledge, imagination, and thought, do not enter, exit, or inhere, but rather denote relationships.

4 For example, knowledge, which is a form acquired by the mind, is an intelligible thing, and to speak of entering into the mind or exiting from it is absurd. Rather, it is a relationship of acquisition, even as images are reflected in a mirror.

Thus, as it is evident and established that intelligible realities do not enter or inhere, it follows that it is in no wise possible for the Holy Spirit to ascend, descend, enter, exit, commingle, or inhere. At most it appears as the sun appears in a mirror. 5

Moreover, in certain passages of the Sacred Scriptures where allusion is made to the Spirit, a specific person is intended, as it is conventionally said in speech and conversation that such-and-such a person is spirit personified, or is the embodiment of mercy and generosity. In this case the focus is not upon the lamp but upon the light. 6

For instance, in reference to the Promised One that must come after Christ, it is said in John 16:12: "I have yet many things to say unto you, but ye cannot bear them now. Howbeit when he, the Spirit of truth, is come, he will guide you into all truth: for he shall not speak of himself; but whatsoever he shall hear, that shall he speak." 7

Now consider carefully that the words "for he shall not speak of himself; but whatsoever he shall hear, that shall he speak" clearly imply that the Spirit of truth is embodied in a Man Who has a soul, Who has ears to hear and a tongue to speak. Likewise Christ is called the "Spirit of God", in the same way that we speak of the light and yet mean both the light and the lamp. 8

26

THE SECOND COMING OF CHRIST
AND THE DAY OF JUDGEMENT

1   IT IS RECORDED in the Sacred Scriptures that Christ will return and that His return is conditioned upon the fulfilment of certain signs: When He returns, He will be attended by those signs. Among them: "The sun shall be darkened, and the moon shall not give her light, and the stars shall fall from heaven." At that time "all the tribes of the earth" shall "mourn" and lament, and "the sign of the Son of man" shall appear "in heaven", "and they shall see the Son of man coming in the clouds of heaven with power and great glory".[85] Bahá'u'lláh has provided a detailed interpretation of these verses in the Kitáb-i-Íqán, and it need not be repeated here. Refer to it and you will grasp their meaning.[86]

2   Now, I would like in turn to say a further word on this subject, which is the following. The first coming of Christ was also from heaven, as has been explicitly stated in the Gospel. Even Christ Himself says that the Son of man came down from heaven, and the Son of man is in heaven; and no man hath ascended up to heaven but He that came down from heaven.[87] Thus it is admitted by all that Christ came down from heaven, whereas to outward seeming He came from the womb of Mary.

Now, just as He came the first time in appearance from the womb but in reality from heaven, so will He come the second time in appearance from the womb but in reality from heaven. The conditions that have been recorded in the Gospel for the second coming of Christ are indeed the same as had been specified for His first coming, as was explained before.

The Book of Isaiah announces that the Messiah will conquer the East and the West, that all the nations of the earth will gather under His shadow, that His kingdom will be established, that He will come from an unknown place, that the sinners will be judged, and that justice will prevail to such a degree that the wolf and the lamb, the leopard and the kid, the sucking child and the asp will all gather at one spring, in one meadow, and in one abode. The first coming was also subject to these conditions, although none of them came to pass outwardly. Thus the Jews cavilled at Christ, and—God forbid!—called Him a monster,[88] regarded Him as the destroyer of the edifice of God and the breaker of the Sabbath and the Law, and sentenced Him to death. Now, each and every one of these conditions had an inner meaning, but the Jews failed to understand and were therefore veiled from recognizing Him.

The second coming of Christ follows a similar pattern. All the signs and conditions that have been indicated have inner meanings and are not to be taken literally. For otherwise it is said, among other things, that the stars will fall upon the earth. Yet the stars are endless and innumerable, and modern mathematicians have established and proven that the mass of the sun is approximately one and a half million times greater than that of the earth, and that each one of the fixed stars is a thousand times larger than the sun. If these stars were to fall upon the surface of the earth, how could there be room for them? It would be as though a thousand million mountains as mighty as the Himalayas were to fall upon a grain of mustard seed. Such a thing is, by reason and by science (and indeed as a matter of simple common sense), utterly impossible. And yet even more astonishing is that Christ said: Perchance I shall come when you are sleeping, for the coming of the Son of man is like the coming of a thief.[89] Perhaps the thief will be in the house and the owner will be unaware.

6   It is therefore clear and evident that these signs have inner meanings and should not be taken literally. These meanings have been fully explained in the Kitáb-i-Íqán: Refer to it.

27

THE TRINITY

QUESTION: WHAT IS the meaning of the Trinity and of its three Persons?

Answer: The reality of the Divinity is sanctified and exalted beyond the comprehension of all created things, can in no wise be imagined by mortal mind and understanding, and transcends all human conception. That reality admits of no division, for division and multiplicity are among the characteristics of created and hence contingent things, and not accidents impinging upon the Necessary Being.

The reality of the Divinity is sanctified above singleness, then how much more above plurality. For that divine reality to descend into stations and degrees would be tantamount to deficiency, contrary to perfection, and utterly impossible. It has ever been, and will ever remain, in the loftiest heights of sanctity and purity. All that is mentioned regarding the manifestation and revelation of God pertains to the effulgence of His light and not to a descent into the degrees of existence.

God is pure perfection and the creation is absolute imperfection. For God to descend into the degrees of existence would be the greatest of imperfections; rather, His manifestation, dawning, and effulgence are even as the appearance of the sun in a clear, bright, and polished mirror.

5   All created things are resplendent signs of God. For instance, the rays of the sun shine upon all earthly things, yet the light that falls upon the plains, the mountains, the trees and fruits is only in such measure as to make them visible, to ensure their growth, and to cause them to attain the object of their existence. The Perfect Man, however, is even as a clear mirror in which the Sun of Truth is revealed and manifested in the fullness of its attributes and perfections. Thus the reality of Christ was a bright and polished mirror of the greatest purity and clarity. The Sun of Truth, the Essence of the Divinity, appeared in that mirror and manifested its light and heat therein, yet it did not descend from the heights of holiness and the heaven of sanctity to reside within it. No, it continues to abide in its loftiness and sublimity, but has been revealed and manifested in the mirror in all its beauty and perfection.

6   Now, if we were to say that we have beheld the Sun in two mirrors—one Christ and the other the Holy Spirit—or, in other words, that we have seen three Suns—one in heaven and two upon the earth—we would be speaking the truth. And if we were to say that there is only one Sun, that it is absolute singleness, and that it has no peer or partner, we would again be speaking the truth.

7   The purport of our words is that the reality of Christ was a clear mirror wherein the Sun of Truth—that is, the divine Essence—appeared and shone forth with infinite perfections and attributes. It is not that the Sun, which is the

Essence of the Divinity, was ever divided or multiplied—for it remains one—but it became manifest in the mirror. That is why Christ said, "The Father is in the Son", meaning that that Sun is manifest and visible in this mirror.

The Holy Spirit is the outpouring grace of God which was revealed and manifested in the reality of Christ. Prophethood is the station of the heart of Christ, and the Holy Spirit is the station of His spirit. It is thus evident and established that the Essence of the Divinity is absolute oneness and has no peer, equal, or likeness. 8

This is the true meaning of the three Persons of the Trinity. Otherwise, the foundations of the religion of God would rest upon an illogical proposition which no mind could ever conceive, and how could the mind be required to believe a thing which it cannot conceive? Such a thing could not be grasped by human reason—how much less be clothed in an intelligible form—but would remain sheer fancy. 9

Now, this explanation clarifies the meaning of the three Persons of the Trinity and establishes at the same time the oneness of God. 10

28

THE PRE-EXISTENCE OF CHRIST

1   QUESTION: WHAT IS the meaning of the verse in the Gospel of John: "And now, O Father, glorify thou me with Thine own self with the glory which I had with Thee before the world was."[90]

2   Answer: Pre-existence is of two kinds. One is essential pre-existence, which is not preceded by a cause but which exists in itself. For example, the sun shines in itself and does not depend on the radiance of the other stars for its light. This is called essential light. But the light of the moon is derived from the sun, for the moon is in need of the sun for its radiance. Thus, with respect to light, the sun is the cause and the moon the effect. The former is ancient, antecedent, and prior, while the latter is preceded by something else.

3   The second kind of pre-existence is temporal pre-existence, which has no beginning. The transcendent Word of God is sanctified beyond time. The past, the present, and the future are all equal in relation to God. Yesterday, today, and tomorrow do not exist in the sun.

4   There is likewise precedence with regard to honour and distinction; that is, the most distinctive precedes the distinctive. Thus the reality of Christ, Who is the Word of God, undoubtedly precedes all created things in essence, in

attributes, and in distinction. Before appearing in human form, the Word of God was in a state of utmost sanctity and glory, abiding in perfect beauty and splendour in the height of its majesty. When, through the wisdom of the Most High, that Word shed its light from the pinnacle of glory upon the corporeal world, it was assaulted through the flesh. Thus it fell into the hands of the Jews, became the captive of the ignorant and the unjust, and was at last crucified. That is why He called upon God, saying: Release Me from the bondage of the corporeal realm and deliver Me from this cage, that I may ascend to the heights of greatness and majesty, regain the former sanctity and glory which I enjoyed before inhabiting the world of the flesh, rejoice in the everlasting dominion, and wing My flight to My true abode, the placeless realm of the unseen Kingdom.

As you have observed, after His ascension the greatness 5 and glory of Christ was established both in the realm of the hearts and across the reaches of the earth, even unto the very dust itself. So long as He dwelt in the corporeal world, He was despised and reviled by the weakest nation on the earth, the Jews, who saw it fit that a crown of thorns be placed upon His blessed brow. But after His ascension the gem-studded crowns of all the kings became humble and submissive before that crown of thorns.

Behold the glory that the Word of God attained even in 6 this world!

29

SIN AND ATONEMENT

1 QUESTION: IN I Corinthians 15:22 it is written: "For as in Adam all die, even so in Christ shall all be made alive." What is the meaning of these words?

2 Answer: Know that there are two natures in man: the material and the spiritual. The material nature is inherited from Adam, while the spiritual nature is inherited from the reality of the Word of God, which is the spirituality of Christ. The material nature is born of Adam, but the spiritual nature is born of the grace of the Holy Spirit. The material nature is the source of every imperfection, and the spiritual nature is the source of all perfection.

3 Christ sacrificed Himself so that mankind might be freed from the imperfections of the material nature and endowed with the virtues of the spiritual nature. This spiritual nature, which has come to exist through the grace of the divine Reality, is the sum of all perfections and proceeds from the breath of the Holy Spirit. It is the divine perfections; it is light, spirituality, guidance, exaltation, high-mindedness, justice, love, generosity, kindness to all, and charitable deeds: It is life upon life. This spiritual nature is an effulgence of the splendours of the Sun of Truth.

4 Christ is the focal centre of the Holy Spirit; He is born

of the Holy Spirit; He has been raised up by the Holy Spirit; He descends from the Holy Spirit—that is, His Reality does not proceed from the lineage of Adam but is born of the Holy Spirit. The meaning of 1 Corinthians 15:22 where it says: "as in Adam all die, even so in Christ shall all be made alive" is therefore as follows: Adam is commonly referred to as the "father of man"; that is, He is the cause of the material life of mankind and holds the position of material fatherhood. He is a living, though not a life-giving, soul, whereas Christ is the cause of the spiritual life of man, and with regard to the spirit He holds the position of spiritual fatherhood. Adam is a living soul; Christ is a life-giving spirit.

In this material world, man is subject to the force of instinctual desires, of which sin is the inevitable consequence, for these desires are not bound by the laws of justice and righteousness. The body of man is a prisoner of nature and will act in accordance with whatsoever nature dictates. It follows that sins—such as wrathfulness, envy, contentiousness, greed, avarice, ignorance, rancour, corruption, pride, and cruelty—must exist in the material world. All these bestial attributes exist in the nature of man. A man who has been deprived of spiritual education is even as an animal, like those inhabitants of Africa whose actions, manners, and morals are purely instinctual and who act according to the dictates of nature, to the point of rending and eating one another. Thus it becomes evident that the material world of man is a world of sin, and that on this plane man is indistinguishable from the animal.

All sin is prompted by the dictates of nature. These

dictates of nature, which are among the hallmarks of corporeal existence, are not sins with respect to the animal but are sins with regard to man. The animal is the source of imperfections such as anger, lust, envy, greed, cruelty, and pride. All these blameworthy qualities are found in the nature of the animal, and do not constitute sins with regard to the animal, whereas they are sins with regard to man.

7   Adam is the cause of man's material life, but the reality of Christ, that is, the Word of God, is the cause of his spiritual life. It is a life-giving spirit, meaning that all the imperfections imposed by the material life of man are, through the instruction and guidance of that Essence of detachment, transmuted into human perfections. Therefore, Christ was a life-giving spirit and the cause of the spiritual life of all mankind.

8   Adam was the cause of material life, and since the material world of man is the realm of imperfections, and since imperfection is tantamount to death, Paul compared the former to the latter.

9   But the majority of the Christians believe that Adam sinned and transgressed by eating from the forbidden tree, that the dire and disastrous consequences of this transgression were inherited for all time by His descendants, and that Adam has thus become the cause of the death of man. This explanation is irrational and clearly mistaken, for it implies that all men, even the Prophets and Messengers of God, through no fault or sin of their own, and for no other reason than their descent from Adam, became guilty sinners and suffered the torments of hell until the day of Christ's

sacrifice. This would be far from the justice of God. If Adam was a sinner, what was the sin of Abraham? What was the fault of Isaac and of Joseph? What was the transgression of Moses?

But Christ, Who was the Word of God, sacrificed Him- 10 self. This has two meanings—an outward meaning and a true meaning. The outward meaning is this: Since Christ intended to promote a Cause that entailed the education of the human race, the quickening of the children of men, and the enlightenment of all humanity, and since promoting such a mighty Cause—a Cause that would antagonize all the peoples of the earth and withstand the opposition of every nation and government—was bound to bring about the spilling of His blood and to lead to His crucifixion and death, therefore at the moment He revealed His mission He offered up His life, welcomed the cross as His throne, regarded every wound as a balm and every poison as sweetest honey, and arose to instruct and guide the people. That is, He sacrificed Himself that He might bestow the spirit of life, and perished in body that He might quicken others in spirit.

However, the second meaning of sacrifice is this: Christ 11 was like a seed, and this seed sacrificed its form so that the tree might grow and develop. Although the form of the seed was destroyed, its reality manifested itself, in perfect majesty and beauty, in the outward form of the tree.

The station of Christ was that of absolute perfection. 12 Those divine perfections shone even as the sun upon all believing souls, and the outpourings of that light became manifest and resplendent in their realities. That is why He says: "I am the bread which came down from heaven; whosoever shall eat of this bread will not die";[91] that is, whosoever partakes of this divine sustenance will gain eternal life. Thus, whoever partook of this grace and acquired a share of these perfections found eternal life, and whoever sought illumination from His ancient grace was delivered from the darkness of error and illumined by the light of guidance.

13   The form of the seed was sacrificed for the tree, but its perfections were revealed and manifested by virtue of this sacrifice: For the tree, its branches, its leaves, and its blossoms were latent and hidden within the seed, but when the form of the seed was sacrificed, its perfections were fully manifested in the leaves, blossoms, and fruit.

30

ADAM AND EVE

QUESTION: WHAT IS the truth of the story of Adam [1] and His eating from the tree?

Answer: It is recorded in the Torah that God placed [2] Adam in the Garden of Eden to work and tend it, and said to Him: "Eat freely of every tree of the garden, save for the tree of good and evil, for if thou wert to eat thereof thou wouldst surely die."[92] Then it is said that God caused Adam to sleep, took a bone from His ribs, and created a woman to be His companion. Further on it is said that the serpent tempted the woman to eat of the tree, saying: "God has forbidden you to eat from the tree, that your eyes may not be opened and that you may not discern good from evil."[93] Then Eve ate from the tree and gave unto Adam, who also ate. Whereupon their eyes were opened, they found themselves naked, and they covered their nakedness with leaves. God then reproached them, saying to Adam: "Hast Thou eaten of the forbidden tree?" Adam answered: "Eve tempted Me." God then reproved Eve, who said: "The serpent tempted me." For this the serpent was cursed, and enmity was established between the serpent and Eve and between their descendants. And God said: "The man is become like unto Us, knowing good and evil. Perhaps He will eat of the tree of life and live forever." So God guarded the tree of life.[94]

3   If we were to take this account according to the literal meaning of the words as indicated by their common usage, it would indeed be exceedingly strange, and human minds would be excused from accepting, affirming, or imagining it. For such elaborate arrangements and details, such statements and reproaches would be implausible even coming from an intelligent person, let alone from the Divinity Himself, Who has arranged this infinite universe in the most perfect form and arrayed its countless beings in the utmost order, soundness, and perfection.

4   One must pause awhile to reflect: If the outward meaning of this account were to be attributed to a wise man, all men of wisdom would assuredly deny it, arguing that such a scheme and arrangement could not possibly have proceeded from such a person. The account of Adam and Eve, their eating from the tree, and their expulsion from Paradise are therefore symbols and divine mysteries. They have all-embracing meanings and marvellous interpretations, but only the intimates of the divine mysteries and the well-favoured of the all-sufficing Lord are aware of the true significance of these symbols.

5   These verses of the Torah have therefore numerous meanings. We will explain one of them and will say that by "Adam" is meant the spirit of Adam and by "Eve" is meant His self. For in certain passages of the Sacred Scriptures where women are mentioned, the intended meaning is the human self. By "the tree of good and evil" is meant the

material world, for the heavenly realm of the spirit is pure goodness and absolute radiance, but in the material world light and darkness, good and evil, and all manner of opposing realities are to be found.

The meaning of the serpent is attachment to the material world. This attachment of the spirit to the material world led to the banishment of the self and spirit of Adam from the realm of freedom to the world of bondage and caused Him to turn from the kingdom of Divine Unity to the world of human existence. When once the self and spirit of Adam entered the material world, He departed from the paradise of freedom and descended into the realm of bondage. He had abided in the heights of sanctity and absolute goodness, and set foot thereafter in the world of good and evil.

By "the tree of life" is meant the highest degree of the world of existence, that is, the station of the Word of God and His universal Manifestation. That station was indeed well guarded, until it appeared and shone forth in the supreme revelation of His universal Manifestation. For the station of Adam, with regard to the appearance and manifestation of the divine perfections, was that of the embryo; the station of Christ was that of coming of age and maturation; and the dawning of the Most Great Luminary[95] was the station of the perfection of the essence and the attributes. That is why in the all-highest Paradise the tree of life alludes to the focal centre of absolute sanctity and purity, that is, the universal Manifestation of God. For from the days of Adam until the time of Christ there was little mention of life eternal and of the all-embracing perfections of the Kingdom on high. This tree of life alludes to the station of the reality of Christ: It was planted in His Dispensation and adorned with everlasting fruits.

8   Now consider how closely this interpretation conforms to reality: For when the spirit and the self of Adam became attached to the material world, they passed from the realm of freedom into the realm of bondage; this condition was perpetuated with each succeeding generation, and this attachment of spirit and self to the material world—which is sin—was inherited by His descendants. This attachment is the serpent which will forever be in the midst of, and at enmity with, the spirits of the descendants of Adam, for attachment to the world has become the cause of the bondage of the spirits. This bondage is that sin which has been transmitted from Adam to His descendants, for it has deprived men of recognizing their essential spirituality and attaining to exalted stations.

9   When the holy breaths of Christ and the sanctified lights of the Most Great Luminary were spread abroad, human realities—that is, those souls who turned towards the Word of God and partook of His manifold grace—were saved from this attachment and sin, were granted eternal life, were delivered from the chains of bondage, and entered the realm of freedom. They were purged of earthly vices and endowed with heavenly virtues. This is the meaning of Christ's words that I gave My blood for the life of the world.[96] That is, I chose to bear all these trials, afflictions, and calamities, even the most great martyrdom, to attain this ultimate objective

and to ensure the remission of sins—that is, the detachment of spirits from the material world and their attraction to the divine realm—that souls may arise who will be the very essence of guidance and the manifestations of the perfections of the Kingdom on high.

Note that if these words were taken literally, as imagined by the people of the Book,[97] it would be sheer injustice and absolute predestination. If Adam sinned in approaching the forbidden tree, what then was the sin of glorious Abraham, the Friend of God, and the error of Moses, Who conversed with God? What was the offence of Noah the Prophet and the transgression of truth-speaking Joseph? What was the fault of the Prophets of God and the failure of John the Chaste? Would divine justice have suffered these luminous Manifestations to endure, by reason of Adam's sin, the torment of hell until such time as Christ should come and by His sacrifice rescue them from the nethermost fire? Such a notion is beyond the pale of every rule and principle, and no rational person can ever accept it. 10

Rather, the meaning is that which was already mentioned: Adam is the spirit of Adam and Eve His self; the tree is the material world and the serpent is attachment to it. This attachment, which is sin, has been transmitted to the descendants of Adam. Through the breaths of holiness, Christ rescued souls from this attachment and delivered them from this sin. 11

This sin in Adam, moreover, is relative to His station: Although this worldly attachment produced substantial results, yet in relation to attachment to the spiritual realm 12 it is nonetheless regarded as a sin, and the truth of the saying, "The good deeds of the righteous are the sins of the near ones" is established. Again, it is like the power of the body, which is imperfect in relation to the power of the spirit—indeed, it is sheer weakness in comparison. Likewise, material life, compared to eternal existence and the life of the Kingdom, is regarded as death. Thus Christ referred to this material life as death and said, "let the dead bury their dead".[98] Although those souls enjoyed material life, yet in His eyes that life was even as death.

13   This is but one of the meanings of the biblical account of Adam. Reflect, that you may discover the others.

31

BLASPHEMY AGAINST THE HOLY SPIRIT

QUESTION: "ALL MANNER of sin and blasphemy shall [1] be forgiven unto men: but the blasphemy against the Holy Ghost shall not be forgiven unto men. And whosoever speaketh a word against the Son of man, it shall be forgiven him: but whosoever speaketh against the Holy Ghost, it shall not be forgiven him, neither in this world, neither in the world to come."[99]

Answer: The sanctified realities of the Manifestations of [2] God have two spiritual stations: One is that of the state of divine manifestation, which can be compared to the orb of the sun, and the other is that of radiance and revelation, which may be likened to the divine light and perfections—the Holy Spirit. For the Holy Spirit is the manifold grace and perfections of God, and these divine perfections are even as the rays and heat of the sun. Now, the sun is the sun by virtue of its effulgent rays; without these rays it would not be the sun. If the perfections of God were not revealed and manifested in Jesus, He would not be Christ. He is a Manifestation of God precisely because the divine perfections are revealed in Him. The Prophets of God are Manifestations, and the divine perfections—that is, the Holy Spirit—are that which is manifested in Them.

3   If a soul distances himself from the Manifestation, he may yet be awakened, for he may have failed to know Him and to recognize Him as the Embodiment of the divine perfections. But if he loathes the divine perfections themselves, which are the Holy Spirit, this shows that, bat-like, he is a hater of the light.

4   This hatred of the light itself is irremediable and unforgivable; that is, it is impossible for such a soul to draw near to God. This lamp here is a lamp because of its light; without the light it would not be a lamp. A soul that abhors the light of the lamp is, as it were, blind and cannot perceive the light, and this blindness is the cause of eternal deprivation.

5   It is evident that souls receive grace from the outpourings of the Holy Spirit which are apparent in the Manifestations of God, and not from the individual personality of the Manifestation. It follows that if a soul fails to partake of the outpourings of the Holy Spirit, it remains deprived of God's grace, and this deprivation itself is equivalent to the denial of divine forgiveness.

6   That is why there have been many souls who opposed the Manifestations of God, not realizing that They were Manifestations, but who became Their friends once they had recognized Them. Thus, enmity towards the Manifestation of God was not the cause of eternal deprivation, for they were enemies of the candleholder and knew not that it was the seat of God's effulgent light. They were not the enemies of the light itself, and once they understood that the candleholder was the seat of the light, they became true friends.

Our meaning is that remoteness from the candleholder 7 is not the cause of eternal deprivation, for one may yet be awakened and guided aright, but that enmity towards the light itself is the cause of eternal deprivation and has no remedy.

32

"MANY ARE CALLED,
BUT FEW ARE CHOSEN"

1   QUESTION: CHRIST SAYS in the Gospel: "many are called, but few are chosen",[100] and in the Qur'án it is written: "He singleth out for His mercy whomsoever He pleaseth."[101] What is the wisdom of this?

2   Answer: Know that the order and perfection of the universe require that existence should appear in countless forms. Created things cannot therefore be realized in a single degree, station, manner, kind, or species: Differences of degree, distinctions in form, and a multiplicity of kinds and species are inevitable. So there must necessarily be mineral, vegetable, animal, and human kingdoms; for through man alone the world of existence could not be adequately arranged, adorned, organized, and perfected. By the same token, with the animals, plants, or minerals alone, this world would not possess such a wondrous appearance, sound arrangement, and subtle adornment: There must be differences of degrees and stations, of kinds and species, for existence to shine forth with the utmost perfection.

3   For example, if this tree were to become entirely fruit, the perfections of the vegetable kingdom could not be

attained, for leaves, blossoms, and fruit are all needed for the tree to appear in the utmost beauty and perfection.

Consider likewise the body of man, which must of necessity be composed of different parts, limbs, and organs. 4 The beauty and perfection of the human body require the existence of the ear, the eye, the brain, and even the nails and hair: If man were all brain, eyes, or ears, this would be tantamount to imperfection. So the absence of hair, eyelashes, teeth, and nails is imperfection itself, for even though in comparison with the eyes the latter are insentient and resemble the mineral and the plant, yet their absence in the body of man is most disagreeable and displeasing.

Now, so long as the degrees of created things are differ-ent, some will naturally rank above the others. Thus, since 5 the election of certain creatures, such as man, for the high-est degree; the maintenance of others, such as plants, in the middle degree; and the relegation of yet others, such as min-erals, to the lowest degree are each and all due to the divine will and purpose, it follows that the singling out of man for the highest degree is through the grace of God, and that the differences among men with regard to spiritual attainments and heavenly perfections are likewise due to the choice of the All-Merciful. For faith, which is life eternal, is a token of grace and not the result of justice. The flame of the fire of love, in this world of earth and water, burns by the power of attraction and not through human effort and striving, although through the latter one may indeed acquire knowl-edge, learning, and other perfections. It is the light of the divine Beauty, then, that must stir up and move the spirit through its attractive power. Wherefore is it said: "many are called, but few are chosen".[102]

6 As for material beings, they are not to be blamed, judged, or held accountable for their own degrees and stations. Thus the mineral, the plant, and the animal are each acceptable in their own degree, but if they were to remain deficient in that degree they would be blameworthy, the degree itself being wholly perfect.

7 Now, the differences among mankind are twofold: One is a difference of degree, and this difference is not blameworthy. The other is a difference with respect to faith and certitude, the absence of which is blameworthy; for the soul must have fallen prey to its own lusts and passions to have been deprived of this bounty and bereft of the attractive power of the love of God. However praiseworthy and acceptable it may be in its human degree, yet as it is deprived of the perfections of that degree, it has become a source of deficiency and is held accountable for that reason.

33

THE RETURN OF THE PROPHETS

QUESTION: WILL YOU explain the subject of Return? Answer: Bahá'u'lláh has set forth a lengthy and detailed explanation of this matter in the Kitáb-i-Íqán.[103] Read it, and the truth of this matter will become clear and manifest. But since you have raised the question, a brief explanation will also be provided here.

We will preface our remarks with the text of the Gospel. It is recorded therein that when John the son of Zacharias appeared and announced unto the people the advent of the Kingdom of God, they asked him, "Who art thou? Art thou the promised Messiah?" He replied, "I am not the Messiah." They then asked him, "Art thou Elias?" He replied, "I am not."[104] These words clearly establish that John the son of Zacharias was not the promised Elias.

But on the day of the transfiguration on Mount Tabor, Christ explicitly said that John the son of Zacharias was the promised Elias. In Mark 9:11 it is said: "And they asked Him, saying, Why say the scribes that Elias must first come? And He answered and told them, Elias verily cometh first, and restoreth all things; and how it is written of the Son of man, that He must suffer many things, and be set at naught. But I say unto you, That Elias is indeed come, and they have done unto him whatsoever they listed, as it is written of him." And in Matthew 17:13 it is said: "Then the disciples understood that He spake unto them of John the Baptist."

5   Now, they asked John the Baptist, "Art thou Elias?" and he answered, "I am not", whereas it is said in the Gospel that John was the promised Elias himself, and Christ clearly stated this as well. If John was Elias, why did he say he was not, and if he was not Elias, why did Christ say he was?

6   The reason is that we consider here not the individuality of the person but the reality of his perfections—that is to say, the very same perfections that Elias possessed were realized in John the Baptist as well. Thus John the Baptist was the promised Elias. What is being considered here is not the essence[105] but the attributes.

7   For example, last year there was a flower, and this year there has also appeared a flower. When I say that the flower of last year has returned, I do not mean that the same flower has returned with the selfsame identity. But since this flower is endowed with the same attributes as last year's flower—as it possesses the same fragrance, delicacy, colour, and form—it is said that last year's flower has returned, and that this is that same flower. Likewise, when spring comes we say that last year's spring has returned, since all that was found in the former is to be found again in the latter. This is why Christ said, "Ye will witness all that came to pass in the days of the former Prophets."[106]

8   Let us give another illustration: Last year's seed was sown, branches and leaves appeared, blossoms and fruit came forth, and in the end a new seed was produced. When this second

seed is planted, it will grow into a tree, and once more those leaves, blossoms, branches, and fruit will return, and the former tree will once again appear. As the beginning was a seed and the end likewise a seed, we say that the seed has returned. When we consider the material substance of the tree, it is different, but when we consider the blossoms, leaves, and fruit, the same fragrance, taste, and delicacy are produced. Hence the perfection of the tree has returned anew.

In the same way, if we consider the individual, it is a different one, but if we consider the attributes and perfections, the same have returned. Thus when Christ said, "This is Elias", He meant: This person is a manifestation of the grace, the perfections, the qualities, the attributes, and the virtues of Elias. And when John the Baptist said, "I am not Elias", he meant, "I am not the same person as Elias." Christ considered their attributes, perfections, qualities, and virtues, and John referred to his own substance and individuality. It is like this lamp: It was here last night, tonight it is lit again, and tomorrow night it will shine as well. When we say that tonight's lamp is the same as last night's and that it has returned, we mean the light and not the oil, the wick, or the holder. 9

These considerations have been explained at length in the Kitáb-i-Íqán. 10

34

PETER AND THE PAPACY

1 QUESTION: IN THE Gospel of Matthew Christ says to Peter: "thou art Peter, and upon this rock I will build My church".[107] What is the meaning of this verse?

2 Answer: This utterance of Christ is an affirmation of Peter's reply, when Christ asked: "Whom do ye believe Me to be?" and Peter answered: "I believe that Thou art the Son of the living God." Then Christ said to him: "thou art Peter"[108]—since "Cephas" in Aramaic means "rock"—"and upon this rock I will build my church". For others, in answer to Christ, had said that He was Elias, or John the Baptist, or Jeremiah, or one of the Prophets.[109]

3 Christ meant, through metaphor and allusion, to affirm the words of Peter. And so, since the latter's name meant "rock", He said: "thou art Peter, and upon this rock I will build my church". That is, your belief that Christ is the Son of the living God will become the foundation of the religion of God, and upon this belief the foundation of the church of God—which is the Law of God—shall be established.

4 As to the existence of Peter's tomb in Rome, it is doubtful and disputed; some say that it is in Antioch.

5 Moreover, let us measure the deeds of certain popes against the religion of Christ. Christ, hungry and destitute,

subsisted on the herbs of the wilderness and would not consent to see any heart saddened. The pope rides in a gilded carriage and passes his days in the utmost majesty, occupied with such pleasures and pursuits as to surpass the opulence and self-indulgence of all the kings of the earth.

Christ did not harm anyone, but certain popes put many 6 innocent souls to death. Refer to the history books. How much blood have the popes spilled merely to secure their temporal authority! How many thousands of servants of humanity, among them learned men who had discovered the mysteries of the universe, have they tortured, imprisoned, and slain, all for mere differences of opinion! How vehemently have they opposed the truth!

Consider the admonitions of Christ and investigate the 7 customs and conduct of the popes: Is there any resemblance between the admonitions of the former and the administration of the latter? We do not like to find fault, but the pages of the history of the Vatican are indeed astounding. Our meaning is that the instructions of Christ are one thing and the conduct of the papal government is quite another: They do not agree in the slightest. See how many Protestants have been slain by order of the popes, what wrongs and cruelties have been countenanced, what tortures and punishments have been inflicted! Can the sweet fragrances of Christ be at all inhaled from these actions? No, by the righteousness of God! Such people did not obey Christ, while Saint Barbara, whose portrait is before us, obeyed Him, walked in His path, and acted upon His admonitions.

8   Among the popes there have indeed been some blessed souls who followed in the footsteps of Christ, particularly in the early centuries of the Christian era when earthly means were lacking and heaven-sent trials were severe. But when the means of temporal sovereignty were secured, and worldly honour and prosperity were obtained, the papal government entirely forgot Christ and occupied itself with earthly dominion and grandeur, with material comforts and luxuries. It put people to death, opposed the diffusion of learning, persecuted men of science, obstructed the light of knowledge, and gave the order to slay and to pillage. Thousands of people, men of science and learning and innocent souls, perished in the prisons of Rome. With such ways and deeds, how can the claim of the vicarship of Christ be accepted?

9   The Holy See has consistently opposed the expansion of knowledge, to such a degree that in Europe it has come to be held that religion is the enemy of science and that science is the destroyer of the foundations of religion. Whereas the religion of God is the promoter of truth, the establisher of science and learning, the supporter of knowledge, the civilizer of the human race, the discoverer of the secrets of existence, and the enlightener of the horizons of the world. How then could it oppose knowledge? God forbid! On the contrary, in the sight of God knowledge is the greatest human virtue and the noblest human perfection. To oppose knowledge is pure ignorance, and he who abhors knowledge and learning is not a human being but a mindless animal. For knowledge is light, life, felicity, perfection,

and beauty, and causes the soul to draw nigh to the divine threshold. It is the honour and glory of the human realm and the greatest of God's bounties. Knowledge is identical to guidance, and ignorance is the essence of error.

Happy are those who spend their days in the pursuit of knowledge, in the discovery of the secrets of the universe, and in the meticulous investigation of truth! And woe to those who content themselves with ignorance, who delight in thoughtless imitation, who have fallen into the abyss of ignorance and unawareness, and who have thus wasted their lives! 10

35

FREE WILL AND PREDESTINATION

1 QUESTION: WHEN AN action which someone will perform becomes the object of God's knowledge and is
recorded in the "Guarded Tablet" of destiny, is it possible to
resist it?

2 Answer: The knowledge of a thing is not the cause of
its occurrence; for the essential knowledge of God encompasses the realities of all things both before and after they
come to exist, but it is not the cause of their existence. This
is an expression of the perfection of God.

3 As to the pronouncements which, through divine revelation, have issued from the Prophets regarding the advent
of the Promised One of the Torah, these likewise were not
the cause of Christ's appearance. But the hidden mysteries
of the days to come were revealed to the Prophets, who
thus became acquainted with future events and who proclaimed them in turn. This knowledge and proclamation
were not the cause of the occurrence of these events. For
instance, tonight everyone knows that in seven hours the
sun will rise, but this common knowledge does not cause
the appearance and rising of the sun.

4 Likewise, God's knowledge in the contingent world does
not produce the forms of things. Rather, that knowledge is

freed from the distinctions of past, present, and future, and is identical with the realization of all things without being the cause of that realization.

In the same way, the record and mention of a thing in 5 the Scriptures is not the cause of its existence. The Prophets of God were informed through divine revelation that certain events would come to pass. For instance, through divine revelation they came to know that Christ would be martyred, which they in turn proclaimed. Now, did their knowledge and awareness cause the martyrdom of Christ? No: This knowledge is a sign of their perfection and not the cause of His martyrdom.

Through astronomical calculations, the mathematicians 6 determine that at a certain time a solar or lunar eclipse will occur. Surely this prediction is not the cause of the eclipse. This of course is merely an analogy and not an exact image.

PART 3

On the Powers and Conditions of the Manifestations of God

36

THE FIVE KINDS OF SPIRIT

K NOW THAT IN general there are five kinds of spirit. 1
First is the vegetable spirit,[110] which is the power that
results from the composition and combination of the elements according to the wisdom and decree of the Most
High, and from their mutual arrangement as well as their
influence upon, and their interconnection with, other created things. When these parts and elements are separated,
the associated power of growth likewise ceases to exist. So,
to give an analogy, electricity results from the composition
of certain constituent parts, and as soon as these parts are
separated, the electrical force is immediately dissipated and
lost. Such is the vegetable spirit.

After this is the animal spirit, which also results from the 2
combination of elements that are brought together in a single composition. But this composition is more complete, and
when by the decree of the almighty Lord it reaches a fuller
degree of combination, the animal spirit, which consists in
the power of the senses, comes to exist. This power perceives
sensible realities—that which can be seen, heard, tasted,
smelled, or touched. After the separation and dissolution of
these composed elements, this spirit will also naturally cease
to exist. It is like this lamp before you: When oil, wick, and

flame are brought together, light is produced; but when the oil is exhausted, the wick consumed, and the constituent parts separated, the light will also be extinguished and lost.

3   As to the human spirit, its likeness is that of a glass and the bounty of the sun. That is, the body of man, which is composed of the elements, is the most perfect form of composition and combination, the soundest arrangement, the noblest composition, and the most perfect of all existing things. It grows and develops through the animal spirit. This perfect body can be compared to a mirror, and the human spirit to the sun: If the glass is shattered or the mirror destroyed, no harm befalls the outpouring grace of the sun, which continues unabated.

4   This spirit is the discovering power that encompasses all things. All the wondrous signs, all the crafts and discoveries, all the mighty undertakings and momentous historical events of which you are aware, have been discovered by this spirit and brought forth from the invisible realm into the visible plane through its spiritual power. Thus it abides upon the earth and yet makes discoveries in the heavens, and deduces that which is unknown from known and visible realities. For example, man is in this hemisphere, but through the power of reason he discovers, as Columbus did, another one—the Americas—which until then was unknown. His body is heavy, but he flies through the air by means of vehicles of his own devising. His movement is slow, but he journeys rapidly through East and West by the aid of the devices which he has fashioned. In short, this power encompasses all things.

But this human spirit has two aspects: one divine and 5 one satanic—that is, it is capable of both the greatest perfection and the greatest deficiency. Should it acquire virtues, it is the noblest of all things; and should it acquire vices, it becomes the most vile.

As to the fourth degree of spirit, it is the heavenly spirit, 6 which is the spirit of faith and the outpouring grace of the All-Merciful. This spirit proceeds from the breath of the Holy Spirit, and through a power born of God it becomes the cause of everlasting life. It is that power which makes the earthly soul heavenly and the imperfect man perfect. It cleanses the impure, unlooses the tongue of the silent, sanctifies the bondslaves of passion and desire, and confers knowledge upon the ignorant.

The fifth degree of spirit is the Holy Spirit, which is 7 the mediator between God and His creation. It is like a mirror facing the sun: Just as a spotless mirror receives the rays of the sun and reflects its bounty to others, so too is the Holy Spirit the mediator of the light of holiness, which it conveys from the Sun of Truth to sanctified souls. This Spirit is adorned with all the divine perfections. Whensoever it appears, the world is revived, a new cycle is ushered in, and the body of humanity is clothed in a fresh attire. It is like the spring: When it arrives, it transports the world from one condition to another. For at the advent of springtide the black earth, the fields, and the meadows become green and verdant; flowers and sweet-scented herbs of every kind spring forth; trees are endowed with a new life; wondrous fruits are produced; and a new cycle is inaugurated.

8   It is the same with the manifestation of the Holy Spirit: Whensoever it appears, it invests the world of humanity with a new life and endows human realities with a new spirit. It clothes all existence with a glorious attire, disperses the darkness of ignorance, and causes the light of human perfections to shine resplendent. It is with such a power that Christ renewed this cycle—whereupon the divine springtide pitched its tent, with utmost vitality and grace, in the realm of humanity and perfumed the senses of the enlightened souls with its life-giving breezes.

9   In the same way, the manifestation of Bahá'u'lláh was a new springtide which appeared with the sweet savours of holiness, with the hosts of everlasting life, and with a power born of the celestial kingdom. He established the throne of God's sovereignty in the midmost heart of the world and, through the power of the Holy Spirit, revived the souls and ushered in a new cycle.

37

THE CONNECTION BETWEEN GOD
AND HIS MANIFESTATIONS

Q UESTION: WHAT IS the reality of the Divinity and   1
its connection to the Daysprings of Lordly splendour
and the Dawning-Places of the light of the All-Merciful?

Answer: Know that the reality of the Divinity and the   2
nature of the divine Essence is ineffable sanctity and absolute holiness; that is, it is exalted above and sanctified beyond
every praise. All the attributes ascribed to the highest degrees
of existence are, with regard to this station, mere imagination. The Invisible and Inaccessible can never be known;
the absolute Essence can never be described. For the divine
Essence is an all-encompassing reality, and all created things
are encompassed. The all-encompassing must assuredly be
greater than that which is encompassed, and thus the latter can in no wise discover the former or comprehend its
reality. No matter how far human minds may advance, even
attaining the highest degree of human comprehension, the
uttermost limit of this comprehension is to behold the signs
and attributes of God in the world of creation and not in
the realm of Divinity. For the essence and the attributes
of the all-glorious Lord are enshrined in the inaccessible
heights of sanctity, and human minds and understandings

will never find a path to that station. "The way is barred, and all seeking rejected."¹¹¹

3   It is evident that whatsoever man understands is a consequence of his existence, and that man is a sign of the All-Merciful: How then can the consequence of the sign encompass the Creator of the sign? That is, how can human understanding, which is a consequence of man's existence, comprehend God? Thus the reality of the Divinity lies hidden from all understanding and is concealed from the minds of all men, and to ascend to that station is in no wise possible.

4   We observe that every lower thing is incapable of comprehending the reality of that which is higher. Thus, no matter how far they may evolve, the stone, the earth, and the tree can never comprehend the reality of man or imagine the powers of sight, hearing, or the other senses, even though the former and the latter alike are created things. How then can man, a mere creature, comprehend the reality of the sanctified Essence of the Creator? No human understanding can approach this station, no utterance can unfold its truth, and no allusion can intimate its mystery. What has the speck of dust to do with the world of sanctity, and what relationship can ever hold between the limited mind and the expanse of the limitless realm? Minds are powerless to comprehend Him, and souls are bewildered as they attempt to describe His reality. "No vision taketh in Him, but He taketh in all vision, and He is the Subtile, the All-Informed!"¹¹²

5   Thus, in this connection, every statement and explanation is deficient, every description and characterization

is unworthy, every conception is unfounded, and every attempt to contemplate its depths is futile. Yet for that Essence of essences, that Truth of truths, that Mystery of mysteries, there are splendours, effulgences, manifestations, and appearances in the world of existence. The Daysprings of those effulgences, the Dawning-places of those revelations, and the Sources of those manifestations are those Exponents of holiness, those universal Realities and divine Beings Who are the true mirrors of the sanctified Essence of the Divinity. All the perfections, bounties, and splendours of the one true God are plainly visible in the realities of His Holy Manifestations, even as the light of the sun is fully reflected with all its perfections and bounties in a clear and spotless mirror. And if it be said that the mirrors are the manifestations of the sun and the dawning-places of the daystar of the world, this is not meant to imply that the sun has descended from the heights of its sanctity or has become embodied in the mirror, or that that limitless Reality has been confined to this visible plane. God forbid! This is the belief of the anthropomorphists. No, all these descriptions, all these expressions of praise and glory, refer to these holy Manifestations; that is, every description, praise, name, or attribute of God that we mention applies to Them. But no soul has ever fathomed the reality of the Essence of the Divinity so as to be able to intimate, describe, praise, or glorify it. Thus all that the human reality knows, discovers, and understands of the names, attributes, and perfections of God refers to these holy Manifestations and leads nowhere else: "The way is cut off, and all seeking rejected."

6   Yet we ascribe certain names and attributes to the reality of the Divinity and praise Him for His sight, His hearing, His power, His life and knowledge. We affirm these names and attributes not to affirm the perfections of God, but to deny that He has any imperfections.

7   When we observe the contingent world, we see that ignorance is imperfection and knowledge is perfection, and thus we say that the sanctified Essence of the Divinity is all-knowing. Weakness is imperfection and power is perfection, and thus we say that that sanctified and divine Essence is all-powerful. It is not that we can understand His knowledge, His sight, His hearing, His power, or His life as they are in themselves: This is assuredly beyond our comprehension, for the essential names and attributes of God are identical with His Essence, and His Essence is sanctified above all understanding. If the essential attributes were not identical with the Essence, then there would be a multiplicity of pre-existences and the distinction between the Essence and the attributes would therefore also be firmly established and pre-existent. But this would imply an infinite chain of pre-existences, which is an evident error.

8   It follows that all these names, attributes, laudations, and praises apply to the Manifestations of God Themselves, and that all that we may construe or conceive besides them is sheer delusion, for we can never find a path to the Invisible and Inaccessible. Thus it is said: "All that ye vainly believe to have discerned and expressed in your subtlest terms is but a creature like unto you and returneth unto your own selves."[113]

It is evident that if we attempt to conceive the reality of the Divinity, that conception would be encompassed and our mind would be that which encompasses it—and assuredly that which encompasses is greater than that which is encompassed! Thus it follows that any reality that we might conceive for the Divinity besides that of the holy Manifestations would be mere delusion, as there is no means of approach to that divine Reality which is entirely beyond the reach of the mind. And all that we might conceive is pure imagination.

Consider then how the peoples of the world are circling round their own vain imaginings and worshipping the idols of their own thoughts and fancies, without the least awareness of doing so. They regard these vain imaginings as that Reality which is sanctified above all understanding and exalted beyond every allusion. They consider themselves to be the proponents of the Divine Unity and all others as worshippers of idols, even though idols at least enjoy a mineral existence, whereas the idols of human thoughts and imaginations are sheer illusion and have not even the existence of stones. "Take ye good heed, O people of insight!"[114]

Know that the attributes of perfection, the outpourings of divine grace, and the effulgences of divine revelation shine resplendent in all the Manifestations of God, but that the all-encompassing Word of God—Christ—and His Most Great Name—Bahá'u'lláh—have appeared with a revelation beyond all conception. For not only do They possess all the perfections of the former Manifestations, but They also evince beyond those such perfections as to make all others even as Their followers. Thus the Prophets of Israel were all recipients of divine revelation, and so too was Christ, but what a difference between the revelation of Him Who was the Word of God and the inspiration of an Isaiah, a Jeremiah, or an Elijah!

12   Consider that light consists in the vibrations of the ether, whereby the nerves of the eye are stimulated and vision is produced. Now, though the vibrations of the ether exist both in the lamp and in the sun, yet what a difference there is between the light of the sun and that of the stars or of the lamp!

13   The human spirit has certain signs and manifestations in the stage of the embryo, and yet other splendours and expressions in the stages of childhood, adolescence, and maturity. The spirit is one, and yet in the embryonic stage it lacks the powers of sight and hearing, whereas in the stages of adolescence and maturity it appears with the utmost splendour and radiance. In the same way, the seed at the beginning of its growth appears only as a leaf, which is the place of appearance of the vegetable spirit; and in the stage of fruition that same spirit, that is, the power of growth, becomes manifest in the plenitude of its perfection—yet how far is the station of the leaf from that of the fruit! For from the fruit a hundred thousand leaves will in time appear, even though they all grow and develop through the same vegetable spirit. Pause then to reflect upon the difference between the virtues and perfections of Christ and the splendours and effulgences of Bahá'u'lláh, on the one hand, and the virtues of the Prophets of the House of Israel, such as

Ezekiel or Samuel, on the other. All were the recipients of divine revelation, but between them there is an immeasurable distance.

38

THE THREE STATIONS OF THE
DIVINE MANIFESTATIONS

1 KNOW THAT, WHILE the Manifestations of God possess infinite virtues and perfections, They occupy only three stations: The first is the material station; the second is the human station, which is that of the rational soul; and the third is that of divine manifestation and heavenly splendour.

2 As for the material station, it has an origin in time, for it is composed of the elements, and every composition must ultimately be decomposed. It is indeed impossible for composition not to be followed by disintegration.

3 The second station is that of the rational soul, which is the human reality. This also has a beginning, and the Manifestations of God share it in common with all humanity.

4 The third station is that of divine manifestation and heavenly splendour, which is the Word of God, the everlasting Grace, and the Holy Spirit. This station has neither beginning nor end; for firstness and lastness pertain to the contingent world and not to the world of God. For God the beginning and the end are one and the same. Similarly, the reckoning of days, weeks, months, and years—of yesterday and today—is made with respect to the earth; but in the sun such things are unknown: There is neither yesterday,

nor today, nor tomorrow, neither months nor years—all are equal. Likewise, the Word of God is sanctified above all these conditions and exalted beyond every law, constraint, or limitation that may exist in the contingent world.

Know that, although human souls have existed upon the 5 earth for a myriad ages and cycles, the human soul is nonetheless originated. And since it is a sign of God, once it has come into being it is everlasting. The human spirit has a beginning but no end: It endures forever. Likewise, the various species found upon the earth have an origin in time; for it is acknowledged by all that there was a time when these species existed nowhere on the face of the earth, and indeed a time when the earth itself did not exist. But the world of existence has always been, for it is not confined to this terrestrial globe.

Our meaning is that, although human souls are origi- 6 nated, they are nevertheless immortal, enduring, and everlasting. For the world of things is a world of imperfection in relation to that of man, and the world of man is a world of perfection in relation to that of things. When imperfect things reach the stage of perfection, they become everlasting. This is meant as an example: Seek to grasp the true intent.

Now, the reality of prophethood, which is the Word of 7 God and the state of perfect divine manifestation, has neither beginning nor end, but its radiance varies like that of the sun. For example, it dawned above the sign of Christ with the utmost splendour and radiance, and this is eternal and everlasting. See how many world-conquering kings, how many wise ministers and rulers have come and gone, each and all fading into oblivion—whereas even now the breezes of Christ still waft, His light still shines, His call is still upraised, His banner is still unfurled, His armies still do battle, His voice still rings sweetly, His clouds still rain down life-giving showers, His lightning still streaks forth, His glory is still clear and indisputable, His splendour is still radiant and luminous; and the same holds true of every soul that abides beneath His shade and partakes of His light.

8   It is therefore evident that the Manifestations of God have three stations: the physical station, the station of the rational soul, and the station of divine manifestation and heavenly splendour. The corporeal station will inevitably perish. As to the station of the rational soul, despite having a beginning, it has no end and is endowed with everlasting life. But as to that holy Reality of which Christ says "the Father is in the Son",[115] it has neither beginning nor end: Its "beginning" refers merely to His revelation of His own station. Thus, by way of analogy, He likens His silence to sleep: A man who is silent is like one who is asleep, and when he speaks, it is as though he has awakened.[116] And yet the sleeping and the wakeful man are one and the same person: No change has taken place in his station, his loftiness, sublimity, inner reality, or innate nature. It is merely that the condition of silence has been likened to sleep, and that of manifestation to wakefulness. A man, whether sleeping or awake, is the same man: Sleep is simply one possible state, and wakefulness another. And so it is that the period of silence is compared to sleep, and the period of manifestation and guidance to wakefulness.

In the Gospel it is said: "In the beginning was the Word,   9
and the Word was with God." It follows then that Christ did
not attain His Messianic station and His perfections at the
moment of His baptism, when the Holy Spirit descended
upon Him in the form of a dove. Rather, the Word of God
has always been, and will ever remain, in the loftiest heights
of sanctity.

39

THE HUMAN AND THE DIVINE STATIONS
OF THE MANIFESTATIONS

1   WE STATED BEFORE that the Manifestations of God
have three stations: first, the material reality, which
pertains to the human body; second, the individual reality, that is, the rational soul; and third, the heavenly manifestation, which consists in the divine perfections and is
the source of the life of the world, the education of the
souls, the guidance of the people, and the enlightenment of
all creation.

2   The corporeal station is human in nature and is subject to disintegration, for it is an elemental composition and
that which is composed of elements must of necessity be
decomposed and dispersed.

3   But the individual reality of the Manifestations of the All-
Merciful is a sanctified reality, and it is so because it surpasses
in essence and in attributes all created things. It is like the
sun, which, by virtue of its inherent disposition, must inevitably produce light, and cannot be compared to any satellite.
For instance, the constituent parts of the sun can in no wise
be compared to those of the moon. The composition and
arrangement of the former necessarily produce rays, whereas
the constituent parts of the latter require the acquisition,

rather than the production, of light. So the other human realities are souls, which, like the moon, acquire their light from the sun, but that sanctified Reality is luminous in and of itself.

The third station is that of divine grace, the revelation of 4 the beauty of the Ancient of Days and the effulgence of the lights of the ever-living and omnipotent Lord. The individual realities of the holy Manifestations cannot be separated from divine grace and revelation any more than the corporeal mass of the sun can be separated from its light. Thus the ascension of the holy Manifestations is simply the abandonment of Their elemental bodies. For example, consider the lamp that lights this niche. Its rays may cease to fall upon the niche if the latter is destroyed, but there is no interruption in the bounty of the lamp itself. The pre-existent grace of the holy Manifestations is even as the light, Their individual realities as the glass globe, and Their human temples as the niche: If the niche is destroyed, the lamp continues to burn. The Manifestations of God are like so many different mirrors, as They each have Their own distinct individuality, but that which is reflected in these mirrors is one and the same sun. Thus, it is evident that the reality of Christ is different from that of Moses.

From the beginning, that sanctified Reality is undoubt- 5 edly aware of the secret of existence, and from childhood the signs of greatness are clearly manifested in Him. How then could He fail, in spite of such bounties and perfections, to be conscious of His own station?

We mentioned the three stations of the Manifestations 6 of God: that of corporeal existence, of individual reality, and of perfect divine manifestation, which can be likened to the sun, its heat, and its light. Other individuals also share the corporeal station and the rational soul—the spirit and mind. Thus the passages that state, "I lay asleep when the breeze of God wafted over Me and roused Me from My slumber"[117] are akin to Christ's saying, "The flesh is full of sorrow but the spirit is rejoiced", or again, "I am afflicted", or "I am at ease", or "I am troubled": All these refer to the corporeal station and have no bearing on the individual reality or on the state of manifestation of the divine Reality. Consider, for example, that thousands of vicissitudes may occur to the body of man of which the spirit remains wholly unaware. It is even possible for certain members of the body to be completely impaired and for the essence of the mind to remain unaffected. A garment may sustain a myriad rents and tears and the wearer may yet remain unharmed. Thus, the words of Bahá'u'lláh, "I lay asleep when a breeze wafted over Me and roused Me from My slumber", refer to the body.

7   In the world of God there is no past, present, or future: All of these are one. So when Christ said, "In the beginning was the Word,"[118] He meant that it was, is, and shall be; for in the world of God there is no time. Time holds sway over the creatures but not over God. So in the prayer where Christ says, "Hallowed be Thy name",[119] the meaning is that Thy name was, is, and shall be hallowed. Again, morning, noon, and evening exist in relation to the earth, but in the sun there is neither morning, nor noon, nor evening.

40

THE KNOWLEDGE OF THE
DIVINE MANIFESTATIONS

QUESTION: WHAT ARE the limitations imposed upon the powers of the Manifestations of God and, in particular, upon Their knowledge?

Answer: Knowledge is of two kinds: existential knowledge and formal knowledge, that is, intuitive knowledge and conceptual knowledge.

The knowledge that people generally have of things consists in conceptualization and observation; that is, either the object is conceived through the rational faculty, or through its observation a form is produced in the mirror of the heart. The scope of this knowledge is quite limited, as it is conditioned upon acquisition and attainment.

The other kind of knowledge, however, which is existential or intuitive knowledge, is like man's knowledge and awareness of his own self.

For example, the mind and the spirit of man are aware of all his states and conditions, of all the parts and members of his body, and of all his physical sensations, as well as of his spiritual powers, perceptions, and conditions. This is an existential knowledge through which man realizes his own condition. He both senses and comprehends it, for the spirit encompasses the body and is aware of its sensations and powers. This knowledge is not the result of effort and acquisition: It is an existential matter; it is pure bounty.

6   Since those sanctified realities, the universal Manifestations of God, encompass all created things both in their essence and in their attributes, since They transcend and discover all existing realities, and since They are cognizant of all things, it follows that Their knowledge is divine and not acquired—that is, it is a heavenly grace and a divine discovery.

7   Let us provide an example merely to illustrate the point. The noblest of all earthly beings is man. In him are realized the animal, the vegetable, and the mineral kingdoms; that is, all these degrees are contained in him in such wise that he is endowed with them all. And, being endowed with all these degrees and stations, he is informed of their mysteries and aware of the secrets of their existence. This is only an example and not an exact analogy.

8   Briefly, the universal Manifestations of God are aware of the truths underlying the mysteries of all created things, and thus They found a religion that is based upon, and consonant with, the prevailing condition of humanity. For religion consists in the necessary relationships deriving from the realities of things. If the Manifestation of God—the divine Lawgiver—were not informed of the realities of things, if He did not understand the necessary relationships deriving from these realities, He would assuredly be incapable of establishing a religion consonant with the needs and conditions of the time. The Prophets of God, the universal Manifestations, are even as skilled physicians; the world of

being is as the body of man; and the divine religions are as the treatment and remedy. The physician must be fully aware and informed of all the parts and organs, the constitution and condition of the patient, in order to prescribe an effective remedy. Indeed, it is from the disease itself that the physician deduces the remedy, for he first diagnoses the ailment and then treats its underlying cause. Until the ailment is properly diagnosed, how can any treatment or remedy be prescribed? The physician must therefore have a thorough knowledge of the constitution, the parts, organs, and condition of the patient, and be likewise well acquainted with every disease and every remedy, in order to prescribe the appropriate cure.

Religion, then, consists in the necessary relationships deriving from the reality of things. The universal Manifestations of God, being aware of the mysteries of creation, are fully informed of these necessary relationships and establish them as the religion of God.

41

UNIVERSAL CYCLES

1   Q UESTION: MENTION HAS been made of universal cycles which occur in the world of existence. Please explain the truth of this matter.

2   Answer: Each of the luminous bodies of this limitless firmament has its cycle of revolution, that period wherein it completes the full circuit of its orbit before beginning a new one. The earth, for example, completes a revolution every 365 days, five hours, forty-eight minutes and a fraction, and then begins anew along the same orbit. In the same way, the entire universe, whether with respect to the realm of nature or the realm of man, proceeds through cycles of major events and occurrences.

3   When a cycle comes to a close, a new one is inaugurated, and the previous cycle, on account of the momentous events which transpire, vanishes so entirely from memory as to leave behind no record or trace. Thus, as you are aware, we have no record of twenty thousand years ago, even though we established before through rational arguments that life on this earth is very ancient—not one or two hundred thousand, or even one or two million years old: It is ancient indeed, and the records and traces of ancient times have been entirely obliterated.

Each of the Manifestations of God has likewise a cycle   4
wherein His religion and His law are in full force and effect.
When His cycle is ended through the advent of a new
Manifestation, a new cycle begins. Thus, cycles are inaugurated, concluded, and renewed, until a universal cycle is
completed in the world of existence and momentous events
transpire which efface every record and trace of the past;
then a new universal cycle begins in the world, for the realm
of existence has no beginning. We have previously presented
proofs and arguments concerning this subject, and there is
no need for repetition.[120]

Briefly, our claim is that a universal cycle in the world   5
of existence comprises a vast span of time and countless
ages and epochs. In such a cycle, the Manifestations of God
shine forth in the visible realm until a universal and supreme
Manifestation makes the world the focal centre of divine
splendours and, through His revelation, brings it to the stage
of maturity. The duration of the cycle He ushers in is very
long indeed. Other Manifestations will arise in the course
of that cycle under His shadow and will renew, according
to the needs of the time, certain laws pertaining to material affairs and transactions, but They will remain under His
shadow. We are in the cycle which began with Adam and
whose universal Manifestation is Bahá'u'lláh.

42

THE POWER AND PERFECTIONS OF
THE DIVINE MANIFESTATIONS

1 QUESTION: HOW FAR do the powers and the perfections of those Thrones of truth, the Manifestations of
God, extend, and what are the limits of Their influence?

2 Answer: Consider the world of existence, that is, the
material creation. The solar system is wrapped in darkness. Within its circumference, the sun is the centre of all
light, and all the associated planets revolve around it and are
illumined by the outpourings of its bounty. The sun is the
source of life and light, and is the cause of the growth and
development of all things within the solar system. Were the
bounty of the sun to cease, no living thing could continue
to exist therein: All things would grow dark and be reduced
to naught. It is therefore clear and evident that the sun is the
centre of all light and the source of the life of all things in
the solar system.

3 In like manner, the holy Manifestations of God are the
focal Centres of the light of truth, the Wellsprings of the
hidden mysteries, and the Source of the effusions of divine
love. They cast Their effulgence upon the realm of hearts
and minds and bestow grace everlasting upon the world
of the spirits. They confer spiritual life and shine with the

splendour of inner truths and meanings. The enlightenment of the realm of thought proceeds from those Centres of light and Exponents of mysteries. Were it not for the grace of the revelation and instruction of those sanctified Beings, the world of souls and the realm of thought would become darkness upon darkness. Were it not for the sound and true teachings of those Exponents of mysteries, the human world would become the arena of animal characteristics and qualities, all existence would become a vanishing illusion, and true life would be lost. That is why it is said in the Gospel: "In the beginning was the Word"; that is, it was the source of all life.[121]

Now consider the pervasive influence of the sun upon all earthly beings, and behold what visible effects and outcomes result from its proximity or remoteness, its rising or setting. At one time it is autumn, at another it is spring. At one time it is summer, at another it is winter. When the sun crosses the equinox, the life-giving spring appears in all its splendour, and when it reaches the summer solstice, the fruits attain their full maturity, grains and plants yield their produce, and earthly things attain the plenitude of their growth and development. 4

In like manner, when the holy Manifestation of God, Who is the Sun of the world of creation, casts His splendour upon the world of hearts, minds, and spirits, a spiritual springtime is ushered in and a new life is unveiled. The power of the matchless springtide appears and its marvellous gifts are beheld. Thus you observe that, with the advent of each of the Manifestations of God, astonishing progress was 5 attained in the realm of human minds, thoughts, and spirits. Consider, for example, the progress that has been achieved in this divine age in the world of minds and thoughts—and this is only the beginning of the dawn! Erelong you will witness how these renewed bounties and heavenly teachings have flooded this darksome world with their light and transformed this sorrow-laden realm into the all-highest Paradise.

6   Were we to fully explain the influence and bounties of each of the Manifestations of God, it would take a very long time. Ponder and reflect upon it yourself in order to grasp the truth of the matter.

43

THE TWO KINDS OF PROPHETS

QUESTION: HOW MANY kinds of Prophets are there 1
in general?

Answer: Prophets are in general of two kinds. Some are 2
independent Prophets Who are followed, while others are
not independent and are themselves followers.

The independent Prophets are each the Author of a 3
divine religion and the Founder of a new Dispensation. At
Their advent the world is clothed in a new attire, a new
religion is established, and a new Book revealed. These
Prophets acquire the outpouring grace of the divine Reality
without an intermediary. Their radiance is an essential radiance like that of the sun, which is luminous in and of itself
and whose luminosity is an essential requirement rather
than being acquired from another star: They are like the sun
and not the moon. These Daysprings of the morn of Divine
Unity are the fountainheads of divine grace and the mirrors
of the Essence of Reality.

The other kind of Prophets are followers and promulga- 4
tors, for their station is contingent rather than independent.
They acquire divine grace from the independent Prophets and seek the light of guidance from the reality of universal prophethood. They are like the moon, which is not

luminous and radiant in and of itself but which receives its light from the sun.

5   The universal Prophets Who have appeared independently include Abraham, Moses, Christ, Muḥammad, the Báb, and Bahá'u'lláh. The second kind, which consists of followers and promulgators, includes Solomon, David, Isaiah, Jeremiah, and Ezekiel. For the independent Prophets are founders; that is, They establish a new religion, recreate the souls, regenerate the morals of society, and promulgate a new way of life and a new standard of conduct. Through Them a new Dispensation appears and a new religion is inaugurated. Their advent is even as the springtime, when all earthly things don a new garment and find a new life.

6   As to the second kind of Prophets, who are followers, they promulgate the religion of God, spread His Faith, and proclaim His Word. They have no power or authority of their own, but derive theirs from the independent Prophets.

7   Question: To which category do Buddha and Confucius belong?

8   Answer: Buddha also established a new religion and Confucius renewed the ancient conduct and morals, but the original precepts have been entirely changed and their followers no longer adhere to the original pattern of belief and worship. The founder of Buddhism was a precious Being Who established the oneness of God, but later His original precepts were gradually forgotten and displaced by primitive customs and rituals, until in the end it led to the worship of statues and images.

Consider, for example, that Christ admonished the peo- 9
ple time and again to heed the Ten Commandments of the
Torah and insisted upon their strict observance. Now, one
of the Ten Commandments forbids the worship of images
and statues.[122] Yet today there are a myriad images and statues in the churches of certain Christian denominations. It
is clear and evident, then, that the religion of God does not
preserve its original precepts among the people, but that
it is gradually changed and altered to the point of being
entirely effaced, and thus a new Manifestation appears and
a new religion is established. For if the former religion had
not been changed and altered, there would be no need
for renewal.

In the beginning, this tree was full of vitality and laden 10
with blossoms and fruit, but gradually it grew old, spent, and
barren, until it entirely withered and decayed. That is why
the True Gardener will again plant a tender sapling of the
same stock, that it may grow and develop day by day, extend
its sheltering shade in this heavenly garden, and yield its
prized fruit. So it is with the divine religions: With the passage of time, their original precepts are altered, their underlying truth entirely vanishes, their spirit departs, doctrinal
innovations spring up, and they become a body without a
soul. That is why they are renewed.

Our meaning is that the followers of Buddha and Con- 11
fucius now worship images and statues and have become
entirely unaware of the oneness of God, believing instead
in imaginary gods, as did the ancient Greeks. But such were

not their original precepts; indeed, their original precepts and conduct were entirely different.

12   Again, consider to what an extent the original precepts of the Christian religion have been forgotten and how many doctrinal innovations have sprung up. For example, Christ forbade violence and revenge and enjoined instead that evil and injury be met with benevolence and loving-kindness. But observe how many bloody wars have taken place among the Christian nations themselves and how much oppression, cruelty, rapacity, and bloodthirstiness have resulted therefrom! Indeed, many of these wars were carried out at the behest of the popes. It is therefore abundantly clear that, with the passage of time, religions are entirely changed and altered, and hence they are renewed.

44

THE REBUKES ADDRESSED BY GOD
TO THE PROPHETS

QUESTION: CERTAIN WORDS of rebuke have been addressed to the Prophets of God in the Sacred Scriptures. To whom are they addressed and to whom do they ultimately refer?

Answer: Every divine utterance that takes the form of a rebuke, though it be outwardly addressed to the Prophets of God, is in reality directed to Their followers. The wisdom of this is naught but unalloyed mercy, that the people might not be dismayed, disheartened, or burdened by such reproaches and rebukes. These words are therefore outwardly addressed to the Prophets, but, even so, they are inwardly intended for the followers and not for the Messenger.

Moreover, the mighty and sovereign monarch of a land represents all who inhabit that land; that is, whatsoever he may utter is the word of all, and whatsoever covenant he may conclude is the covenant of all, for the will and purpose of all his subjects is subsumed in his own. Likewise, every Prophet is the representative of the entire body of His followers. Therefore, the covenant that God makes with Him and the words that He addresses to Him apply to all His people.

4   Now, the divine reproach and rebuke tends to burden and afflict the hearts of the people, and the consummate wisdom of God demands, therefore, such a form of address. For example, it appears from the Torah itself that the Israelites rebelled against Moses, saying: "We cannot fight the Amalekites, for they are mighty, fierce, and courageous." God then spoke with rebuke to Moses and Aaron, although Moses was in complete obedience and not in rebellion.[123] Surely such a glorious Being, Who is the channel of God's grace and the champion of His law, must be obedient to the divine command.

5   These holy Souls are like the leaves of a tree which are stirred into motion by the breeze and not of Their own accord, for They are attracted by the breaths of the love of God and have forsaken Their own will. Their word is the word of God; Their commandment is the commandment of God; Their prohibition is the prohibition of God. They are even as this glass globe whose light comes from the flame of the lamp. Although the light appears to emanate from the glass, in reality it proceeds from the flame. Similarly, the movement and repose of the Prophets of God, Who are His Manifestations, proceed from revelation and not from mere human whim. Were it not so, how could the Prophet act as a faithful representative and chosen envoy of God? How could He promulgate God's commandments and prohibitions? All the shortcomings ascribed to the Manifestations of God in the Sacred Scriptures must therefore be understood in this light.

6   Praise be to God that you have come here and met the

servants of God! Have you inhaled from them aught save the fragrance of the good-pleasure of the Lord? Indeed, no! You have seen with your own eyes how they strive night and day to no other end but to exalt the Word of God, to foster the education of the souls, to rehabilitate the fortunes of mankind, to ensure spiritual progress, to promote universal peace, to show forth kindliness and goodwill to all peoples and nations, to sacrifice themselves for the common good, to forsake their own material advantage, and to promote the virtues of the world of humanity.

Let us return to our subject. In the Torah it is said in Isaiah 48:12: "Hearken unto Me, O Jacob and Israel, My called; I am He; I am the first, I also am the last." It is evident that the intended meaning is not Jacob who was called Israel, but the Israelites. Also in Isaiah 43:1 it is said: "But now thus saith the Lord that created thee, O Jacob, and He that formed thee, O Israel, Fear not: for I have redeemed thee, I have called thee by thy name; thou art Mine." 7

Furthermore, in Numbers 20:23–4 it is said: "And the Lord spake unto Moses and Aaron in mount Hor, by the coast of the land of Edom, saying, Aaron shall be gathered unto his people: for he shall not enter into the land which I have given unto the children of Israel, because ye rebelled against My word at the water of Meribah"; and in 20:13: "This is the water of Meribah; because the children of Israel strove with the Lord, and He was sanctified in them." 8

Observe that it was the people of Israel who had rebelled, but the reproach was outwardly addressed to Aaron and Moses, as it is said in Deuteronomy 3:26: "But the Lord was 9 wroth with me for your sakes, and would not hear me: and the Lord said unto me, Let it suffice thee; speak no more unto Me of this matter."

10 Now, this reproach and rebuke was in reality addressed to the children of Israel, who, on account of their rebellion against the commandments of God, were made to dwell for a long period in the barren desert beyond the Jordan, until the time of Joshua. This reproach and rebuke appeared to be addressed to Moses and Aaron, but in reality it was directed to the people of Israel.

11 Similarly, in the Qur'án it is said to Muḥammad: "We have granted thee a manifest victory, that God may forgive thee thy past and future sins."[124] Now, these words, though apparently addressed to Muḥammad, were in reality meant for all His people; and this proceeds from the consummate wisdom of God, as we said previously, so that hearts might not be troubled, perplexed, or dismayed.

12 How often have the Prophets of God and His universal Manifestations confessed in Their prayers to Their sins and shortcomings! This is only to instruct other souls, to inspire and encourage them to be humble and submissive before God, and to acknowledge their own sins and shortcomings. For these holy Souls are sanctified above every sin and freed from every fault. For example, it is said in the Gospel that a man came to Christ and called Him "Good Master". Christ answered, "Why callest thou me good? there is none good but one, that is, God."[125] Now, this did not mean—God forbid!—that Christ was a sinner, but rather His intention was to teach humility, lowliness, meekness, and modesty to the

man He was addressing. These blessed Souls are light, and light cannot be united with darkness. They are life everlasting, and life cannot be gathered in with death. They are guidance, and guidance cannot be brought together with waywardness. They are the very essence of obedience, and obedience cannot join hands with rebellion.

In brief, our meaning is that the rebukes recorded in the 13 Sacred Scriptures, though outwardly addressed to the Prophets—the Manifestations of God—are in reality intended for the people. Were you to peruse the Bible, this matter would become clear and evident.

45

THE MOST GREAT INFALLIBILITY

1   IT IS SAID in the blessed verse: "He Who is the Dawning-place of God's Cause hath no partner in the Most Great Infallibility. He it is Who, in the kingdom of creation, is the Manifestation of 'He doeth whatsoever He willeth'. God hath reserved this distinction unto His own Self, and ordained for none a share in so sublime and transcendent a station."[126]

2   Know that infallibility is of two kinds: infallibility in essence and infallibility as an attribute. The same holds true of all other names and attributes: For example, there is the knowledge of the essence of a thing and the knowledge of its attributes. Infallibility in essence is confined to the universal Manifestations of God; for infallibility is an essential requirement of Their reality, and the essential requirement of a thing is inseparable from the thing itself. The rays are an essential requirement of the sun and are inseparable from it; knowledge is an essential requirement of God and is inseparable from Him; power is an essential requirement of God and is likewise inseparable from Him. If it were possible to separate these from Him, He would not be God. If the rays could be separated from the sun, it would not be the sun. Therefore, were one to imagine the Most Great Infallibility

being separated from the universal Manifestation of God, He would not be a universal Manifestation and would lack essential perfection.

But infallibility as an attribute is not an essential requirement; rather, it is a ray of the gift of infallibility which shines from the Sun of Truth upon certain hearts and grants them a share and portion thereof. Although these souls are not essentially infallible, yet they are under the care, protection, and unerring guidance of God—which is to say, God guards them from error. Thus there have been many sanctified souls who were not themselves the Daysprings of the Most Great Infallibility, but who have nevertheless been guarded and preserved from error under the shadow of divine care and protection. For they were the channels of divine grace between God and man, and if God did not preserve them from error they would have led all the faithful to fall likewise into error, which would have wholly undermined the foundations of the religion of God and which would be unbefitting and unworthy of His exalted Reality.

To summarize, infallibility in essence is confined to the universal Manifestations of God, and infallibility as an attribute is conferred upon sanctified souls. For instance, the Universal House of Justice, if it be established under the necessary conditions—that is, if it be elected by the entire community—that House of Justice will be under the protection and unerring guidance of God. Should that House of Justice decide, either unanimously or by a majority, upon a matter that is not explicitly recorded in the Book, that decision and command will be guarded from error. Now, the members of the House of Justice are not essentially infallible as individuals, but the body of the House of Justice is under the protection and unerring guidance of God: This is called conferred infallibility.

5 Briefly, Bahá'u'lláh says that "He Who is the Dawning-place of God's Cause" is the manifestation of "He doeth whatsoever He willeth", that this station is reserved to that sanctified Being, and that others receive no share of this essential perfection. That is, since the essential infallibility of the universal Manifestations of God has been established, whatsoever proceeds from Them is identical with the truth and conformable to reality. They are not under the shadow of the former religion. Whatsoever They say is the utterance of God, and whatsoever They do is a righteous deed, and to no believer is given the right to object; rather must he show forth absolute submission in this regard, for the Manifestation of God acts with consummate wisdom, and human minds may be incapable of grasping the hidden wisdom of certain matters. Therefore, whatsoever the universal Manifestation of God says and does is the very essence of wisdom and conformable to reality.

6 Now, if certain souls fail to grasp the mysteries concealed within a given commandment or action of the True One, they should raise no objection, for the universal Manifestation of God "doeth whatsoever He willeth". How often has it happened that a wise, accomplished, and sagacious person took a course of action, and those who were incapable of grasping its wisdom objected and questioned why he said or did thus. This objection is prompted by ignorance,

and the wisdom of that wise man is free and sanctified from error.

In like manner, a skilled physician "doeth whatsoever 7 he willeth" in treating the patient, and the latter has no right to object. Whatsoever the physician may say or do, the same is sound and true, and he must be regarded by all as the embodiment of "He doeth whatsoever He willeth, and ordaineth whatsoever He pleaseth." The physician will doubtless prescribe remedies that are at variance with popular notions, but is it permissible for those who have no knowledge of science and medicine to object? No, by God! On the contrary, they must all acquiesce and follow whatsoever the skilled physician prescribes. Thus, the skilled physician "doeth whatsoever he willeth", and the patients have no share in this station. First, the skill of the physician must be ascertained, and once this has been done, he "doeth whatsoever he willeth".

Likewise, a general who is unrivalled in the art of war 8 "doeth whatsoever he willeth" in all that he says or commands, and the same holds true of the ship's captain who masters the art of seafaring, and of the True Educator Who possesses all human perfections: They do whatsoever they will in all that they say and command.

In sum, the meaning of "He doeth whatsoever He willeth" is that if the Manifestation of God issues a command, 9 enforces a law, or performs an action whose wisdom His followers cannot grasp, they should not think for a moment of questioning His words or actions. All souls are under the shadow of the universal Manifestation, must submit to the authority of the religion of God, and are not to deviate so much as a hairsbreadth. Rather, they must conform their every act and deed to the religion of God, and should they deviate from it they will be reproved and held accountable before God. It is certain that they have no share of the station "He doeth whatsoever He willeth", for it is confined to the universal Manifestation of God.

10   Thus Christ—may my soul be a sacrifice for His sake!— was the embodiment of the words "He doeth whatsoever He willeth", but His disciples had no share of this station, for they abided under His shadow and were not granted leave to deviate from His will and command.

PART 4

On the Origin, Powers, and Conditions of Man

46

EVOLUTION AND THE TRUE
NATURE OF MAN

W E NOW COME to the question of the transforma- 1
tion of species and the evolutionary development
of organs, that is, whether man has come from the animal
kingdom.[127]

This idea has entrenched itself in the minds of certain 2
European philosophers, and it is very difficult now to make
its falsity understood; but in the future it will become clear
and evident, and the European philosophers will themselves
recognize it. For in reality it is an evident error. When one
examines creation with a penetrating eye, when one grasps
the intricacies of created things and witnesses the condition,
the order, and the completeness of the world of existence,
one is convinced of the truth that "there is naught in creation more wondrous than that which already exists".[128] For
all existing things, whether on earth or in the heavens, even
this limitless firmament and all that it contains, have been
most befittingly created, arranged, composed, ordered, and
completed, and suffer no imperfection. To such an extent
is this true that if all beings were to become pure intelligence and to reflect until the end that has no end, they

could not possibly imagine anything better than that which already exists.

3   If in the past, however, the creation had lacked such completeness and adornment, if it had been in an inferior state, then existence would have necessarily been wanting and imperfect and, as such, incomplete. This matter requires the utmost attention and thought. Imagine, for example, the entire contingent world—the realm of existence—as resembling the body of man. If the composition, the arrangement, the completeness, the beauty, and the perfection which now exist in the human body were in any way different, the result would be imperfection itself.

4   So if we were to imagine a time when man belonged to the animal kingdom, that is, when he was merely an animal, existence would have been imperfect. This means that there would have been no man, and this chief member, which in the body of the world is like the mind and the brain in a human being, would have been lacking, and the world would thus have been utterly imperfect. This is sufficient proof in itself that if there had been a time when man belonged to the animal realm, the completeness of existence would have been destroyed; for man is the chief member of the body of this world, and a body without its chief member is undoubtedly imperfect. We regard man as the chief member because, among all created things, he encompasses all the perfections of existence.

5   Now, what we mean by "man" is the complete human being, the foremost person in the world, who is the sum of all spiritual and material perfections, and who is like the sun

among all created things. Imagine, then, a time when the sun did not exist as such, in other words, when the sun was merely another celestial body. Undoubtedly, at such a time the relationships between existing things would have been disrupted. How can such a thing be imagined? Were one to carefully examine the world of existence, this argument alone would suffice.

Let us give another, more subtle proof: The innumerable created things that are found in the world of existence—be they man, animal, plant, or mineral—must each be composed of elements. There is no doubt that the completeness seen in each and every thing arises, by divine creation, from the component elements, their appropriate combination, their proportionate measure, the manner of their composition, and the influence of other created things. For all beings are linked together like a chain; and mutual aid, assistance, and interaction are among their intrinsic properties and are the cause of their formation, development, and growth. It is established through numerous proofs and arguments that every single thing has an effect and influence upon every other, either independently or through a causal chain. In sum, the completeness of each and every thing—that is, the completeness which you now see in man, or in other beings, with regard to their parts, members, and powers—arises from their component elements, their quantities and measures, the manner of their combination, and their mutual action, interaction, and influence. When all these are brought together, then man comes into existence.

7   As the completeness of man stems entirely from the component elements, their measure, their manner of combination, and the mutual action and interaction of other beings—and since man was produced ten or a hundred thousand years ago from the same earthly elements, with the same measures and quantities, the same manner of composition and combination, and the same interactions with other beings—it follows that man was exactly the same then as exists now. This is a self-evident truth and cannot be doubted. And if a thousand million years hence, the component elements of man are brought together, measured out in the same proportion, combined in the same manner, and subjected to the same interaction with other beings, exactly the same man will come into existence. For example, if a hundred thousand years hence one were to bring together oil, flame, wick, lamp, and a lighter of the lamp—briefly, if all that is needed now be combined then—exactly the same lamp will be produced.

8   This matter is evident and these arguments conclusive. But those which the European philosophers have adduced are speculative and inconclusive.

47

THE ORIGIN OF THE UNIVERSE AND
THE EVOLUTION OF MAN

K NOW THAT IT is one of the most abstruse questions 1
of divinity that the world of existence—that is, this
endless universe—has no beginning.

We have already explained that the very names and attri- 2
butes of Divinity require the existence of created things.
Although a detailed explanation of this matter was already
provided,[129] a brief mention will again be made here. Know
that a lord without vassals cannot be imagined; a sovereign
without subjects cannot exist; a teacher without pupils cannot be designated; a creator without a creation is impossible;
a provider without those provided for is inconceivable—
since all the divine names and attributes call for the existence of created things. If we were to imagine a time when
created things did not exist, it would be tantamount to
denying the divinity of God.

Apart from this, absolute non-existence lacks the capac- 3
ity to attain existence. If the universe were pure nothingness, existence could not have been realized. Thus, as that
Essence of Oneness, or divine Being, is eternal and everlasting—that is, as it has neither beginning nor end—it follows
that the world of existence, this endless universe, likewise

has no beginning. To be sure, it is possible for some part of creation—one of the celestial globes—to be newly formed or to disintegrate, but the other countless globes would continue to exist and the world of existence itself would not be disrupted or destroyed. On the contrary, its existence is perpetual and unchanging. Now, as each globe has a beginning, it must inevitably have an end as well, since every composition, whether universal or particular, must of necessity be decomposed. At most, some disintegrate quickly and others slowly, but it is impossible for something that is composed not to ultimately decompose.

4   We must know, then, what each one of the great existent things was in the beginning. There is no doubt that initially there was a single origin: There cannot have been two origins. For the origin of all numbers is one and not two; the number two is itself in need of an origin. It is therefore evident that originally matter was one, and that one matter appeared in a different form in each element. Thus various forms appeared, and as they appeared, they each assumed an independent form and became a specific element. But this distinction attained its full completion and realization only after a very long time. Then these elements were composed, arranged, and combined in infinite forms; in other words, from the composition and combination of these elements countless beings appeared.

5   This composition and arrangement arose, through the wisdom of God and His ancient might, from one natural order. Thus, as this composition and combination has been produced according to a natural order, with perfect

soundness, following a consummate wisdom, and subject to a universal law, it is clear that it is a divine creation and not an accidental composition and arrangement. That is why from every natural composition a living thing comes into existence, but from a chance composition no living thing will appear. So, for example, if man, with all his astuteness and intelligence, were to gather together and combine certain elements, a living being will not be brought into existence as it would not be according to the natural order. This is the answer to the implicit question that might arise, that since these beings come into existence through the composition and combination of these elements, then can we not also gather together and combine the very same elements and thus create a living thing? This idea is mistaken; for the original composition is a divine composition, and the combination is produced by God according to the natural order, and it is for this reason that a living being is created from this composition and an existence is realized. But a composition made by man produces nothing because man cannot create life.

Briefly, we have said that from the composition of the elements; from their combination, manner, and proportion; and from their interaction with other beings countless forms and realities and innumerable beings have come to exist. But it is clear that this terrestrial globe in its present form did not come into existence all at once, but that this universal existent gradually traversed different stages until it appeared in its present completeness. Universal existences can be likened and compared to particular ones, for both

6

are subject to one natural order, one universal law, and one divine arrangement. For instance, you will find the smallest atoms to be similar in their general structure to the greatest entities in the universe, and it is clear that they have proceeded from one laboratory of might according to one natural order and one universal law, and can therefore be compared to one another.

7 For example, the human embryo grows and develops gradually in the womb of its mother and assumes different forms and conditions until it reaches maturity with the utmost beauty and appears in a consummate form with the utmost grace. In like manner, the seed of this flower which you see before you was, in the beginning, a small and insignificant thing, but it grew and developed in the womb of the earth and assumed different forms until it appeared with such perfect vitality and grace in this degree. It is likewise clear and evident that this terrestrial globe came to exist, grow, and develop in the matrix of the universe and assumed different forms and conditions until it gradually attained its present completeness, became adorned with countless beings, and appeared in such a consummate form.

8 It is therefore evident that the original matter, which is like unto the embryo, initially took the form of composed and combined elements, and that composition gradually grew and developed over a myriad ages and centuries, passing from one shape and form to another until, through the consummate wisdom of God, it appeared with such completeness, order, arrangement, and soundness.

Let us return to our subject. From the beginning of exis- 9
tence in the womb of the terrestrial globe, man gradually
grew and developed like the embryo in the womb of its
mother, and passed from one shape and form to another
until he appeared with this beauty and perfection, this power
and constitution. It is certain that initially he did not possess
such loveliness, grace, and refinement, and that he has only
gradually attained such form, disposition, comeliness, and
grace. There is no doubt that, like the embryo in the womb
of the mother, the embryo of humankind did not appear
all at once in this form and become the embodiment of
the words "Hallowed be the Lord, the most excellent of all
creators!"¹³⁰ Rather, it gradually attained various conditions
and assumed divers forms until it attained this appearance
and beauty, this perfection, refinement, and grace. It is therefore clear and evident that the growth and development of
man on this planet unto his present completeness, even as
the growth and development of the embryo in the womb of
the mother, has been by degrees and through passing from
state to state, and from one shape and form to another, for
this is according to the requirements of the universal order
and the divine law.

That is, the human embryo assumes different conditions 10
and traverses numerous stages until it reaches that form in
which it manifests the reality of the words "Hallowed be the
Lord, the most excellent of all creators!" and shows forth
the signs of full development and maturity. In like manner, from the beginning of man's existence on this planet
until he assumed his present shape, form, and condition, a

long time must have elapsed, and he must have traversed many stages before reaching his present condition. But from the beginning of his existence man has been a distinct species. This is similar to the embryo of man in the womb of the mother: It possesses at first a strange appearance; then this body passes from shape to shape and from form to form until it appears in the utmost beauty and perfection. But even when it possesses, in the womb of the mother, a strange form entirely different from its present shape and appearance, it is the embryo of a distinct species and not of an animal: The essence of the species and the innate reality undergo no transformation at all.

11   Now, were one to establish the existence of vestigial organs, this would not disprove the independence and originality of the species. At most it would prove that the form, appearance, and organs of man have evolved over time. But man has always been a distinct species; he has been man, not an animal. Consider: If the embryo of man in the womb of the mother passes from one form to another which in no way resembles the former, is this a proof that the essence of the species has undergone transformation? That it was at first an animal and that its organs developed and evolved until it became a man? No, by God! How feeble and unfounded is this thought! For the originality of the human species and the independence of the essence of man are clear and evident.

48

THE DIFFERENCE BETWEEN
MAN AND ANIMAL

WE HAVE ALREADY had one or two conversations on
the subject of the spirit, but they were not written
down. [1]

Know that the people of the world are of two kinds; that
is, they belong to two groups. One group denies the human
spirit and says that man is a kind of animal. Why? Because
we see that man and animal share in common the same
powers and senses. The simple and individual elements that
fill the space around us are brought together in countless
combinations, each of which gives rise to a different being.
Among these are sentient beings possessed of certain powers
and senses. The more complete the combination, the nobler
the being. The combination of the elements in the body
of man is more complete than in any other being, and its
elements have been combined in perfect equilibrium, and
thus it is more noble and more perfect. It is not, they say,
that man has a special power and spirit of which the other
animals are deprived: Animals too have sensory perceptions,
but man's powers are simply more acute in certain respects
(although with respect to the outer senses, such as hearing,
sight, taste, smell, and touch, and even with regard to inner [2]

powers such as memory, the animal is more richly endowed than man). The animal, they say, possesses the powers of intelligence and understanding. All they will concede is that man's intelligence is greater.

3   Such are the claims of the present-day philosophers. Such are their words, such are their claims, and such are the dictates of their imaginations. And so, after extensive research and armed with powerful arguments, they place man in the lineage of the animal, saying that at one time man was an animal, and that the species gradually changed and evolved until it reached the human degree.

4   But the divine philosophers say: No, this is not so. Although man shares the same outward powers and senses in common with the animal, there exists in him an extraordinary power of which the animal is deprived. All sciences, arts, inventions, crafts, and discoveries of realities proceed from this singular power. This is a power that encompasses all created things, comprehends their realities, unravels their hidden mysteries, and brings them under its control. It even understands things that have no outward existence, that is, intelligible, imperceptible, and unseen realities such as the mind, the spirit, human attributes and qualities, love and sorrow—all of which are intelligible realities. Moreover, all the existing sciences and crafts, all the great undertakings and myriad discoveries of man were at one time hidden and concealed mysteries, and it is that all-encompassing human power that has discovered them and brought them forth from the invisible into the visible realm. So the telegraph, the photograph, the phonograph—all such great inventions

and crafts were once hidden mysteries which that human reality discovered and brought forth from the invisible to the visible realm. There was even a time when this piece of iron before you, and indeed every mineral, was a hidden mystery. The human reality discovered this mineral and wrought its metal into this finished form. The same holds true for all the other discoveries and inventions of man, which are innumerable. This matter is irrefutable and there is no point in denying it.

If we were to claim that all these effects proceed from the powers of the animal nature and the physical senses, then we see plainly and clearly that, with regard to these powers, the animals are superior to man. For example, the sight of animals is much keener than that of man, their hearing is more acute, and likewise with their powers of smell and taste. Briefly, in the powers which man and animal share in common, the animal often has the advantage. Take the power of memory: If you carry a pigeon from here to a faraway country, and there set it free, it will remember the way and return home. Take a dog from here to the heart of Asia, set it free, and it will return home without ever losing its way. And so is it with the other powers, such as hearing, sight, smell, taste, and touch. It is clear then that if man did not possess a power beyond the animal powers, the animal would perforce surpass man in significant discoveries and in the comprehension of realities. It follows from this argument that man is endowed with a gift, and possesses a perfection, which is not present in the animal.

6   Moreover, the animal perceives sensible things but cannot perceive conceptual realities. For example, the animal sees that which is within the range of its vision but cannot comprehend or conceive that which lies beyond it. Thus it is not possible for the animal to comprehend that the earth has a spherical shape. But man can deduce the unknown from the known and discover hidden realities. So, for example, from observing the inclination of the heavens man infers the curvature of the earth. The Pole Star at 'Akká, for instance, is at 33 degrees; that is, it is inclined 33 degrees above the horizon. When one goes towards the North Pole, the Pole Star rises one degree above the horizon for every degree of distance travelled; that is, the inclination of the Pole Star will reach 34 degrees, then 40, 50, 60, and 70 degrees. When one reaches the North Pole, the inclination of the Pole Star will be 90 degrees and the star will be seen at the zenith, that is, directly overhead.

7   Now, the Pole Star is a sensible reality, and so too is its ascension, that is, the fact that the closer one goes to the Pole, the higher the Pole Star rises. And from these two known realities an unknown reality is discovered, namely, that the heavens are inclined, meaning that the sky above the horizon at each latitude is different from that at another latitude. Man comprehends this relation and reasons from it a previously unknown thing, namely, the curvature of the earth. But this comprehension is impossible for the animal. It is likewise impossible for the animal to comprehend that the sun is the centre and that the earth revolves around it. The animal is a prisoner of the senses and is circumscribed

by them: It cannot comprehend anything that lies beyond the reach or control of the senses, even though it excels man in the outward powers and senses. It is therefore clearly established that man is endowed with a power of discovery that distinguishes him from the animal, and this power is none but the human spirit.

Praise be to God! Man ever aspires to greater heights 8 and loftier goals. He ever seeks to attain a world surpassing that which he inhabits, and to ascend to a degree above that which he occupies. This love of transcendence is one of the hallmarks of man. I am astonished that certain philosophers in Europe and America have consented to lower themselves to the animal realm and so to regress, whereas all existence must ever aspire towards exaltation. And yet, were you to call one of them an animal, he would be most hurt and offended.

What a difference between the world of man and the 9 world of the animal! What a difference between the loftiness of man and the abasement of the animal, between the perfections of man and the ignorance of the animal, between the light of man and the darkness of the animal, between the glory of man and the degradation of the animal! An Arab child of ten years can subdue two or three hundred camels in the desert and lead them about with his mere voice. A feeble Indian can so subdue a mighty elephant as to compel it to move in strict obedience. All things are subdued by the hand of man, who withstands nature itself.

All other beings are captives of nature and cannot free 10 themselves from its exigencies: Man alone can withstand nature. So nature attracts all bodies to the centre of the earth, but through mechanical means man moves away from it and soars in the air; nature prevents man from crossing the sea, but man builds ships and traverses the heart of the great ocean, and so forth—the subject is endless. For example, man traverses mountains and plains in vehicles and gathers in one place the news of the events of East and West. This is how man withstands nature. The sea in all its vastness cannot deviate one iota from the rule of nature; the sun in all its greatness cannot stray so much as a needle's point from the rule of nature, nor can it ever comprehend the states, conditions, properties, movements, and nature of man. What then is the power residing in man's puny form that encompasses all this? What conquering power is this that subdues all things?

11   One more point remains. Modern philosophers say: "Nowhere do we see a spirit in man, and, although we have investigated the inmost recesses of the human body, nowhere do we perceive a spiritual power. How then are we to imagine a power which is not sensible?" The divine philosophers reply: "The spirit of the animal is not sensible either and cannot be perceived through our material powers: How do you infer its existence? There is no doubt that it is from its effects that you infer in the animal the existence of a power which is lacking in the plant, and that is the power of the senses—sight, hearing, and the other powers. It is from these that you infer that there is an animal spirit. Infer, likewise, from the aforementioned signs and arguments the existence of a human spirit. Thus, since there are signs in the animal

that cannot be found in the plant, you say that this sensory power is one of the hallmarks of the animal spirit. You see likewise in man signs, powers, and perfections that do not exist in the animal: Infer then that there is a power in him of which the animal is bereft."

If we were to deny all that is not accessible to the senses, then we would be forced to deny realities which undoubtedly exist. For example, the ether is not sensible, although its reality can be proven. The power of gravity is not sensible, although its existence is likewise undeniable. Whence do we affirm their existence? From their signs. For instance, this light consists in the vibrations of the ether, and from these vibrations we infer its existence.

49

EVOLUTION AND THE
EXISTENCE OF MAN

1 QUESTION: WHAT DO you say regarding the theory of the evolution of beings to which certain European philosophers subscribe?

2 Answer: We discussed this matter the other day, but we will speak of it again. Briefly, this question comes down to the originality or non-originality of the species, that is, whether the essence of the human species was fixed from the very origin or whether it subsequently came from the animals.

3 Certain European philosophers hold that species evolve and can even change and transform into other species. Among the proofs they advance for this claim is that, through careful geological research and investigation, it has become clear and evident to us that the existence of the plants preceded that of the animals, and that the existence of the animals preceded that of man. They hold, moreover, that both vegetable and animal kingdoms have undergone transformation; for in certain strata of the earth, plants have been discovered which existed in the past but which have since disappeared, meaning that they evolved, became hardier, and changed in form and appearance, and thus the

species have changed. Likewise, in the strata of the earth there are certain animal species which have changed and altered. One of these is the snake, which has vestigial limbs, that is, signs indicating that it once had feet, which have disappeared over time and left behind only a remnant. In like manner, there is in man's vertebral column a vestige indicating that like other animals he once had a tail, of which, they assert, traces still remain. At one point that member was useful, but as man evolved, it lost its utility and hence it gradually disappeared. Likewise, as snakes came to live beneath the ground and became creeping animals, they were no longer in need of feet and so the latter disappeared, leaving behind a remnant. Their principal proof is that these vestigial limbs are evidence of the existence of earlier limbs that have gradually disappeared for want of use, and that they no longer have any benefit or reason to exist. Thus, the fit and necessary limbs have remained, while the unnecessary ones have gradually disappeared as a result of the transformation of the species, but have left behind a remnant.

The first answer to this argument is that the antecedence 4 of animals to man is not a proof that the essence of the human species was altered or transformed or that man came from the animal kingdom. For so long as it is acknowledged that these different beings have appeared in time, it is possible that man simply came into existence after the animal. Thus we observe in the vegetable kingdom that the fruits of different trees do not appear all at once; on the contrary, some appear earlier in the season and others later. This priority is not a proof that the later fruit of one tree was produced from the earlier fruit of another.

5 Secondly, these minor traces and vestigial limbs might have some great underlying wisdom which the human mind has so far been unable to fathom. How many things are found in this world whose underlying wisdom to this day has not been grasped! Thus, it is said in physiology—the science of the relations of the body's organs—that the underlying wisdom and cause of the differences in the colouration of animals and of human hair, or of the redness of the lips, or of the variety of the colours of birds, are still unknown and remain hidden and concealed. But it has been discovered that the blackness of the pupil of the eye is due to its absorbing the rays of the sun, for if it were of another colour—say, uniformly white—it would not absorb these rays. Now, so long as the wisdom underlying the things that we have mentioned is unknown, one may well imagine that the reason and wisdom of the vestigial limbs, whether in the animal or in man, is also unknown. Such an underlying wisdom of course exists, even though it may not be known.

6 Thirdly, even if we were to suppose that certain animals, or even man, once possessed limbs which have now disappeared, this would not be a sufficient proof of the transformation of the species. For man, from the conception of the embryo until the attainment of maturity, assumes different forms and appearances. His appearance, form, features, and colour change; that is, he passes from form to form and from appearance to appearance. Yet, from the formation of the embryo he belongs to the human species; that is, it is the

embryo of a man and not of an animal. But at first this fact is not apparent; only later does it become plain and visible.

For example, let us suppose that man once bore a resemblance to the animal and that he has since evolved and transformed. Accepting this statement does not prove the transformation of species, but could instead be likened to the changes and transformations that the human embryo undergoes before reaching its full development and maturity, as was earlier mentioned. To be more explicit, let us suppose that man once walked on all fours or had a tail: This change and transformation is similar to that of the fetus in the womb of the mother. Even though the fetus develops and evolves in every possible way before it reaches its full development, from the beginning it belongs to a distinct species. The same holds true in the vegetable kingdom, where we observe that the original and distinctive character of the species does not change, while its form, colour, and mass do change, transform, and evolve.

To summarize: Just as man progresses, evolves, and is transformed from one form and appearance to another in the womb of the mother, while remaining from the beginning a human embryo, so too has man remained a distinct essence—that is, the human species—from the beginning of his formation in the matrix of the world, and has passed gradually from form to form. It follows that this change of appearance, this evolution of organs, and this growth and development do not preclude the originality of the species. Now, even accepting the reality of evolution and progress, nevertheless, from the moment of his appearance man has possessed perfect composition, and has had the capacity and potential to acquire both material and spiritual perfections and to become the embodiment of the verse, "Let Us make man in Our image, after Our likeness."[131] At most, he has become more pleasing, more refined and graceful, and by virtue of civilization he has emerged from his wild state, just as the wild fruits become finer and sweeter under the cultivation of the gardener, and acquire ever greater delicacy and vitality.

9   The gardeners of the world of humanity are the Prophets of God.

50

SPIRITUAL PROOFS OF THE
ORIGINALITY OF MAN

THE ARGUMENTS WE have adduced thus far for the originality of the human species have been rational ones. Now we will provide spiritual arguments, which are indeed the fundamental ones. For we established the existence of God through rational arguments, and it was likewise established through rational arguments that man has been man from his very inception and origin, and that the essence of his species has existed from eternity. We will now present spiritual proofs that human existence—that is, the human species—is a necessary existence and that without man the perfections of Divinity would not shine forth. But these are spiritual and not rational arguments.

We have established time and again through proofs and arguments that man is the noblest of all beings and the sum of all perfections. Indeed, all existing things are the seat of the revelation of the divine splendours; that is, the signs of the divinity of God are manifest in the realities of all things. Just as the earth is the place where the rays of the sun are reflected—meaning that the light, heat, and influence of the sun are plain and manifest in all the atoms of the earth— so too does each one of the atoms of the universe in this infinite space proclaim one of the perfections of God. Nothing is deprived of this: Each is either a sign of the mercy of God, or of His power, or His greatness, or His justice, or His sustaining providence, or His generosity, or His sight, or His hearing, or His knowledge, or His grace, and so on.

3   Our meaning is that every existing thing is of necessity the seat of the revelation of the divine splendours; that is, the perfections of God are manifested and revealed therein. It is even as the sun which shines upon the desert, the sea, the trees, the fruits, the blossoms—upon all earthly things. Now, the world of existence, indeed every created thing, proclaims but one of the names of God, but the reality of man is an all-encompassing and universal reality which is the seat of the revelation of all the divine perfections. That is, a sign of each one of the names, attributes, and perfections that we ascribe to God exists in man. If such were not the case, he would be unable to imagine and comprehend these perfections. For example, we say that God is all-seeing. The eye is the sign of His sight: If this faculty were lacking in man, how could we imagine the sight of God? For one born blind cannot imagine what it is to see, any more than one born deaf can imagine what it is to hear, or the lifeless what it is to be alive.

4   Thus, the divinity of God, which is the totality of all perfections, reveals itself in the reality of man—that is, the divine Essence is the sum total of all perfections, and from this station it casts a ray of its splendour upon the human reality. In other words, the Sun of Truth is reflected in this mirror. Thus man is a perfect mirror facing the Sun of Truth

and is the seat of its reflection. The splendour of all the divine perfections is manifest in the reality of man, and it is for this reason that he is the vicegerent and apostle of God. If man did not exist, the universe would be without result, for the purpose of existence is the revelation of the divine perfections. We cannot say, then, that there was a time when man was not. At most we can say that there was a time when this earth did not exist, and that at the beginning man was not present upon it.

But from the beginning that has no beginning to the end 5
that has no end, a perfect Manifestation has always existed. This Man of Whom we speak here is not just any man: That which we intend is the Perfect Man. For the noblest part of the tree, and the fundamental purpose of its existence, is the fruit. A tree without fruit is of no use. Therefore, it cannot be imagined that the world of existence, whether in the realms above or below, was once populated by cows and donkeys, cats, and mice, and yet was deprived of the presence of man. What a false and vacuous notion!

The word of God is as clear as the sun. This is a spiri- 6
tual argument, but it cannot be presented to the material philosophers at the outset. Rather, we must first present the rational arguments and only afterwards the spiritual ones.

51

THE APPEARANCE OF THE SPIRIT
AND THE MIND IN MAN

1 QUESTION: DID THE mind and the spirit appear in the human species from the very beginning of its growth and development on earth, or was it a gradual process? And, if the latter, was this achieved over a short span of time or over a long period?

2 Answer: The beginning of the formation of man on the terrestrial globe is like the formation of the human embryo in the womb of the mother. The embryo gradually grows and develops until it is born, and thereafter it continues to grow and develop until it reaches the stage of maturity. Although in infancy the signs of the mind and the spirit are already present in man, they do not appear in a state of perfection, and remain incomplete. But when man attains maturity, the mind and the spirit manifest themselves in the utmost perfection.

3 Likewise, at the beginning of his formation in the matrix of the world, man was like an embryo. He then gradually progressed by degrees, and grew and developed until he reached the stage of maturity, when the mind and the spirit manifested themselves in the utmost perfection. From the beginning of his formation, the mind and the

spirit existed, but they were hidden and appeared only later. In the world of the womb, too, the mind and the spirit exist in the embryo but are concealed and appear only afterwards. It is even as the seed: The tree exists within it but is hidden and concealed; when the seed grows and develops, the tree appears in its fullness. In like manner, the growth and development of all beings proceeds by gradual degrees. This is the universal and divinely ordained law and the natural order. The seed does not suddenly become the tree; the embryo does not at once become the man; the mineral substance does not in a moment become the stone: No, all these grow and develop gradually until they attain the limit of perfection.

All beings, whether universal or particular, were created 4 perfect and complete from the beginning. The most one can say is that their perfections only become apparent gradually. The law of God is one; the evolution of existence is one; the divine order is one. All beings great and small are subject to one law and one order. Every seed has, from the beginning, all the perfections of the plant. For example, all the vegetable perfections existed in this seed at the outset but were invisible and appeared only gradually. So it is the shoot which first appears from the seed, then the branches, leaves, and blossoms, and finally the fruit. But from the beginning of its formation, all of these existed potentially, albeit invisibly, in the seed. Likewise, from the beginning the embryo possesses all perfections, such as the spirit, the mind, sight, smell, and taste—in a word, all the powers—but they are invisible and become apparent only gradually.

5   Similarly, the terrestrial globe was created, from the beginning, with all its elements, substances, minerals, parts, and components, but these appeared only gradually: first the minerals, then the plants, then the animals, and finally man. But from the beginning, these kinds and species were latent in the earthly realm and appeared gradually thereafter. For the supreme law of God and the universal natural order encompasses all things and subjects them to its rule. When you consider this universal order, you see that not a single thing reaches the limit of perfection immediately upon coming into existence, but grows and develops gradually until it reaches that stage.

52

THE APPEARANCE OF THE SPIRIT
IN THE BODY

Q UESTION: WHAT IS the wisdom of the appearance 1
of the spirit in the body?

Answer: The wisdom of the appearance of the spirit in 2
the body is this: The human spirit is a divine trust which
must traverse every degree, for traversing and passing
through the degrees of existence is the means of its acquiring perfections. So, for example, when a man travels in
an orderly and methodical manner through many different countries and regions, this will most certainly be the
means of acquiring perfections, for he will see at first hand
various sites, scenes, and regions; learn about the affairs and
circumstances of other nations; become familiar with the
geography of other lands; acquaint himself with their arts
and wonders; become informed of the customs, conduct, and
character of their inhabitants; witness the civilization and
the advancements of the time; and be apprised of the
manner of government, the capacity, and the receptivity
of each country. In the same way, when the human spirit
traverses the degrees of existence and attains each degree
and station—even that of the body—it will assuredly acquire
perfections.

3   Moreover, it is necessary that the signs of the perfections of the spirit appear in this world, that the realm of creation may bring forth endless fruits, and that this body of the contingent world may receive life and manifest the divine bounties. So, for example, the rays of the sun must shine upon the earth and its heat must nurture all earthly beings; if the rays and heat of the sun were not to reach the earth, it would remain idle and desolate and its development would be arrested. Likewise, were the perfections of the spirit not to appear in this world, it would become dark and wholly animalistic. It is through the appearance of the spirit in the material body that this world is illumined. Just as the spirit of man is the cause of the life of his body, so is the whole world even as a body and man as its spirit. If man did not exist, if the perfections of the spirit were not manifested and the light of the mind were not shining in this world, it would be like a body without a spirit.

4   By another token, this world is even as a tree and man as the fruit; without the fruit the tree would be of no use.

5   Beyond this, the members, constituent parts, and composition that are found within man attract and act as a magnet for the spirit: The spirit is bound to appear in it. Thus, when a mirror is polished, it is bound to attract the rays of the sun, to be illumined, and to reflect splendid images. That is, when these physical elements are gathered and combined together, according to the natural order and with the utmost perfection, they become a magnet for the spirit, and the spirit will manifest itself therein with all its perfections.

From this perspective one does not ask, "Why is it nec- 6
essary for the rays of the sun to fall upon the mirror?"; for
the relationships that bind together the realities of all things,
whether spiritual or material, require that when the mirror is polished and turned towards the sun it should manifest the rays thereof. In like manner, when the elements are
composed and combined according to the noblest order,
arrangement, and manner, the human spirit will appear
and manifest itself therein. Such is the decree of the All-
Glorious, the All-Wise.

53

THE CONNECTION BETWEEN
GOD AND HIS CREATION

1   QUESTION: WHAT IS the nature of the connection between God and His creation, between the Absolute and Inaccessible One and all other beings?

2   Answer: The connection between God and His creation is that of the originator and the originated, of the sun and the dark bodies of the universe, of the craftsman and his handiwork. Not only is the sun sanctified in its very essence above all the bodies that receive its illumination, but its light is also, in its essence, sanctified from and independent of the earth. So, though the earth is nurtured by the sun and is the recipient of its light, the sun and its rays are nonetheless sanctified above it. But were it not for the sun, the earth and all terrestrial life could not exist.

3   The procession of creation from God is a procession through emanation. That is, creation emanates from God; it does not manifest Him. The connection is that of emanation and not of manifestation. The light of the sun emanates from the sun; it does not manifest it. Appearance through emanation[132] is like the appearance of the rays from the sun: The sanctified Essence of the Sun of Truth cannot be divided or descend into the condition of the creation. In the

same way, the sun does not divide itself or descend upon the earth, but its rays—the outpourings of its grace—emanate from it and illumine the dark bodies.

But appearance through manifestation is like the mani- 4
festation of the branches, leaves, blossoms, and fruit from the seed; for the seed itself becomes the branches and fruit, and its reality descends into them. This manifestational appearance would be sheer imperfection and utterly impossible for the Most High, for this would require unconditioned pre-existence to take on the attributes of the originated, absolute independence to become abject poverty, and the essence of existence to become pure non-existence; and this is in no wise possible.

It follows that all things have emanated from God; that 5
is, it is through God that all things have been realized, and through Him that the contingent world has come to exist. The first thing to emanate from God is that universal reality which the ancient philosophers termed the "First Intellect" and which the people of Bahá call the "Primal Will". This emanation, with respect to its action in the world of God, is not limited by either time or place and has neither beginning nor end, for in relation to God the beginning and the end are one and the same. The pre-existence of God is both essential and temporal, while the origination of the contingent world is essential but not temporal, as we have already explained another day at table.[133]

Though the First Intellect is without beginning, this 6
does not mean that it shares in the pre-existence of God, for in relation to the existence of God the existence of that

universal Reality is mere nothingness—it cannot even be said to exist, let alone to partake of the pre-existence of God. An explanation of this matter was provided on a previous occasion.

7   As for created things, their life consists in composition, and their death in decomposition. But matter and the universal elements cannot be entirely destroyed and annihilated. No, their annihilation is merely transformation. For instance, when man dies, his body becomes dust, but it does not become absolute non-existence: It retains a mineral existence, but a transformation has taken place, and that composition has been subjected to decomposition. It is the same with the annihilation of all other beings; for existence does not become absolute non-existence, and absolute non-existence does not acquire existence.

54

THE PROCESSION OF THE
HUMAN SPIRIT FROM GOD

QUESTION: IN WHAT manner does the human spirit proceed from God, since in the Torah it is said that God breathed the spirit into the body of man?[134]

Answer: Know that procession is of two kinds: procession and appearance through emanation, and procession and appearance through manifestation. Emanational procession is like the procession of the handiwork from its author. For example, the writing proceeds from the writer. Now, just as the writing emanates from the writer and the discourse from the speaker, so does the human spirit emanate from God. But it does not manifest Him; that is, no part has been separated from the divine Reality to enter into the body of man. No, the human spirit has emanated, just as speech emanates from the speaker, and become manifested in the body of man.

As for manifestational procession, it is the manifestation of the reality of a thing in other forms, like the procession of this tree or this flower from their seeds, for it is the seed itself that has become manifested in the form of the branches, leaves, and flowers. This is called manifestational procession.

4   The spirits of men proceed from God by emanation, in the same way as the discourse proceeds from the speaker and the writing from the writer; that is, the speaker himself does not become the speech, any more than the writer becomes the writing: The connection is rather one of emanational procession. For the speaker remains in an absolute state of ability and power, as the discourse emanates from him, even as the action emanates from its author. The true Speaker, the divine Essence, ever remains in the same condition and experiences no change or alteration, no transformation or vicissitude. It has neither beginning nor end. The procession of human spirits from God is therefore an emanational procession. When it is said in the Torah that God breathed His spirit into man, this spirit is even as speech that has emanated from the true Speaker and taken effect in the reality of man.

5   Now, if we were to understand manifestational procession as "appearance" rather than "division into parts", we have already stated that this is the manner of the procession and appearance of the Holy Spirit and the Word, which are from God. As it is said in the Gospel of John, "In the beginning was the Word, and the Word was with God."[135] It follows then that the Holy Spirit and the Word are the appearance of God and consist in the divine perfections that shone forth in the reality of Christ. And these perfections were with God, even as the sun which manifests the fullness of its glory in a mirror. For by "the Word" is not meant the body of Christ but the divine perfections that were manifested in Him. Thus Christ was like a spotless mirror which was

turned towards the Sun of Truth, and the perfections of that Sun—that is, its light and heat—were plainly manifest in that mirror. If we look into the mirror, we see the sun and we say it is the sun. Therefore, the Word and the Holy Spirit, which consist in the perfections of God, are the divine appearance. This is the meaning of the verse in the Gospel which says: "the Word was with God, and the Word was God",[136] for the divine perfections cannot be distinguished from the divine Essence. The perfections of Christ are called the Word since all created things are like individual letters, and individual letters do not convey a complete meaning, while the perfections of Christ are even as an entire word, for from a word a complete meaning can be inferred. As the reality of Christ was the manifestation of the divine perfections, it was even as a word. Why? Because it comprised a complete meaning, and that is why it has been called the Word.

And know that the procession of the Word and the 6 Holy Spirit from God, which is a manifestational procession and appearance, should not be taken to mean that the reality of the Divinity has been divided or multiplied, or has descended from its heights of purity and sanctity. God forbid! If a clear and spotless mirror were placed before the sun, the light and heat, the form and image of the sun would appear therein with such a manifestational appearance that if a beholder were to say, "This is the sun", he would be speaking the truth. But the mirror is the mirror and the sun is the sun. The sun is but one sun, and remains one even if it appears in numerous mirrors. There is no place here for inherence, egress, commingling, or descent; for egress, regress, inherence, descent, and commingling are among the characteristics and requirements of bodies, not of spirits—how much less of the holy and sanctified Reality of the Divinity. Glorified is God above all that ill beseems His holiness and sanctity, and exalted is He in the heights of His sublimity!

7   The Sun of Truth, as we have said, has ever remained in the same condition and undergoes neither change nor alteration, neither transformation nor vicissitude. It has neither beginning nor end. But the sanctified Reality of the Word of God is even as a clear, spotless, and shining mirror wherein the heat and light, the form and image of the Sun of Truth—that is to say, all its perfections—are reflected. That is why Christ says in the Gospel, "The Father is in the Son",[137] meaning that the Sun of Truth shines resplendent in this mirror. Glorified be He Who has cast His splendour upon this Reality that is sanctified above all created things!

55

SPIRIT, SOUL, AND MIND

QUESTION: WHAT IS the difference between mind, spirit, and soul?

Answer: It was already explained that, in general, spirit is divided into five categories: the vegetable spirit, the animal spirit, the human spirit, the spirit of faith, and the Holy Spirit.[138]

The vegetable spirit is that power of growth which is brought about in the seed through the influence of other created things.

The animal spirit is that all-embracing sensory power which is realized through the composition and combination of the elements. When this composition disintegrates, that spirit likewise perishes and becomes non-existent. It may be likened to this lamp: When oil, wick, and flame are brought together and combined, it is lit; and when this combination disintegrates—that is, when the constituent parts are separated from one another—the lamp also is extinguished.

The human spirit, which distinguishes man from the animal, is the rational soul, and these two terms—the human spirit and the rational soul—designate one and the same thing. This spirit, which in the terminology of the philosophers is called the rational soul, encompasses all things and, as far as human capacity permits, discovers their realities and becomes aware of the properties and effects, the characteristics and conditions of earthly things. But the human spirit, unless it be assisted by the spirit of faith, cannot become acquainted with the divine mysteries and the heavenly realities. It is like a mirror which, although clear, bright, and polished, is still in need of light. Not until a sunbeam falls upon it can it discover the divine mysteries.

6   As for the mind, it is the power of the human spirit. The spirit is as the lamp, and the mind as the light that shines from it. The spirit is as the tree, and the mind as the fruit. The mind is the perfection of the spirit and a necessary attribute thereof, even as the rays of the sun are an essential requirement of the sun itself.

7   This explanation, however brief, is complete. Reflect upon it and, God willing, you will grasp the details.

56

THE OUTWARD AND THE
INWARD POWERS OF MAN

THERE ARE FIVE outward material powers in man
which are the means of perception—that is, five powers whereby man perceives material things. They are sight,
which perceives sensible forms; hearing, which perceives
audible sounds; smell, which perceives odours; taste, which
perceives edible things; and touch, which is distributed
throughout the body and which perceives tactile realities.
These five powers perceive external objects.

Man has likewise a number of spiritual powers: the power
of imagination, which forms a mental image of things;
thought, which reflects upon the realities of things; comprehension, which understands these realities; and memory,
which retains whatever man has imagined, thought, and
understood. The intermediary between these five outward
powers and the inward powers is a common faculty, a sense
which mediates between them and which conveys to the
inward powers whatever the outward powers have perceived. It is termed the common faculty as it is shared in
common between the outward and inward powers.

For instance, sight, which is one of the outward powers,
sees and perceives this flower and conveys this perception

to the inward power of the common faculty; the common faculty transmits it to the power of imagination, which in turn conceives and forms this image and transmits it to the power of thought; the power of thought reflects upon it and, having apprehended its reality, conveys it to the power of comprehension; the comprehension, once it has understood it, delivers the image of the sensible object to the memory, and the memory preserves it in its repository.

4   The outward powers are five: the power of sight, of hearing, of taste, of smell, and of touch. The inward powers are also five: the common faculty and the powers of imagination, thought, comprehension, and memory.

57

THE DIFFERENCES
IN HUMAN CHARACTER

QUESTION: HOW MANY kinds of character are there ₁ in man and what are the causes of the differences and variations among them?

Answer: There are the innate character, the inher- ₂ ited character, and the acquired character, which is gained through education.

As to the innate character, although the innate nature ₃ bestowed by God upon man is purely good, yet that character differs among men according to the degrees they occupy: All degrees are good, but some are more so than others. Thus every human being possesses intelligence and capacity, but intelligence, capacity, and aptitude differ from person to person. This is self-evident.

For example, take a number of children from the same ₄ place and family, attending the same school and instructed by the same teacher, raised on the same food and in the same climate, wearing the same clothing and studying the same lessons: It is certain that among these children some will become skilled in the arts and sciences, some will be of average ability, and some will be dull. It is therefore clear that in man's innate nature there is a difference in degree, aptitude, and capacity, but it is not a matter of good or evil—it is merely a difference of degree. One occupies the highest degree, another the middle degree, and yet another the lowest degree. Thus man, the animal, the plant, and the mineral all exist, but the existence of these four kinds of beings is different. Indeed, what a difference there is between the existence of man and that of the animal! Yet all these do exist, and it is evident that in existence there are differences of degree.

5   As to differences in inherited character, they arise from the strength and weakness of man's constitution; that is, if the parents are of weak constitution, then the children will be likewise, and if they are strong, then the children will also be robust. Moreover, the excellence of the bloodline exerts a major influence; for the goodly seed is like the superior stock that exists, likewise, among plants and animals. For example, you see that children born of a weak and sickly mother and father will naturally have a weak constitution and nerves, will lack patience, endurance, resolution, and perseverance, and will be impulsive, for they have inherited the weakness and frailty of their parents.

6   Aside from this, certain families and lineages have been singled out for a special blessing. Thus the descendants of Abraham received the special blessing that all the Prophets of the House of Israel were raised up from among their ranks. This is a blessing that God bestowed upon that lineage. Moses, through both His father and His mother; Christ, through His mother; Muḥammad; the Báb; and all the Prophets and Holy Ones of Israel belong to that lineage.

Bahá'u'lláh too is a lineal descendant of Abraham, for Abraham had other sons besides Ishmael and Isaac who in those days emigrated to the regions of Persia and Afghanistan, and the Blessed Beauty is one of their descendants.

Hence it is evident that inherited character also exists, 7 to such a degree that if one's character does not conform to that of one's forebears, one would not be accounted among that lineage in spirit even if one were a descendant in body. Such is the case of Canaan, who is not reckoned among the descendants of Noah.[139]

As to the differences of character arising from education, 8 they are great indeed, for education exerts an enormous influence. Through education the ignorant become learned, the cowardly become courageous, the crooked branch becomes straight, the acrid and bitter fruit of the mountains and woods becomes sweet and succulent, and the five-petalled flower puts forth a hundred petals. Through education barbarous nations become civilized and even animals take on human-like manners. Education must be accorded the greatest importance; for just as diseases are highly communicable in the world of bodies, so is character highly communicable in the realm of hearts and spirits. The differences caused by education are enormous and exert a major influence.

Now, someone might say that, since the capacity and 9 aptitude of souls differ, such difference in capacity must inevitably lead to a difference in character.[140] But this is not so, for capacity is of two kinds: innate and acquired. The innate capacity, which is the creation of God, is wholly and entirely good—in the innate nature there is no evil. The acquired capacity, however, can become the cause of evil. For example, God has created all men in such a fashion, and has given them such a capacity and disposition, that they are benefited by sugar and honey and are harmed or killed by poison. This is an innate capacity and disposition that God has bestowed equally upon all men. But man may begin little by little to take poison by ingesting a small quantity every day and gradually increasing it until he reaches the point where he would perish if he were not to consume several grams of opium every day, and where his innate capacities are completely subverted. Consider how the innate capacity and disposition can be so completely changed, through variation of habit and training, as to be entirely perverted. It is not on account of their innate capacity and disposition that one reproaches the wicked, but rather on account of that which they themselves have acquired.

10   In the innate nature of things there is no evil—all is good. This applies even to certain apparently blameworthy attributes and dispositions which seem inherent in some people, but which are not in reality reprehensible. For example, you can see in a nursing child, from the beginning of its life, the signs of greed, of anger, and of ill temper; and so it might be argued that good and evil are innate in the reality of man, and that this is contrary to the pure goodness of the innate nature and of creation. The answer is that greed, which is to demand ever more, is a praiseworthy quality provided that it is displayed under the right circumstances. Thus, should a person show greed in acquiring science and knowledge, or in the exercise of compassion, high-mindedness, and justice,

this would be most praiseworthy. And should he direct his anger and wrath against the bloodthirsty tyrants who are like ferocious beasts, this too would be most praiseworthy. But should he display these qualities under other conditions, this would be deserving of blame.

It follows therefore that in existence and creation there 11 is no evil at all, but that when man's innate qualities are used in an unlawful way, they become blameworthy. Thus if a wealthy and generous person gives alms to a poor man to spend on his necessities, and if the latter spends that sum in an improper way, that is blameworthy. The same holds true of all the innate qualities of man which constitute the capital of human life: If they are displayed and employed in an improper way, they become blameworthy. It is clear then that the innate nature is purely good.

Consider that the worst of all qualities and the most odi- 12 ous of all attributes, and the very foundation of all evil, is lying, and that no more evil or reprehensible quality can be imagined in all existence. It brings all human perfections to naught and gives rise to countless vices. There is no worse attribute than this, and it is the foundation of all wickedness. Now, all this notwithstanding, should a physician console a patient and say, "Thank God, you are doing better and there is hope for your recovery", although these words may be contrary to the truth, yet sometimes they will ease the patient's mind and become the means of curing the illness. And this is not blameworthy.

This question has now been elucidated most clearly. 13

58

THE EXTENT AND LIMITATION OF HUMAN COMPREHENSION

1   QUESTION: HOW FAR does human comprehension extend, and what are its limitations?

2   Answer: Know that comprehension varies. Its lowest degree consists in the senses of the animal realm, that is, the natural sensations which arise from the powers of the outward senses. This comprehension is common to man and animals, and indeed certain animals surpass man in this regard. In the human realm, however, comprehension differs and varies in accordance with the different degrees occupied by man.

3   The foremost degree of comprehension in the world of nature is that of the rational soul. This power and comprehension is shared in common by all men, whether they be heedless or aware, wayward or faithful. In the creation of God, the rational soul of man encompasses and is distinguished above all other created things: It is by virtue of its nobility and distinction that it encompasses them all. Through the power of the rational soul, man can discover the realities of things, comprehend their properties, and penetrate the mysteries of existence. All the sciences, branches of learning, arts, inventions, institutions, undertakings, and

discoveries have resulted from the comprehension of the rational soul. These were once impenetrable secrets, hidden mysteries, and unknown realities, and the rational soul gradually discovered them and brought them out of the invisible plane into the realm of the visible. This is the greatest power of comprehension in the world of nature, and the uttermost limit of its flight is to comprehend the realities, signs, and properties of contingent things.

But the universal divine Intellect, which transcends 4 nature, is the outpouring grace of the pre-existent Power. It encompasses all existing realities and receives its share of the lights and mysteries of God. It is an all-knowing power, not a power of investigation and sensing. The spiritual power associated with the world of nature is the power of investigation, and it is through investigation that it discovers the realities and properties of things. But the heavenly intellectual power, which is beyond nature, encompasses, knows, and comprehends all things; is aware of the divine mysteries, truths, and inner meanings; and discovers the hidden verities of the Kingdom. This divine intellectual power is confined to the holy Manifestations and the Daysprings of prophethood. A ray of this light falls upon the mirrors of the hearts of the righteous, that they may also receive, through the holy Manifestations, a share and benefit of this power.

The holy Manifestations have three stations: the corpo- 5 real station, the station of the rational soul, and the station of perfect divine manifestation and heavenly splendour. Their bodies perceive things only according to the capacity of the material world, and so it is that They have at certain times expressed physical weakness. For example: "I was asleep and unconscious; the breeze of God wafted over Me, awoke Me and summoned Me to voice His call";[141] or when Christ was baptized in His thirtieth year and the Holy Spirit descended upon Him, having not manifested itself in Him before this time. All these things refer to the corporeal station of the Manifestations, but Their heavenly station encompasses all things, is aware of all mysteries, is informed of all signs, and rules supreme over all things. And this is equally true both before and after the intimation of Their mission. That is why Christ said: "I am Alpha and Omega, the first and the last"[142]—that is, there has never been, nor shall there ever be, any change or alteration in Me.

59

MAN'S COMPREHENSION OF GOD

QUESTION: TO WHAT extent can human perception comprehend God?

Answer: This subject requires ample time, and to explain it at table will be difficult. Nevertheless, a brief explanation will be given.

Know that there are two kinds of knowledge: the knowledge of the essence of a thing and the knowledge of its attributes. The essence of each thing is known only through its attributes; otherwise, that essence is unknown and unfathomed.

As our knowledge of things, even of created and limited ones, is of their attributes and not of their essence, how then can it be possible to understand in its essence the unbounded Reality of the Divinity? For the inner essence of a thing can never be known, only its attributes. For example, the inner reality of the sun is unknown, but it is understood through its attributes, which are heat and light. The inner essence of man is unknown and unfathomed, but it is known and characterized by its attributes. Thus everything is known by its attributes and not by its essence: Even though the human mind encompasses all things, and all outward things are in turn encompassed by it, yet the latter are unknown with regard to their essence and can only be known with regard to their attributes. How then can the ancient and everlasting Lord, Who is sanctified above all comprehension and imagining, be known in His Essence? That is, as created things can only be known through their attributes and not in their essence, the reality of the Divinity, too, must be unknown with regard to its essence and known only with respect to its attributes.

5   Furthermore, how can a reality that is originated encompass that Reality which has existed from all eternity? For comprehension is the result of encompassing—the latter must take place in order that the former may occur—and the divine Essence is all-encompassing and can never be encompassed.

6   Moreover, differences of degree in the world of creation are a barrier to knowledge. For example, as this mineral belongs to the mineral kingdom, however far it may rise, it can never comprehend the power of growth. The plants and trees, however far they may progress, cannot imagine the powers of sight or of the other senses. The animal cannot imagine the human degree, that is, the spiritual powers. Thus, differences of degree are a barrier to knowledge: The inferior degree cannot comprehend the superior. How then can a reality which is originated comprehend that Reality which has existed from all eternity?

7   Knowing God, therefore, means the comprehension and knowledge of His attributes and not of His Reality. And even this knowledge of His attributes extends only so far as human power and capacity permit, and remains wholly

inadequate. Philosophy consists in comprehending, so far as human power permits, the realities of things as they are in themselves. The originated reality has no recourse but to comprehend the pre-existent attributes within the intrinsic limits of human capacity. The invisible realm of the Divinity is sanctified and exalted above the comprehension of all beings, and all that can be imagined is mere human understanding. The power of human understanding does not encompass the reality of the divine Essence: All that man can hope to achieve is to comprehend the attributes of the Divinity, the light of which is manifest and resplendent in the world and within the souls of men.

When we examine the world and the souls of men, the perspicuous signs of the perfections of the Divinity appear clear and manifest, for the realities of all things attest to the existence of a universal Reality. The reality of the Divinity is even as the sun, which from the heights of its sanctity shines upon every land, and of whose radiance every land and every soul receives a share. Were it not for this light and this radiance, nothing could exist. Now, all created things tell of this light, partake of its rays, and receive their portion thereof, but the full splendour of the perfections, bounties, and attributes of the Divinity shines forth from the reality of the Perfect Man, that is, that unique Individual Who is the universal Manifestation of God. For the other beings have each received only a portion of that light, but the universal Manifestation of God is the mirror held before this Sun, and the latter manifests itself therein with all its perfections, attributes, signs, and effects.

8

9   The knowledge of the reality of the Divinity is in no wise possible, but the knowledge of the Manifestations of God is the knowledge of God, for the bounties, splendours, and attributes of God are manifest in Them. Thus, whoso attains to the knowledge of the Manifestations of God attains to the knowledge of God, and whoso remains heedless of Them remains bereft of that knowledge. It is therefore clearly established that the Holy Manifestations are the focal centres of the heavenly bounties, signs, and perfections. Blessed are those who receive the light of divine bounties from those luminous Daysprings!

10   We cherish the hope that the loved ones of God, like unto an attractive force, will draw these bounties from their very source and arise with such radiance and exert such influence as to become the perspicuous signs of the Sun of Truth.

60

THE IMMORTALITY OF THE SPIRIT (1)

HAVING ESTABLISHED THE existence of the human spirit,[143] we must now establish its immortality.

In the heavenly Books, mention is made of the immortality of the spirit, which is the very foundation of the divine religions. For rewards and punishments are said to be of two kinds—one being existential rewards and punishments and the other, ultimate rewards and punishments. Existential paradise and hell are to be found in all the worlds of God, whether in this world or in the heavenly realms of the spirit, and to gain these rewards is to attain life eternal. That is why Christ said: Act in such a manner that you may find eternal life, be born of water and of the spirit, and thus enter into the Kingdom.[144]

Existential rewards consist in the virtues and perfections that adorn the human reality. For example, man was immersed in darkness and becomes luminous; he was ignorant and becomes informed; he was heedless and becomes aware; he was asleep and is awakened; he was dead and is quickened to life; he was blind and begins to see; he was deaf and begins to hear; he was earthly and becomes heavenly; he was material and becomes spiritual. Through these rewards he is reborn in spirit, is created anew, and becomes the manifestation of the verse in the Gospel that says that the Apostles "were born, not of blood, nor of the flesh, nor of the will of man, but of God"[145]—that is, they were delivered from the animal characteristics and qualities that are inherent to human nature, and acquired divine attributes, which are the outpouring grace of God. This is the true meaning of being born again. For such souls, there is no greater torment than to be veiled from God, and no worse punishment than selfish qualities, evil attributes, baseness of character, and engrossment in carnal desires. When these souls are delivered from the darkness of these vices through the light of faith, when they are illumined by the rays of the Sun of Truth and endowed with every human virtue, they reckon this as the greatest reward and regard it as the true paradise. In like manner, they consider spiritual punishment—that is, existential torment and chastisement—to consist in subjection to the world of nature; in being veiled from God; in ignorance and unawareness; in engrossment with covetous desires; in absorption in animal vices; in being marked by evil attributes, such as falsehood, tyranny, and iniquity; in attachment to worldly things; and in immersion in satanic fancies—all of which they reckon to be the greatest of torments and punishments.

4   The ultimate rewards, which consist in life everlasting, have been explicitly recorded in all the heavenly Scriptures. They are divine perfections, eternal bounty, and everlasting joy. The ultimate rewards are the gifts and perfections that man attains in the spiritual realms after his ascension from this world, while the existential rewards

are those true and luminous perfections which are attained while still abiding in this world, and which are the cause of everlasting life. For the existential rewards are the advancement of existence itself and are analogous to the passage of man from the stage of the embryo to that of maturity and becoming the embodiment of the verse, "Hallowed be the Lord, the most excellent of all creators!"[146] The ultimate rewards consist in spiritual bounties and bestowals, such as the manifold gifts of God that are vouchsafed after the ascension of the soul, the attainment of the heart's desire, and reunion with Him in the everlasting realm. Similarly, ultimate retributions and punishments consist in being deprived of the special bounties and unfailing bestowals of God and sinking to the lowest degrees of existence. And whoso is deprived of these favours, though he continue to exist after death, is accounted as dead in the eyes of the people of truth.

A rational proof for the immortality of the spirit is this, 5 that no effect can be produced by a non-existent thing; that is, it is impossible that any effect should appear from absolute nothingness. For the effect of a thing is secondary to its existence, and that which is secondary is conditioned upon the existence of that which is primary. So from a non-existent sun no rays can shine; from a non-existent sea no waves can surge; from a non-existent cloud no rain can fall; from a non-existent tree no fruit can appear; from a non-existent man nothing can be manifested or produced. Therefore, so long as the effects of existence are visible, they prove that the author of that effect exists.

6   Consider how, to this day, the sovereignty of Christ has endured. How can a sovereignty of such greatness be manifested by a non-existent sovereign? How can such waves surge from a non-existent sea? How can such heavenly breezes waft from a non-existent garden? Consider that as soon as the constituent parts of anything, be it mineral, plant, or animal, are disintegrated and its elemental composition is dissolved, all effect, influence, and trace thereof vanish. But it is not so with the human spirit and reality, which continues to manifest its signs, to exert its influence, and to sustain its effects even after the dissociation and decomposition of the various parts and members of the body.

7   This question is very subtle: Consider it attentively. This is a rational proof that we are providing, that rational minds may weigh it in the balance of reason and fair-mindedness. But if the human spirit be rejoiced and attracted to the Kingdom, if the inner eye be opened and the spiritual ear attuned, and if spiritual feelings come to predominate, the immortality of the spirit will be seen as clearly as the sun, and heavenly tidings and intimations will encompass that spirit.

8   Tomorrow we will give other proofs.

61

THE IMMORTALITY OF THE SPIRIT (2)

YESTERDAY WE WERE discussing the immortality of 1
the spirit. Know that the influence and perception of
the human spirit is of two kinds; that is, the human spirit
has two modes of operation and understanding. One mode
is through the mediation of bodily instruments and organs.
Thus it sees with the eye, hears with the ear, speaks with
the tongue. These are actions of the spirit and operations
of the human reality, but they occur through the mediation of bodily instruments. Thus, it is the spirit that sees,
but by means of the eye; it is the spirit that hears, but by
means of the ear; it is the spirit that speaks, but by means of
the tongue.

The other mode of the spirit's influence and action is 2
without these bodily instruments and organs. For example,
in the state of sleep, it sees without eyes, it hears without
ears, it speaks without a tongue, it runs without feet—in
brief, all these powers are exerted without the mediation of
instruments and organs. How often it happens that the spirit
has a dream in the realm of sleep whose purport comes to be
exactly materialized two years hence! Likewise, how often
it happens that in the world of dreams the spirit solves a
problem that it could not solve in the realm of wakefulness.

Awake, the eye sees only a short distance, but in the realm of dreams one who is in the East may see the West. Awake, he sees only the present; in sleep he beholds the future. Awake, by the fastest means he travels at most seventy miles in an hour; in sleep he traverses East and West in the blink of an eye. For the spirit has two modes of travel: without means, or spiritual travel, and with means, or material travel—as birds that fly, or as being carried in a vehicle.

3   While asleep, this physical body is as dead: It neither sees, nor hears, nor feels, and it has neither consciousness nor perception—its powers are suspended. Yet the spirit is not only alive and enduring but also exerts a greater influence, soars to loftier heights, and possesses a deeper understanding. To hold that the spirit is annihilated upon the death of the body is to imagine that a bird imprisoned in a cage would perish if the cage were to be broken, though the bird has nothing to fear from the breaking of the cage. This body is even as the cage and the spirit is like the bird: We observe that this bird, unencumbered by its cage, soars freely in the world of sleep. Therefore, should the cage be broken, the bird would not only continue to exist but its senses would be heightened, its perception would be expanded, and its joy would grow more intense. In reality, it would be leaving a place of torment for a delightsome paradise; for there is no greater paradise for the grateful birds than to be freed from their cage. So it is that the martyrs hasten to the field of sacrifice with the utmost joy and elation.

4   In wakefulness the eye of man sees, at most, as far as one hour's distance; for the influence of the spirit through the

intermediary of the body extends only so far, but with the mind's eye it sees America, understands that land, is apprised of its condition, and arranges affairs accordingly. Now, if the spirit were identical with the body, its power of vision would extend no further. It is therefore evident that the spirit is different from the body, that the bird is different from the cage, and that the power and influence of the spirit is more pronounced without the intermediary of the body. Now, if the instrument becomes idle, its wielder continues to exist. For example, if the pen is abandoned or broken, the writer remains alive and well; if a house is destroyed, its owner lives on. This is one of the rational arguments proving the immortality of the soul.

Another proof is this: Man's body may become weak or [5] robust, sick or healthy, tired or rested; it may suffer the loss of a hand or leg; it may decline in material powers; it may become blind, deaf, dumb, or paralysed—in short, it may become gravely impaired. And yet, despite this, the spirit maintains its original condition and spiritual perceptions, suffering no impairment or disruption. But when the body is afflicted with a major illness or calamity, it is deprived of the grace of the spirit, like a mirror that is broken or covered with dust, and that can no longer reflect the light of the sun or manifest its bounty.

We have already explained that the spirit of man is not [6] contained within the body, for it is freed and sanctified from egress and regress, which are among the properties of material bodies. Rather, the connection of the spirit with the body is like that of the sun with the mirror. Briefly, the human spirit is always in one condition. It neither falls ill with the illness of the body nor is made healthy by the latter's health; it does not become weak or incapacitated, wretched or downtrodden, diminished or lessened—that is, it suffers no harm or ill effect on account of the infirmities of the body, even if the body were to waste away, or if the hands, feet, and tongue were to be cut off, or if the powers of sight and hearing were to be disrupted. It is therefore evident and established that the spirit is different from the body and that its immortality is not conditioned upon the latter's, but that the spirit rules supreme in the world of the body, and that its power and influence are as plain and visible as the bounty of the sun in a mirror. But when the mirror is covered with dust or broken, it will be deprived of the rays of the sun.

62

THE INFINITE PERFECTIONS
OF EXISTENCE AND THE PROGRESS OF
THE SOUL IN THE NEXT WORLD

K NOW THAT THE degrees of existence are finite—the
degrees of servitude, of prophethood, and of Divinity—but that the perfections of God and of creation are
infinite. If you examine the matter with care, you will see
that even in their most outward sense the perfections of
existence are infinite; for it is impossible to find any created
thing such that nothing superior to it can be imagined. For
example, one cannot find in the mineral kingdom a ruby, or
in the vegetable kingdom a rose, or in the animal kingdom
a nightingale, such that an even better specimen cannot
be imagined.

As the grace of God is limitless, so too are the perfections of man. If it were possible for the reality of anything to
reach the very summit of perfection, then it would become
independent of God and the contingent reality would attain
to the station of the necessary reality. But every created thing
has been assigned a degree which it can in no wise overpass.
So he who occupies the degree of servitude, no matter how
far he may progress and acquire endless perfections, can

never reach the degree of divine Lordship. The same holds true of all other created things. No matter how far a mineral may progress, it can never acquire the power of growth in the mineral kingdom. No matter how far this flower may progress, it can never manifest the power of sensation while it is in the vegetable kingdom. So this silver mineral can never gain sight or hearing; at most it can progress in its own degree and become a perfect mineral, but it cannot acquire the power of growth or sensation and can never become living: It can only progress in its own degree.

3   For example, Peter cannot become Christ. At most, he can attain infinite perfections in the degrees of servitude, for every existing reality is capable of progress. As the spirit of man lives forever after casting off this elemental frame, it is, like all existing things, undoubtedly capable of progress, and thus one may pray for a departed soul to advance, to be forgiven, or to be made the recipient of divine favours, bounties, and grace. That is why, in the prayers of Bahá'u'lláh, the forgiveness and pardon of God are implored for those who have ascended to the next world. Moreover, just as people are in need of God in this world, so too are they in need of Him in the next. The creatures are ever in need, and God is ever completely independent of them, whether in this world or in the world to come.

4   The wealth of the next world consists in nearness to God. It is certain therefore that those who enjoy near access to the divine threshold are permitted to intercede, and that this intercession is approved in the sight of God. But intercession in the next world bears no resemblance to intercession

in this world. It is an altogether different condition and reality, which cannot be expressed in words.

Should a wealthy man choose to bequeath, upon his 5 death, a portion of his wealth to the poor and needy, perchance this action will bring about divine pardon and forgiveness and result in his progress in the Kingdom of the All-Merciful.

Likewise, parents endure the greatest toil and trouble 6 for their children, and often, by the time the latter have reached the age of maturity, the former have hastened to the world beyond. Rarely do the mother and father enjoy in this world the rewards of all the pain and trouble they have endured for their children. The children must therefore, in return for this pain and trouble, make charitable contributions and perform good works in their name, and implore pardon and forgiveness for their souls. You should therefore, in return for the love and kindness of your father, give to the poor in his name and, with the utmost lowliness and fervour, pray for God's pardon and forgiveness and seek His infinite mercy.[147]

It is even possible for those who have died in sin and 7 unbelief to be transformed, that is, to become the object of divine forgiveness. This is through the grace of God and not through His justice, for grace is to bestow without desert, and justice is to give that which is deserved. As we have the power to pray for those souls here, so too will we have the same power in the next world, the world of the Kingdom. Are not all the creatures in that world the creation of God? They must therefore be able to progress in that world as well. And just as they can seek illumination here through supplication, so too can they plead there for forgiveness and seek illumination through prayer and supplication. Thus, as souls can progress in this world through their entreaties and supplications, or through the prayers of holy souls, so too after death can they progress through their own prayers and supplications, particularly if they become the object of the intercession of the holy Manifestations.

63

THE PROGRESS OF ALL THINGS
WITHIN THEIR OWN DEGREE

KNOW THAT NOTHING that exists remains in a state 1
of repose—that is, all things are in motion. They are
either growing or declining, either coming from non-existence into existence or passing from existence into non-
existence. So this flower, this hyacinth, was for a time coming from non-existence into existence and is now passing
from existence into non-existence. This is called essential or
natural motion, and it can in no wise be dissociated from
created things, for it is one of their essential requirements,
just as it is an essential requirement of fire to burn.

It is therefore clearly established that motion, whether 2
advancing or declining, is necessary to existence. Now, as the
human spirit continues after death, it must either advance
or decline, and in the next world to cease to advance is the
same as to decline. But the human spirit never transcends
its own degree: It progresses only within that degree. For
example, no matter how far the spirit and reality of Peter
may progress, it will never reach the degree of the reality of
Christ but will progress only within its own inherent limits.

Thus, you see that however much this mineral may prog- 3
ress, its progress remains within its own degree; you cannot

possibly bring this crystal, for example, to a state where it gains the power of sight. The moon, howsoever it may progress, can never become the shining sun, and its apogee and perigee will always remain within its own degree. And however far the Apostles might have progressed, they could never have become Christ. It is true that coal can become a diamond, but both are in the mineral degree and their constituent parts are the same.

64

THE STATION OF MAN AND
HIS PROGRESS AFTER DEATH

W HEN WE EXAMINE all things with the eye of dis- 1
cernment, we observe that they are generally confined to three categories: mineral, vegetable, and animal.
Thus there are three classes of beings and each class has its
associated species. Man is the most distinguished species in
that he combines the perfections of all three classes—that
is, he possesses a material body, the power of growth, and
the power of sensation. Beyond the mineral, vegetable, and
animal perfections, however, he also possesses a special perfection of which other created things are bereft, namely, the
perfections of the mind. Thus man is the noblest of all existing things.

Man is in the ultimate degree of materiality and the 2
beginning of spirituality; that is, he is at the end of imperfection and the beginning of perfection. He is at the fur-
thermost degree of darkness and the beginning of the light.
That is why the station of man is said to be the end of night
and the beginning of day, meaning that he encompasses all
the degrees of imperfection and that he potentially possesses
all the degrees of perfection. He has both an animal side and
an angelic side, and the role of the educator is to so train

human souls that the angelic side may overcome the animal. Thus, should the divine powers, which are identical with perfection, overcome in man the satanic powers, which are absolute imperfection, he becomes the noblest of all creatures, but should the converse take place, he becomes the vilest of all beings. That is why he is the end of imperfection and the beginning of perfection.

3   In no other species in the world of existence can such difference, distinction, contrast, and contradiction be seen as in man. For instance, it is upon man that the effulgent light of the Divinity has been shed, as it was with Christ—see how glorious and noble man is! At the same time, he worships stones, trees, and lumps of clay—see how wretched he is, that the object of his worship should be the basest degrees of existence, that is, lifeless stones and clods of earth, mountains, woods, and trees! What greater wretchedness can there be for man than to worship the lowliest of all things?

4   Moreover, knowledge is a human attribute but so is ignorance; truthfulness is a human attribute but so is falsehood; and the same holds true of trustworthiness and treachery, justice and tyranny, and so forth. In brief, every perfection and virtue, as well as every vice, is an attribute of man. Consider, likewise, the differences that exist among the members of the human race. Christ was in the form of a man and so was Caiaphas; Moses was a man and so was Pharaoh; Abel was a man and so was Cain; Bahá'u'lláh was a man and so was Yaḥyá.[148] That is why man is said to be the greatest sign of God—that is, he is the Book of Creation—for all the mysteries of the universe are found in him. Should he come under the shadow

of the true Educator and be rightly trained, he becomes the gem of gems, the light of lights, and the spirit of spirits; he becomes the focal centre of divine blessings, the wellspring of spiritual attributes, the dawning-place of heavenly lights, and the recipient of divine inspirations. Should he, however, be deprived of this education, he becomes the embodiment of satanic attributes, the epitome of animal vices, and the source of all that is oppressive and dark.

This is the wisdom of the appearance of the Prophets: 5 to educate humanity, that this lump of coal may become a diamond and this barren tree may be grafted and yield fruit of the utmost sweetness and delicacy. And after the noblest stations in the world of humanity have been attained, further progress can be made only in the degrees of perfection, not in station, for the degrees are finite but the divine perfections are infinite.

Both before and after casting off this elemental frame, 6 the human soul progresses in perfections but not in station. The progression of all created things culminates in perfect man, and no greater being than him exists: Man, having reached the human station, can progress only in perfections and not in station, for there is no higher station to which he can find passage than that of a perfect man. He can progress solely within the human station, as human perfections are infinite. Thus, however learned a man may be, it is always possible to imagine one even more learned.

And as the perfections of man are infinite, he can also 7 advance in these perfections after his ascension from this world.

65

FAITH AND WORKS

1 QUESTION: IT IS said in the Kitáb-i-Aqdas: "...whoso is deprived thereof, hath gone astray, though he be the author of every righteous deed".[149] What is the meaning of this verse?

2 Answer: The meaning of this blessed verse is that the foundation of success and salvation is the recognition of God, and that good deeds, which are the fruit of faith, derive from this recognition.

3 When this recognition is not attained, man remains veiled from God and, as he is veiled, his good works fail to achieve their full and desired effect. This verse does not mean that those who are veiled from God are all equal, whether they be doers of good or workers of iniquity. It means only that the foundation is the recognition of God and that good deeds derive from this knowledge. Nevertheless, it is certain that among those who are veiled from God there is a difference between the doer of good and the sinner and malefactor. For the veiled soul who is endowed with good character and conduct merits the forgiveness of God, while the veiled sinner possessed of bad character and conduct will be deprived of the bounties and bestowals of God. Herein lies the difference.

This blessed verse means, therefore, that good deeds 4 alone, without the recognition of God, cannot lead to eternal redemption, to everlasting success and salvation, and to admittance into the Kingdom of God.[150]

66

THE SUBSISTENCE OF THE RATIONAL SOUL
AFTER THE DEATH OF THE BODY

1 QUESTION: AFTER THE body has been cast off and the spirit has taken flight, through what will the rational soul subsist? Let us suppose that those souls who are aided by the outpourings of the Holy Spirit attain true existence and everlasting life. But what becomes of those rational souls who are veiled from God?

2 Answer: Some hold that the body is the substance and that it subsists by itself, and that the spirit is an accident which subsists through the substance of the body. The truth, however, is that the rational soul is the substance through which the body subsists. If the accident—the body—is destroyed, the substance—the spirit—remains.

3 Secondly, the rational soul, or the human spirit, does not subsist through this body by inherence—that is to say, it does not enter it; for inherence and entrance are characteristics of bodies, and the rational soul is sanctified above this. It never entered this body to begin with, that it should require, upon leaving it, some other abode. No, the connection of the spirit with the body is even as the connection of this lamp with a mirror. If the mirror is polished and perfected, the light of the lamp appears therein,

and if the mirror is broken or covered with dust, the light remains concealed.

The rational soul—the human spirit—did not descend 4 into this body or subsist through it to begin with, that it should require some substance to depend upon after the constituent parts of the body have decomposed. On the contrary, the rational soul is the substance upon which the body depends. The rational soul is endowed from the beginning with individuality; it does not acquire it through the intermediary of the body. At most, what can be said is that the individuality and identity of the rational soul may be strengthened in this world, and that the soul may either progress and attain to the degrees of perfection or remain in the lowest abyss of ignorance and be veiled from and deprived of beholding the signs of God.

Question: Through what means can the spirit of man— 5 the rational soul—progress after departing from this mortal world?

Answer: The progress of the human spirit in the divine 6 world, after its connection with the physical body has been severed, is either purely through the grace and bounty of the Lord, or through the intercession and prayers of other human souls, or through the significant contributions and charitable deeds which are offered in its name.

Question: What happens to children who die before 7 reaching the age of maturity or before the appointed time of birth?

Answer: These children abide under the shadow of the 8 Divine Providence, and, as they have committed no sin and are unsullied by the defilements of the world of nature, they will become the manifestations of divine bounty and the glances of the eye of divine mercy will be directed towards them.

67

ETERNAL LIFE AND ENTRANCE
INTO THE KINGDOM OF GOD

YOU HAVE ASKED concerning eternal life and entrance 1
into the Kingdom. The Kingdom is outwardly referred
to as "heaven", but this is an expression and likeness and
not a factual statement or reality. For the Kingdom is not a
material location but is sanctified above time and place. It
is a spiritual realm, a divine world, and it is the seat of the
sovereignty of the almighty Lord. It is exalted above bodies
and all that is corporeal, and it is freed and sanctified from
the idle conjectures of men. For to be confined to place is
a characteristic of bodies and not of spirits: Time and place
encompass the body, not the mind and the soul.

Observe that the body of man abides in a limited space 2
and occupies no more than two spans of earth. But the spirit
and mind of man traverses all countries and regions and
even the limitless expanse of the heavens; it encompasses all
existence and makes discoveries in the spheres above and in
the infinite reaches of the universe. This is because the spirit
has no place: It is a placeless reality, and for the spirit earth
and heaven are the same, since it makes discoveries in both.
But the body is confined in space and is unaware of that
which lies beyond.

3   Now, life is of two kinds: that of the body and that of the spirit. The life of the body consists in material life, but the life of the spirit is a heavenly existence which consists in receiving the grace of the Divine Spirit and being quickened through the breath of the Holy Spirit. Although material life has existence, yet in the eyes of holy and spiritually minded souls it is utter non-existence and death. Thus man exists and so does this stone, but what a difference between the existence of man and that of the stone! Although the stone exists, in relation to the existence of man it is non-existent.

4   What is meant by "eternal life" is receiving the grace of the Holy Spirit, even as a flower partakes of the gifts and breezes of spring. Observe that in the beginning this flower had a purely mineral life, yet through the advent of spring-time, the outpouring of its vernal showers, and the heat of its shining sun, it found another life and appeared with the utmost vitality, delicacy, and fragrance. Compared to its latter life, the former life of the flower was even as death.

5   Our meaning is that the life of the Kingdom is the life of the spirit, and that it is eternal and sanctified above time and place, even as the human spirit, which is placeless. For were you to search throughout the human body, you would be unable to find a specific place or location for the spirit. The spirit is absolutely placeless and immaterial, but it has a connection with the body, even as the sun has a connection with this mirror: The sun occupies no place within the mirror, but it has a connection with it. In the same way, the world of the Kingdom is sanctified above all that can

be seen by the eye or perceived by the other senses, such as hearing, smell, taste, or touch.

Where then can one find in man this mind that resides 6 in him and whose existence is beyond doubt? Were you to examine the human body with the eye, the ear, or the other senses, you would fail to find it, even though it clearly exists. The mind, therefore, has no place, although it is connected with the brain. So it is with the Kingdom. Likewise, love has no place, but it is connected with the heart. And in the same way, the Kingdom has no place, but it is connected with the human reality.

Entrance into the Kingdom is through the love of God, 7 through detachment, through sanctity and holiness, through truthfulness and purity, through steadfastness and faithfulness, and through self-sacrifice.

It follows clearly from these explanations that man is 8 immortal and everlasting. Those who believe in God, who cherish His love, and who have attained certitude, enjoy that blessed life which we call life eternal; but those who are veiled from God, though they be endowed with life, yet they live in darkness and their life, in comparison with that of the believers, is non-existence.

Thus, the eye is alive and so too is the fingernail, but the 9 life of the fingernail in relation to that of the eye is non-existence. The stone and the man both exist, but in relation to man the stone has no existence or being. For when man dies and his body is disintegrated and destroyed, it becomes like the stone, the earth, and the mineral. It is therefore clear that even though the mineral exists, it is non-existent in relation to man.

10   Likewise, those souls who are veiled from God, although they exist both in this world and in the world to come, are non-existent and forgotten in relation to the sanctified existence of the children of the divine Kingdom.

68

TWO KINDS OF FATE

Q UESTION: IS FATE, which is mentioned in the Holy
Books, an irrevocable thing? If so, what use or benefit
will come from seeking to avoid it?

Answer: Fate is of two kinds: One is irrevocable and the
other is conditional, or, as it is said, impending. Irrevocable
fate is that which cannot be changed or altered, while conditional fate is that which may or may not occur. Thus, the
irrevocable fate for this lamp is that its oil will be burnt and
consumed. Its eventual extinction is therefore certain, and it
is impossible to change or alter this outcome, for such is its
irrevocable fate. Likewise, a power has been created in the
body of man whose depletion and exhaustion leads inevitably to the disintegration of the body. It is even as the oil in
this lamp: After it has been burnt and consumed, the lamp
will assuredly be extinguished.

But conditional fate may be likened to this: While some oil
yet remains, a strong wind blows and extinguishes the lamp.
This fate is conditional. It is expedient to avoid this fate, to
guard oneself against it, and to be cautious and prudent. But
the irrevocable fate, which is like the depletion of the oil of
the lamp, cannot be changed, altered, or delayed. It is bound
to occur, and the lamp will undoubtedly be extinguished.

69

THE INFLUENCE OF THE STARS
AND THE INTERCONNECTEDNESS
OF ALL THINGS

1 QUESTION: DO THE stars of the heavens have a spiritual influence upon human souls or not?

2 Answer: Certain celestial bodies exert a physical influence upon the earth and its creatures which is clear and apparent and which requires no explanation. Consider the sun, which, through the help of divine grace, nurtures the earth and all its creatures. Indeed, were it not for the light and heat of the sun, all earthly things would entirely cease to exist.

3 As to spiritual influences, although it might seem strange that these stars should exert a spiritual influence upon the human world, yet were you to reflect deeply upon this matter you would not be greatly surprised by it. My meaning, however, is not that the deductions that the astrologers of old made from the motions of the stars and planets were true, for these were mere figments of the imagination which had their origin with the Egyptian, Assyrian, and Chaldean priests, or rather stemmed from the idle conjectures of the Hindus and the superstitions of the Greeks, the Romans, and the other star worshippers. My meaning,

instead, is that this endless universe is like the human body, and that all its parts are connected one with another and are linked together in the utmost perfection. That is, in the same way that the parts, members, and organs of the human body are interconnected, and that they mutually assist, reinforce, and influence each other, so too are the parts and members of this endless universe connected with, and spiritually and materially influenced by, one another. For example, the eye sees and the entire body is affected; the ear hears and every limb and member is stirred. Of this there is no doubt, for the world of existence is also like a living person. Thus, the interconnection that exists between the various parts of the universe requires mutual influences and effects, whether material or spiritual.

For those who deny the spiritual influence of material 4
things, we mention this brief example: Beautiful sounds, wondrous tones, and harmonious melodies are accidents which affect the air; for sound consists in vibrations of the air, and through these vibrations the nerves of the tympanum are excited and hearing results. Now consider how the vibrations of the air, which are an accident among accidents and which are accounted as naught, attract and exhilarate the spirit of man and move him to the utmost: They cause him to laugh and to weep, and can even induce him to throw himself in harm's way. Observe, then, what a connection exists between the spirit of man and the vibrations of the air, that the latter can transport him to another state and so overwhelm him as to entirely deprive him of patience and composure. Consider how strange this is, for nothing

comes forth from the singer and enters into the listener, and yet great spiritual effects are produced. This intimate relationship between all created things is therefore bound to give rise to spiritual influences and effects.

5   It was already mentioned that the parts and members of the human body mutually influence one another. For instance, the eye sees and the heart is affected. The ear hears and the spirit is influenced. The heart finds peace, the thoughts expand, and all the members of the body experience a state of well-being. What a connection and relationship this is! And if such relationships, such spiritual influences and effects, are found among the various members of the body of man, which is only one particular being among many, then there must assuredly exist both spiritual and material relationships among the countless universal beings. And although our present methods and sciences cannot detect these relationships among the universal beings, their existence is nonetheless clear and indisputable.

6   In sum, all beings, whether universal or particular, are mutually connected in accordance with God's consummate wisdom and mutually influence one another. Were it not so, the all-embracing organization and universal arrangement of existence would become disordered and disrupted. And as all created things are most soundly connected one with another, they are well ordered, arranged, and perfected.

7   This matter deserves close examination and calls for careful attention and deep reflection.

70

FREE WILL AND ITS LIMITS

QUESTION: IS MAN free and unconstrained in all his actions, or is he compelled and constrained?

Answer: This is one of the most important questions of divinity, and it is most abstruse. God willing, another day we will explain this matter at length from the beginning of our lunch. For now, we will briefly say a few words, as follows.

Certain matters are subject to the free will of man, such as acting with justice and fairness, or injustice and iniquity—in other words, the choice of good or evil actions. It is clear and evident that the will of man figures greatly in these actions. But there are certain matters where man is forced and compelled, such as sleep, death, sickness, failing powers, misfortune, and material loss: These are not subject to the will of man and he is not accountable for them, for he is compelled to endure them. But he is free in the choice of good and evil actions, and it is of his own accord that he performs them.

For example, should he so wish, he can pass his days in praise of God, and should he so desire, he can occupy himself with that which is other than Him. He can light the candle of his heart with the flame of the love of God and become a well-wisher of the world, or he can become an enemy of all mankind or set his affections on worldly things; he can choose to be just or iniquitous. All these deeds and actions are under his own control, and he is therefore accountable for them.

5   But another question arises: Man's condition is one of utter helplessness and absolute poverty. All might and power belong to God alone, and man's exaltation and abasement depend on the will and purpose of the Most High. Thus it is said in the Gospel that God is like a potter who makes "one vessel unto honour, and another unto dishonour".[151] Now, the dishonoured vessel has no right to reproach the potter, saying, "Why did you not make me a precious cup that would be passed from hand to hand?" The meaning of these words is that souls occupy different stations. That which occupies the lowest station of existence, like the mineral, has no right to object, saying, "O God, why have you denied me the perfections of the plant?" Likewise, the plant has no right to protest that it has been deprived of the perfections of the animal realm. And, similarly, it is not befitting for the animal to complain of the want of human perfections. No, all these things are perfect in their own degree and must pursue the perfections of that degree. As we have said previously, that which is inferior in rank has no right or qualification to aspire to the station and perfections of that which is superior, but must progress within its own degree.[152]

6   Moreover, man's stillness or motion itself is conditioned upon the aid of God. Should this assistance fail to reach him, he can do neither good nor evil. But when the assistance

of the all-bounteous Lord confers existence upon man, he is capable of both good and evil. And should that assistance be cut off, he would become absolutely powerless. That is why the aid and assistance of God are mentioned in the Sacred Scriptures. This condition can be likened to that of a ship that moves by the power of wind or steam. Should this power be cut off, the ship would become entirely unable to move. Nevertheless, in whatever direction the rudder is turned, the power of the steam propels the ship in that direction. If the rudder is turned to the east, the ship moves eastward, and if it is directed to the west, the ship moves west. This motion does not arise from the ship itself, but from the wind or steam.

In like manner, all the doings of man are sustained by the power of divine assistance, but the choice of good or evil belongs to him alone. It is like when the king appoints an individual as governor of a city, grants him full authority, and shows him that which is just and unjust according to the law. Now, should the governor commit injustice, even though he acts by the power and authority of the king, yet the king would not condone his injustice. And should the governor act with justice, this too would be through the royal authority, and the king would be well pleased and satisfied with his justice. 7

Our meaning is that the choice of good and evil belongs to man, but that under all circumstances he is dependent upon the life-sustaining assistance of Divine Providence. The sovereignty of God is great indeed, and all are held 8 captive in the grasp of His power. The servant can do nothing of his own will alone: God is almighty and all-powerful and bestows His assistance upon all creation.

9   This question has been clearly explained and elucidated.

71

SPIRITUAL DISCLOSURES

QUESTION: SOME PEOPLE believe that they have spir- 1
itual disclosures, that is, that they converse with spirits.
How is this?

Answer: Spiritual disclosures are of two kinds: One, 2
which is commonly referred to among other peoples, is
mere imagination, while the other is true spiritual visions
such as the revelations of Isaiah, of Jeremiah, and of John.

Consider that man's contemplative powers produce two 3
kinds of conceptions. One kind consists in sound and
true conceptions, which, when combined with resolution, become outwardly realized, such as proper arrangements, wise opinions, scientific discoveries, and technologi-
cal inventions. The other consists in false ideas and baseless
imaginations, which yield no fruit and have no reality. They
surge like the waves of the sea of delusion and fade away
like idle dreams.

In like manner, spiritual disclosures are of two kinds. 4
One is the visions of the Prophets and the spiritual disclosures of the chosen ones of God. The visions of the Prophets are not dreams but true spiritual disclosures. Thus when
they say, "I saw someone in such a form, and I spoke such
words, and he gave such a reply", this vision takes place in

a state of wakefulness and not in the realm of sleep. It is a spiritual discovery that is expressed in the form of a vision.

5 The other kind of spiritual disclosures is mere illusion, but these illusions take such a tangible form in the mind that many simple-hearted people imagine them to be real. The obvious proof of this is that no concrete result or outcome ever follows from this supposed compelling or summoning of spirits. No, these are mere fables and fictions.

6 Know, therefore, that the human reality encompasses the realities of all things and discovers their true nature, their properties, and their mysteries. For instance, all the existing crafts, inventions, sciences, and branches of learning have been discovered by the human reality. At one time they were all hidden and concealed mysteries, but the reality of man gradually discovered them and brought them forth from the invisible world into the visible realm. It is therefore evident that the reality of man encompasses all things. Thus it is in Europe and discovers America; it is on the earth and makes discoveries in the heavens. It unravels the mysteries of all things and apprehends the realities of all beings. These true disclosures which conform to reality are similar to visions—which consist in spiritual understanding, heavenly inspiration, and the close communion of human spirits—and thus the recipient will say that he saw, or said, or heard such a thing.

7 It is therefore clear that the spirit has powerful perceptions that are not mediated by the organs of the five senses, such as the eyes and the ears. And, with respect to spiritual understandings and inner disclosures, there exists

among spiritual souls a unity that surpasses all imagination and comparison and a communion that transcends time and place. So, for example, when it is written in the Gospel that Moses and Elijah came to Christ on Mount Tabor, it is clear that this was not a material communion but a spiritual condition that has been expressed as a physical meeting.

The other kind of summoning of, and conversation and communication with, spirits is vain imagination and pure illusion, although it may appear to be real. The mind and thought of man at times discovers certain truths, and this thought and discovery produce definite results and benefits. Such thoughts have a solid foundation. But many things come to mind that are like the waves of the sea of delusion; they bear no fruit and produce no result. In the world of sleep, too, one may have a dream which exactly comes true, while on another occasion one will have a dream which has absolutely no result. 8

Our meaning is that this condition which we call conversation or communication with spirits is of two kinds: One is sheer delusion, and the other, which consists in the visions mentioned in the Bible, such as those of Isaiah and John and the meeting of Christ with Moses and Elijah, is real. The latter exert a marvellous effect upon minds and thoughts and produce powerful attractions in the hearts. 9

72

HEALING WITHOUT MEDICINE

1 QUESTION: SOME HEAL the sick by spiritual means—that is, without medicine. How is this?

2 Answer: A detailed explanation of this matter was provided earlier. If you have not fully grasped it, we will repeat it so that you may. Know that there are four kinds of treatment and healing without medicine. Two are due to material causes and two to spiritual ones.

3 As to the two material kinds, one is due to the fact that in reality both health and sickness are contagious. The contagiousness of disease is rapid and violent, whereas that of health is exceedingly slow and weak. If two bodies are brought into contact with each other, it is certain that microbial particles will be transmitted from one to the other. In the same way that disease is rapidly and violently transmitted from one body to another, the strong health of a healthy person may also alleviate a very slight condition in a sick person. Our meaning is that the contagiousness of disease is rapid and violent, while that of health is very slow and of limited effect, and it is only in minor ills that this modest effect can be felt. In such cases, the strength of the healthy body overcomes the slight weakness of the sick body and brings about its health. This is one kind of healing.

Another kind of healing is through the force of bodily 4 magnetism, where the magnetic force of one body affects another body and brings about the cure. This force, too, has only a slight effect. Thus someone may lay his hand upon the head or stomach of a patient and perchance the latter will benefit from this. Why? Because the effect of the magnetism, and the impression made upon the psyche of the patient, may dispel the disease. But this effect is also very slight and weak.

The two other kinds are spiritual; that is, the means of 5 healing is a spiritual power. One is when a healthy person focuses his whole attention upon a sick person, and the latter in turn fully expects to be healed through the spiritual power of the former and is wholly convinced thereof, to such an extent that a strong connection is created between their hearts. Should the healthy individual then bend every effort to heal the sick one, and should the latter have full faith that health will be attained, an excitement may be produced in his nerves from these soul-to-soul influences and bring about the cure. So, for example, when a sick person is suddenly given the good news that his most ardent wish and desire has been realized, a nervous excitement may result that will entirely dispel the ailment. In the same way, when a terrifying event suddenly comes to pass, such an excitement may be produced in the nerves of a healthy person that he immediately falls ill. The cause of the illness is not a material thing, for that person has not ingested or come into contact with anything: The nervous excitement alone has brought about the illness. Likewise, the sudden realization of a most cherished desire may impart such joy as to excite the nerves and restore health.

6   In brief, a complete and perfect connection between the spiritual physician and the patient—that is, one where the physician concentrates his entire attention on the patient and where the patient likewise concentrates all his attention on the spiritual physician and anticipates healing—causes a nervous excitement whereby health is regained. But this is effective only to a point and not in all cases. For instance, should someone contract a grave illness or be physically injured, these means will neither dispel the illness nor soothe and heal the injury—that is, these means have no sway over grave illnesses unless assisted by the constitution of the patient, for a strong constitution will often ward off an illness. This is the third kind of healing.

7   But the fourth kind is when healing is brought about through the power of the Holy Spirit. This depends neither upon physical contact, nor upon sight, nor even upon presence: It is not dependent upon any condition. Whether the disease be mild or severe, whether there be contact between the bodies or not, whether a connection be established between patient and physician or not, whether the patient be present or not, this healing takes place through the power of the Holy Spirit.

73

HEALING BY MATERIAL MEANS

YESTERDAY AT TABLE we mentioned, in connection with the question of spiritual medicine and healing, how illnesses can be cured through spiritual powers. 1

Now we will speak of material healing. The science 2 of medicine is still in its infancy and has not yet reached maturity. But when it reaches that stage, treatments will be administered with things that are not repulsive to the senses of taste and smell, that is, through foods, fruits, and plants that have an agreeable taste and a pleasant smell. For the cause of the intrusion of illness into the human body is either a physical agent or a nervous excitement and stimulation.

As to physical agents, which are the primary cause of 3 illness, their effect is due to the following: The human body is composed of numerous elements according to a particular state of equilibrium. So long as this equilibrium is maintained, man is preserved from sickness, but should this fundamental balance, which is the central requirement of a sound constitution, be upset, the constitution will be disrupted and illnesses will supervene.

For instance, if there is a deficiency in one of the com- 4 ponent parts of the body and a surfeit of another, the state of equilibrium is disturbed and illness occurs. So, for example, equilibrium may require one component to be a thousand grams and another to be five grams. Should the former fall to seven hundred grams and the latter increase in such wise that the state of equilibrium is disturbed, then illness will supervene; and should equilibrium be restored through medicines and treatments, the illness will be overcome. Thus if the sugar component becomes excessive, the health is impaired; and when the physician forbids sweet and starchy foods, the sugar component diminishes, equilibrium is restored, and the illness is banished.

5   Now, the equilibration of these bodily components can be accomplished by one of two means, either through medicines or with foods, and when the constitution has recovered its equilibrium, the illness is banished. Since all the constituent elements of the human body are also found in plants, if one of these components were to become deficient, and if one were to partake of foods that are rich in that component, then equilibrium would be restored and the cure realized. So long as the aim is the equilibration of the component parts of the body, this can be equally effected through medicines or various foods.

6   The majority of the illnesses that afflict man also afflict animals, but the animal does not treat them through medicines. The animal's physician in the mountains and the wilderness is its powers of taste and smell. The sick animal smells the plants that grow in the wilderness, eats those that its smell and taste find to be sweet and fragrant, and is cured. The reason is this: When, for example, the sugar component in its body becomes deficient, it craves sweet things and thus

eats of sweet-tasting plants, for nature so urges and guides it. Thus, as the animal eats things that are pleasing to its smell and taste, the sugar component increases and it regains its health.

It is therefore evident that it is possible to cure illnesses 7 by means of fruits and other foods. But as the science of medicine has not yet been perfected, this fact has not been fully understood. When this science reaches perfection, treatments will be administered with fragrant fruits and plants as well as with other foods, and with hot and cold waters of various temperatures.

This is only a brief explanation. God willing, and the 8 occasion permitting, we will provide a more detailed explanation another time.

PART 5

Miscellaneous Subjects

74

ON GOOD AND EVIL

TO EXPLAIN THE truth of this matter is difficult indeed. 1
Know that created things are of two kinds: material
and spiritual, sensible and intelligible. That is, some are per-
ceptible to the senses, while others are only perceived by
the mind.

Sensible realities are those which are perceived by the 2
five outer senses: So, for example, those outward things
which the eye sees are called sensible. Intelligible realities are
those which have no outward existence but are perceived
by the mind. For example, the mind itself is an intelligible
reality and has no outward existence. Likewise, all human
virtues and attributes have an intelligible rather than a sensible existence; that is, they are realities that are perceived by
the mind and not by the senses.

Briefly, intelligible realities such as the praiseworthy 3
attributes and perfections of man are purely good and have
a positive existence. Evil is simply their non-existence. So
ignorance is the want of knowledge, error is the want of
guidance, forgetfulness is the want of remembrance, foolish-
ness is the want of understanding: All these are nothing in
themselves and have no positive existence.

4   As for sensible realities, these are also purely good, and evil is merely their non-existence; that is, blindness is the want of sight, deafness is the want of hearing, poverty is the want of wealth, illness is the want of health, death is the want of life, and weakness is the want of strength.

5   Now, a doubt comes to mind: Scorpions and snakes are poisonous—is this good or evil, for they have a positive existence? Yes, it is true that scorpions and snakes are evil, but only in relation to us and not to themselves, for their venom is their weapon and their sting their means of defence. But as the constituent elements of their venom are incompatible with those of our bodies—that is, as these constituent elements are mutually opposed—the venom is evil, or rather, those elements are evil in relation to each other, while in their own reality they are both good.

6   To summarize, one thing may be evil in relation to another but not evil within the limits of its own being. It follows therefore that there is no evil in existence: Whatsoever God has created, He has created good. Evil consists merely in non-existence. For example, death is the absence of life: When man is no longer sustained by the power of life, he dies. Darkness is the absence of light: When light is no more, darkness reigns. Light is a positively existing thing, but darkness has no positive existence; it is merely its absence. Likewise, wealth is a positively existing thing but poverty is merely its absence.

7   It is thus evident that all evil is mere non-existence. Good has a positive existence; evil is merely its absence.

75

TWO KINDS OF TORMENT

K NOW THAT THERE are two kinds of torment: subtle 1
and palpable. For example, ignorance is itself a torment, but it is a subtle torment; indifference to God is itself
a torment; falsehood is itself a torment; iniquity and treachery are torments. Indeed, all the human imperfections are
torments, but they are subtle torments. A person endowed
with a conscience will certainly prefer to be killed rather
than to sin, and to have his tongue cut out rather than to
slander and lie.

The other kind of torment is palpable and consists in 2
physical punishments such as imprisonment, beating, expulsion, and banishment. But for the people of God, to be veiled
from Him is still more grievous than all these torments.

76

THE JUSTICE AND MERCY OF GOD

1   KNOW THAT JUSTICE consists in rendering to each his due. For example, when a workman labours from morning till evening, justice requires that he be paid his wage, but bounty consists in rewarding him even when he has done no work and expended no effort. So when you give alms to a poor man who has made no effort and done nothing for your benefit to deserve it, this is bounty. Thus, Christ besought forgiveness for those responsible for His death: This is called bounty.

2   Now, the question of the excellence or baseness of things is determined either by reason or by religious law. Some believe that it is based on religious law: Such is the case with the Jews, who believe that all the commandments of the Torah are binding and that they are matters of religious law rather than of reason. Thus they say that one of the commandments of the Torah is that meat and butter cannot be eaten together, for this is "trefah" (and "trefah" in Hebrew means unclean, while "kosher" means clean). This they say is a question of religious law and not of reason.

3   But the divine philosophers hold that the excellence or baseness of things depends upon both reason and religious law. Thus, the prohibitions on murder, theft, treachery,

falsehood, hypocrisy, and iniquity are based on reason: Every rational mind can grasp that these are all vile and reprehensible. For if you merely prick a man with a thorn he will cry out in pain: How well must he realize then that murder, according to reason, is vile and reprehensible. And were he to commit such a crime, he would be held accountable for it whether the prophetic message had reached him or not, for reason itself grasps the reprehensible character of this deed. Thus, when such a person commits such base actions, he will assuredly be held to account.

But if the prophetic injunctions have not reached a place 4 and the people fail, as a result, to act in conformity with the divine teachings, then they are not held accountable according to the laws of religion. For instance, Christ enjoined that cruelty should be met with kindness. If a person remains unaware of this injunction and acts according to the promptings of nature, that is, if he returns injury for injury, then he is not held accountable according to the laws of religion, for this divine injunction has not been conveyed to him. Although such a person is not deserving of divine bounty and favour, God will nevertheless deal with him in His mercy and grant him forgiveness.

Now, vengeance is reprehensible even according to rea- 5 son, for it is of no benefit to the avenger. If a man strikes another, and the victim chooses to exact revenge by return-ing the blow, what advantage will he gain? Will this be a balm to his wound or a remedy for his pain? No, God for-bid! In truth the two actions are the same: Both are injuries; the only difference is that one preceded the other. Therefore, if the victim forgives, or better still, if he acts in the opposite manner, this is praiseworthy.

6   As for the body politic, it punishes the aggressor but not to exact revenge. The purpose of this punishment, rather, is to deter and dissuade, and to oppose iniquity and aggression, so as to prevent others from extending their hand likewise in oppression. But if the victim chooses to forgive and to show instead the greatest mercy, this is most approved in the sight of God.

77

THE PUNISHMENT OF CRIMINALS

QUESTION: SHOULD A criminal be punished, or should he be forgiven and his crime overlooked?

Answer: There are two kinds of retributive actions: One is revenge and retaliation, and the other—punishment and requital. An individual has no right to seek revenge, but the body politic has the right to punish the criminal. Such punishment is intended to dissuade and deter others from committing similar crimes. It is for the protection of the rights of man and does not constitute revenge, for revenge is that inner gratification that results from returning like for like. This is not permissible, for no one has been given the right to seek revenge. And yet, if criminals were entirely left to their own devices, the order of the world would be disrupted. So while punishment is one of the essential requirements of the body politic, the wronged and aggrieved party has no right to seek revenge. On the contrary, he should show forgiveness and magnanimity, for this is that which befits the human world.

The body politic, however, must punish the oppressor, the murderer, and the assailant, to dissuade and deter others from committing similar crimes. But that which is essential is to so educate the masses that no crimes will be committed in the first place; for a people can be so educated as to shrink entirely from any crime, and indeed regard the crime itself as the greatest chastisement and the most grievous torment and punishment. Thus no crimes would occur in the first place such that punishments would be required.

4   We must speak only of that which is practically feasible in the world. There is indeed an abundance of lofty ideals and sentiments that cannot be put into effect. Therefore we must confine ourselves to that which is practicable.

5   For example, if someone wrongs, injures, and assaults another, and the latter retaliates in kind, this constitutes revenge and is blameworthy. If Peter kills the son of Paul, Paul has no right to kill the son of Peter. Were he to do so, it would be an act of vengeance and blameworthy in the extreme. Rather, he must act in the opposite manner and show forgiveness, and, if possible, even be of some assistance to his aggressor. This indeed is that which is worthy of man; for what advantage does one gain from revenge? The two actions are indeed one and the same: If one is reprehensible, so too is the other. The only difference is that one preceded the other.

6   But the body politic has the right to preserve and to protect. It holds no grudge and harbours no enmity towards the murderer, but chooses to imprison or punish him solely to ensure the protection of others. The purpose is not revenge but a punishment through which the body politic is protected. Otherwise, were both the victim's heirs and the community to forgive and return good for evil, the wrongdoers would never cease their onslaught and a murder would be

committed at every moment—nay, bloodthirsty individuals would, like wolves, entirely destroy the flock of God. The body politic is not prompted by ill will in meting out its punishment; it acts without prejudice and does not seek to gratify a sense of vengeance. Its purpose in inflicting the punishment is to safeguard others and to prevent the future commission of such vile actions.

Thus when Christ said, "Whosoever shall smite thee on thy right cheek, turn to him the left one also",[153] the purpose was to educate the people, not to imply that one should assist a wolf that has fallen upon a flock of sheep and is intent upon devouring them all. No, if Christ had known that a wolf had entered the fold and was about to destroy the sheep, He most certainly would have prevented it.

Just as forgiveness is one of the attributes of God's mercy, so is justice one of the attributes of His lordship. The canopy of existence rests upon the pole of justice and not of forgiveness, and the life of mankind depends on justice and not on forgiveness. Thus, if a decree of amnesty were to be enacted henceforth in all countries, the whole world would soon be thrown into disarray and the foundations of human life would be shattered. Likewise, if the powers of Europe had not resisted the notorious Attila, he would not have left a single soul alive.

Some men are like bloodthirsty wolves: If they were to see no punishment ahead, they would kill others solely for the sake of their own pleasure and diversion. One of the tyrants of Persia killed his tutor for mere amusement. Mutavakkil, the famous Abbasid caliph, would summon his ministers, deputies, and trustees to his presence, have a box full of scorpions let loose among them, and, forbidding anyone to move, would burst into boisterous laughter whenever one of them was stung.

10   In sum, the proper functioning of the body politic depends upon justice and not forgiveness. So what Christ meant by forgiveness and magnanimity is not that if another nation were to assail you; burn your homes; plunder your possessions; assault your wives, children, and kin; and violate your honour, you must submit to that tyrannical host and permit them to carry out every manner of iniquity and oppression. Rather, the words of Christ refer to private transactions between two individuals, stating that if one person assaults another, the injured party should forgive. But the body politic must safeguard the rights of man. Thus, if someone were to attack, injure, oppress, and wound me, I would in no wise oppose him but would show forgiveness. But if someone were to attack Siyyid Manshádí here,[154] I would of course prevent him. Although to the assailant non-interference would appear as kindness, it would be sheer oppression towards Manshádí. So if a savage Arab were to enter the room at this moment brandishing a sword and bent upon assaulting, wounding, or killing you, I would of course prevent him. Were I to abandon you to that man, this would be oppression, not justice. But if he were to harm me personally, I would forgive him.

11   One final point: The body politic is engaged day and night in devising penal laws and in providing for ways and means of punishment. It builds prisons, acquires chains

and fetters, and ordains places of exile and banishment, of torment and hardship, seeking thereby to reform the criminal, whereas in reality this only brings about the degradation of morals and the subversion of character. The body politic should instead strive night and day, bending every effort to ensure that souls are properly educated, that they progress day by day, that they advance in science and learning, that they acquire praiseworthy virtues and laudable manners, and that they forsake violent behaviour, so that crimes might never occur. At the present time the contrary prevails: The body politic is ever seeking to strengthen penal laws and securing means of punishment, instruments of death and chastisement, and places of imprisonment and exile, and then waiting for crimes to be committed. This has a most detrimental effect.

But if the masses were educated so that knowledge and 12 learning increased day by day, understanding was broadened, perceptions were refined, morals were rectified and manners reformed—in a word, that progress was made with respect to every degree of perfection—then the occurrence of crime would subside.

Experience has shown that crime is less prevalent among 13 civilized peoples—that is, among those who have acquired true civilization. And true civilization is divine civilization, the civilization of those who combine material and spiritual perfections. As ignorance is the root cause of crime, the more knowledge and learning advance, the less crime will be committed. Consider the lawless tribes of Africa: How often they kill one another and even consume each other's flesh and blood! Why do such savageries not take place in Switzerland? The reason, clearly, is education and virtue.

14   Therefore, the body politic must seek to prevent crimes from being committed in the first place, rather than devise harsh punishments and penalties.

78

STRIKES

YOU HAVE ASKED about strikes. Great difficulties have ₁
arisen and will continue to arise from this issue. The
origin of these difficulties is twofold: One is the excessive
greed and rapacity of the factory owners, and the other is
the gratuitous demands, the greed, and the intransigence of
the workers. One must therefore seek to address both.

Now, the root cause of these difficulties lies in the law ₂
of nature that governs present-day civilization, for it results
in a handful of people accumulating vast fortunes that far
exceed their needs, while the greater number remain naked,
destitute, and helpless. This is at once contrary to justice, to
humanity, and to fairness; it is the very height of inequity
and runs counter to the good-pleasure of the All-Merciful.

This disparity is confined to the human race: Among ₃
other creatures, that is, among the animals, a certain kind of
justice and equality prevails. Thus there is equality within a
shepherd's flock, or within a herd of deer in the wilderness,
or among the songbirds that dwell in the mountains, plains,
and orchards. The animals of every species enjoy a measure
of equality and do not differ greatly from one another in
their means of existence, and thus they live in perfect peace
and joy.

4   It is quite otherwise with the human race, where the greatest oppression and injustice are to be found. Thus you can observe, on the one hand, a single person who has amassed a fortune, made an entire country his personal dominion, acquired immense wealth, and secured an unceasing flow of gains and profits, and, on the other, a hundred thousand helpless souls—weak, powerless, and wanting even a mouthful of bread. There is neither equality here nor benevolence. Observe how, as a result, general peace and happiness have become so wanting, and the welfare of humanity so undermined, that the lives of a vast multitude have been rendered fruitless! For all the wealth, power, commerce, and industry are concentrated in the hands of a few individuals, while all others toil under the burden of endless hardships and difficulties, are bereft of advantages and benefits, and remain deprived of comfort and peace. One must therefore enact such laws and regulations as will moderate the excessive fortunes of the few and meet the basic needs of the myriad millions of the poor, that a degree of moderation may be achieved.

5   However, absolute equality is just as untenable, for complete equality in wealth, power, commerce, agriculture, and industry would result in chaos and disorder, disrupt livelihoods, provoke universal discontent, and undermine the orderly conduct of the affairs of the community. For unjustified equality is also fraught with peril. It is preferable, then, that some measure of moderation be achieved, and by moderation is meant the enactment of such laws and regulations as would prevent the unwarranted concentration of wealth

in the hands of the few and satisfy the essential needs of the many. For instance, the factory owners reap a fortune every day, but the wage the poor workers are paid cannot even meet their daily needs: This is most unfair, and assuredly no just man can accept it. Therefore, laws and regulations should be enacted which would grant the workers both a daily wage and a share in a fourth or fifth of the profits of the factory in accordance with its means, or which would have the workers equitably share in some other way in the profits with the owners. For the capital and the management come from the latter and the toil and labour from the former. The workers could either be granted a wage that adequately meets their daily needs, as well as a right to a share in the revenues of the factory when they are injured, incapacitated, or unable to work, or else a wage could be set that allows the workers to both satisfy their daily needs and save a little for times of weakness and incapacity.

If matters were so arranged, neither would the factory 6 owners amass each day a fortune which is absolutely of no use to them—for should one's fortune increase beyond measure, one would come under a most heavy burden, become subject to exceeding hardships and troubles, and find the administration of such an excessive fortune to be most difficult and to exhaust one's natural powers—nor would the workers endure such toil and hardship as to become incapacitated and to fall victim, at the end of their lives, to the direst need.

It is therefore clearly established that the appropriation of 7 excessive wealth by a few individuals, notwithstanding the needs of the masses, is unfair and unjust, and that, conversely, absolute equality would also disrupt the existence, welfare, comfort, peace, and orderly life of the human race. Such being the case, the best course is therefore to seek moderation, which is for the wealthy to recognize the advantages of moderation in the acquisition of profits and to show regard for the welfare of the poor and the needy, that is, to fix a daily wage for the workers and also to allot them a share of the total profits of the factory.

8   In brief, insofar as the mutual rights of the factory owners and the workers are concerned, laws must be enacted that would enable the former to make reasonable profits and the latter to be provided with their present necessities and their future needs, so that if they become incapacitated, grow old, or die and leave behind small children, they or their children will not be overcome by dire poverty but will receive a modest pension from the revenues of the factory itself.

9   For their part, the workers should not make excessive demands, be recalcitrant, ask for more than they deserve, or go on strike. They should obey and comply and make no demands for exorbitant wages. Rather, the mutual and equitable rights of both parties should be officially fixed and established according to the laws of justice and compassion, and any party that violates them should be condemned after a fair hearing and be subject to a definitive verdict enforced by the executive branch, so that all affairs may be appropriately ordered and all problems adequately resolved.

10   The intervention of the government and the courts in the problems arising between owners and workers is fully

warranted, since these are not such particular matters as are ordinary transactions between two individuals, which do not concern the public and in which the government should have no right to interfere. For problems between owners and workers, though they may appear to be a private matter, are detrimental to the common good, since the commercial, industrial, and agricultural affairs, and even the general business of the nation, are all intimately linked together: An impairment to one is a loss to all. And since the problems between owners and workers are detrimental to the common good, the government and the courts have therefore the right to intervene.

Even in the case of differences that arise between two individuals with regard to particular rights, a third party, namely the government, is needed to resolve the dispute. How, then, can the problem of strikes, which entirely disrupt the country—whether they arise from the inordinate demands of the workers or the excessive greed of the factory owners—remain neglected? 11

Gracious God! How can one see one's fellow men hungry, destitute, and deprived, and yet live in peace and comfort in one's splendid mansion? How can one see others in the greatest need and yet take delight in one's fortune? That is why it has been decreed in the divine religions that the wealthy should offer up each year a portion of their wealth for the sustenance of the poor and the assistance of the needy. This is one of the foundations of the religion of God and is an injunction binding upon all. And since in this regard one is not outwardly compelled or obliged by the 12 government, but rather aids the poor at the prompting of one's own heart and in a spirit of joy and radiance, such a deed is most commendable, approved, and pleasing.

13   This is the meaning of the righteous deeds mentioned in the heavenly Books and Scriptures.

79

THE REALITY OF THE
WORLD OF BEING

THE SOPHISTS HOLD that all existence is illusory, 1
indeed, that each and every being is an absolute illusion that has no existence whatsoever—in other words, that
the existence of created things is like a mirage, or like the
reflection of an image in water or in a mirror, which is
merely an appearance devoid of any basis, foundation, or
ascertainable reality.

This notion is false, for although the existence of things 2
is an illusion compared to the existence of God, yet in the
contingent world it is established, proven, and undeniable.
For example, the existence of the mineral is non-existence
compared to that of man—since man's body becomes mineral when he physically dies—but the mineral indeed exists
within the mineral realm. It is therefore clear that dust is
non-existent or has an illusory existence compared to that
of man, but that within the mineral realm it exists.

In like manner, the existence of created things is sheer 3
illusion and utter non-existence compared to that of God
and consists in a mere appearance, like an image seen in a
mirror. But although this image is an illusion, its source and
reality is the person reflected, whose image has appeared in

the mirror. Briefly, the reflection is an illusion compared to that which is reflected. It is therefore evident that although created things have no existence compared to that of God, being instead like a mirage or an image reflected in a mirror, yet in their own degree they exist.

4   That is why Christ referred to those who were heedless of God and denied His truth as dead, even though to outward seeming they were alive; for in relation to the faithful they were indeed dead, blind, deaf, and dumb. That is what Christ meant when He said, "let the dead bury their dead". [155]

80

PRE-EXISTENCE AND ORIGINATION

QUESTION: HOW MANY kinds of pre-existence and 1
origination are there?

Answer: Certain sages and philosophers hold that there 2
are two kinds of pre-existence—essential and temporal—
and that there are likewise two kinds of origination—essential and temporal.

Essential pre-existence is an existence which is not 3
preceded by a cause; essential origination is preceded by a
cause. Temporal pre-existence has no beginning; temporal
origination has both a beginning and an end. For the existence of each and every thing depends upon four causes: the
efficient cause, the material cause, the formal cause, and the
final cause.[156] So this chair has a creator who is a carpenter,
a matter which is wood, a form which is that of a chair, and
a purpose which is to serve as a seat. Therefore, this chair
is essentially originated, for it is preceded by, and its existence is conditioned upon, a cause. This is called essential or
intrinsic origination.

The world of existence, in relation to its Creator, is intrin- 4
sically originated. Likewise, since the body depends upon and
is sustained by the spirit, it is, in relation to the spirit, essentially originated. Conversely, the spirit can dispense with the

body and is therefore essentially pre-existent in relation to the body. Although the rays are always inseparable from the sun, the sun is pre-existent and the rays are originated; for the existence of the rays depends upon that of the sun, but the converse does not hold true: The sun is the bestower of grace and the rays are the grace itself.

5   The second consideration is that existence and non-existence are both relative. If it be said that a certain thing was brought forth from non-existence, the intent is not absolute non-existence; rather, it is meant that the former condition was non-existence in relation to the present one. For absolute non-existence cannot become existence, as it lacks the very capacity to exist. Man exists, and the mineral likewise exists, but the existence of the mineral is non-existence in relation to that of man; for when the body of man is destroyed, it becomes dust and mineral, and when dust progresses into the human world, and that inanimate body of matter becomes living, man comes into existence. Though the dust—the mineral—enjoys existence in its own station, yet in relation to man it is non-existence. Our meaning is that both exist, but the existence of dust and mineral, in relation to man, is non-existence, for when man dies he becomes dust and mineral.

6   Therefore, although the contingent world exists, in relation to the existence of God it is non-existence and nothingness. Man and dust both exist, but how great the difference between the existence of the mineral and that of man! The one in relation to the other is non-existence. Likewise, the existence of creation is non-existence in relation to that

of God. Thus, even though the universe has existence, in relation to God it is non-existence.

Thus it is clear and evident that although created things 7 exist, in relation to God and to His Word they are non-existent. This is the firstness and the lastness of the Word of God, Who says, "I am the Alpha and the Omega", for He is both the source of grace and its ultimate goal. The Creator has ever had a creation, and the rays have ever emanated and shone forth from the Sun of Truth; for a lightless sun would be impenetrable darkness. The names and attributes of God require the existence of things, and no cessation in the out-pouring of God's ancient grace can ever be contemplated, for this would be contrary to the divine perfections.

81

REINCARNATION

1   Q UESTION: WHAT IS to be said about reincarnation, which is a belief upheld by the followers of certain religions?

2   Answer: Our purpose in what we are about to say is to express the truth and not to denigrate the beliefs of others: It is merely to explain the facts of the matter and nothing more. Otherwise, we are neither inclined to dispute anyone's deeply held beliefs, nor do we sanction such conduct.

3   Know, then, that the reincarnationists are of two kinds. The first do not believe in spiritual rewards and punishments in the next world. They hold instead that man receives his punishment or recompense through reincarnation and return to this world; they regard heaven and hell to be confined to this material realm, and they do not believe in the world beyond. This group is itself divided in two: One division holds that, as a severe punishment, man may at times assume an animal form in returning to this world, and that after enduring this painful torment he proceeds from the animal realm into the human world, and this they call transmigration. The other division holds that man returns to the same human world whence he departed, and that the rewards and punishments of the former life are experienced

in his return, and this they call reincarnation. Neither of these divisions believes in a world beyond this one.

The second group of reincarnationists believe in the next 4 world and see reincarnation as the means of becoming perfect, in that man gradually acquires perfections by departing from and returning again to this world until he attains to the very heart of perfection. That is, man is composed of matter and energy: In the beginning, or in the first cycle, the matter is imperfect, but upon returning repeatedly to this world it progresses and acquires refinement and subtlety until it becomes like a polished mirror; and then the energy, which consists in the spirit, is fully realized therein with all its perfections.

Such is a brief account of the beliefs of the reincarna- 5 tionists and transmigrationists. Were we to enter into the details, much time would be lost—this summary will suffice. Such persons have no rational proofs or arguments for their belief, which is based on mere conjecture and circumstantial inference and not on conclusive proofs. It is proofs that one must demand from the reincarnationists and not inference, conjecture, and presentiment.

But you have asked me for proofs and arguments of the 6 impossibility of reincarnation, and we must therefore explain the reasons for its impossibility. The first proof is that the outward is the expression of the inward: The earthly realm is the mirror of the heavenly Kingdom, and the material world is in accordance with the spiritual world. Now observe that in the sensible world the divine appearances are not repeated, for no created thing can be identical with another in every way. The sign of Divine Unity is present and visible in all things. If all the granaries of the world were filled with grain, you would be hard-pressed to find two grains that are absolutely identical and indistinguishable in every respect: Some difference or distinction is bound to remain between them. Now, as the proof of the Divine Unity exists within all things, and the oneness and singleness of God is visible in the realities of all beings, the recurrence of the same divine appearance is in no wise possible. Therefore reincarnation, which is the repeated manifestation in this world of the same spirit with its former essence and conditions, would be the selfsame appearance and is thus impossible. And since the recurrence of the same divine appearance is impossible for material beings, the repeated assumption of the same station, whether on the arc of descent or on the arc of ascent, is likewise impossible for spiritual beings, for the material world corresponds to the spiritual world.

7   With respect to the species, however, return and recurrence are plainly visible in material realities; that is, the trees which in years past bore leaves, blossoms, and fruit will in the years to come bear the same leaves, blossoms, and fruit. This is called recurrence of species. Were anyone to object that the leaf, the blossom, and the fruit have decomposed, have descended from the vegetable to the mineral world, and have returned again to the former, and that there has thus been a recurrence, we would reply that the blossom, the leaf, and the fruit of last year were decomposed, and their component elements were disintegrated and dispersed. It is not that the same particles of last year's leaf and

fruit that had decomposed have recombined and returned, but that the essence of the species has returned through the combination of new elements. Likewise, the human body is fully disintegrated after the decomposition and dispersion of its constituent parts. Were this body to return from the mineral or vegetable world, it would not comprise the selfsame constituents as the former person, for its elements were decomposed, disintegrated, and dispersed in space. Afterwards other elemental constituents were combined and another body was formed. And while it may be the case that certain constituents of the former body entered into the composition of the latter, those constituents have not been exactly and completely conserved, without any addition or diminution, so as to be composed again and to give rise through their composition and combination to another individual. One cannot deduce, then, that this body has returned with all its constituent parts, that the former individual has become the latter, and hence that a recurrence has taken place—that the very same spirit, like the body, has returned and that after death its essence has regained this world.

And were we to claim that reincarnation is intended to 8 bring about perfection, so that matter might gain in purity and refinement and that the light of the spirit might appear therein with the utmost perfection, this too would be mere imagination. For even if we granted such an assumption, the renewal of an object's existence cannot bring about the transformation of its essence. For the substance of imperfection, by returning, will not become the reality of perfection;

total darkness will not become a source of light; abject weakness will not become power and strength; and an earthly essence will not become a heavenly reality. However often it may return, the infernal tree[157] will never bring forth a sweet fruit, nor will the good tree bear a bitter one. It is thus clear that recurrence and return to the material world are not the means of attaining perfection, and that this supposition rests on no proof or evidence; it is merely a conjecture. No, the attainment of perfection is in reality dependent upon the grace of God.

9   The Theosophists believe that man will return time and again on the arc of ascent until he reaches the Supreme Centre, where matter becomes as a spotless mirror, the light of the spirit shines forth in the plenitude of its power, and essential perfection is attained. However, those who have thoroughly investigated the questions of divinity know of a certainty that the material worlds terminate at the end of the arc of descent; that the station of man lies at the end of the arc of descent and the beginning of the arc of ascent, which is opposite the Supreme Centre; and that from the beginning to the end of the arc of ascent the degrees of progress are of a spiritual nature. The arc of descent is called that of "bringing forth" and the arc of ascent that of "creating anew". The arc of descent ends in material realities and the arc of ascent in spiritual realities. The point of the compass in describing a circle does not reverse its motion, for this would be contrary to the natural movement and the divine order and would disrupt the regularity of the circle.

Moreover, this material world is not of such worth or 10
advantage that one who has been freed from its cage should
seek once again to be caught in its snare. No: By God's
eternal grace the true capacity and receptivity of the human
reality is made clear and manifest through traversing the
degrees of existence and not through recurrence and return.
When the shell is opened but once, it is made plain and
clear whether it conceals a shining pearl or worthless matter. When a plant has grown but once, it puts forth either
flowers or thorns: It need not grow again. Apart from this,
advancing and moving through the worlds in a direct line
and according to the natural order is the cause of existence,
and moving against the natural order and arrangement of
things is the cause of extinction. The return of the spirit
after death is incompatible with the natural movement and
contrary to the divine order.

Thus it is in no wise possible to attain existence through 11
returning: It is as if man, after being freed from the world of
the womb, were to return to it. Consider how unfounded
the conceptions of the reincarnationists and transmigrationists are! They conceive of the body as a vessel and the spirit as
its contents, like water and cup, with the water being emptied from one cup and poured into another. This is indeed a
childish notion: They do not reflect deeply enough to realize that the spirit is an entirely incorporeal thing, that it does
not enter or exit, and that, at most, it is connected with the
body as the sun is with the mirror. If the spirit could indeed
traverse all the degrees and attain to essential perfection by
repeatedly returning to the material world, then it would

have been better if God had prolonged the life of the spirit in this material world in order for it to acquire virtues and perfections, and hence there would be no need for it to taste of the cup of death and enter this life a second time.

12   This idea has its origin in the fact that certain reincarnationists imagine existence to be confined to this fleeting world, and deny the other worlds of God, whereas in reality the latter are infinite. If the worlds of God were to culminate in this material world, then all creation would be in vain and existence itself would be a childish game. For the ultimate result of this endless universe, the most noble reality of man, would go hither and thither for a few days in this ephemeral abode and receive his rewards and punishments. In the end, all would attain perfection, the creation of God with its infinite beings would be completed and consummated, and thus the divinity of the Lord and the names and attributes of God would cease to have any effect and influence upon the spiritual beings which now exist. "Far from the glory of thy Lord, the All-Glorious, be that which His creatures affirm of Him!"[158]

13   The limited minds of the philosophers of old, such as Ptolemy and others, held that the realm of life and existence was confined to this terrestrial globe, and imagined that this infinite space was contained within the nine celestial spheres, all of which were void and empty. Witness how limited were their thoughts and how deficient their reasoning! The reincarnationists likewise imagine the spiritual worlds to be confined to those realms that the human mind can conceive. Some of them, such as the Druze and the

Nuṣayrís, even imagine existence to be confined to this material world. What an ignorant supposition this is! For in this universe of God's, which appears in the utmost perfection, beauty, and grandeur, the luminous bodies of the material universe are infinite. Pause to infer, then, how infinite and unbounded the spiritual realms of God, which are the very foundation, must be! "Take ye good heed, O people of insight!"[159]

But let us return to our original theme. In the Holy 14 Books and Sacred Scriptures there is mention of a "return", but the ignorant have failed to grasp its meanings and have imagined it to refer to reincarnation. For what the Prophets of God meant by "return" is not the return of the essence but of the attributes; it is not the return of the Manifestation Himself but of His perfections. In the Gospel it is said that John the son of Zacharias is Elijah. By these words is not meant the return of the rational soul and personality of Elijah in the body of John, but rather that the perfections and attributes of Elijah became plain and manifest in him.[160]

A lamp was lit in this room last night: When another 15 lamp is lit tonight, we say that the light of last night is shining again. When the water that had ceased to flow from a fountain flows a second time, we say that it is the same water flowing once again, or we say that this light is the same as the former light. Likewise, last spring flowers and sweet-scented herbs bloomed and delicious fruits produced; next year we say that those delicious fruits and those blossoms, flowers, and sweet herbs have returned. It is not that the very same constituents of last year's flowers, after decomposing, have recombined and returned. No, the meaning is that the same freshness and delicacy, the same pleasing fragrance and wondrous colour that characterized last year's flowers are to be exactly found in the flowers of this year. Briefly, the point is the resemblance and similarity between the former and the latter flowers. This is the "return" which is mentioned in the heavenly Scriptures. It is fully explained by Bahá'u'lláh in the Kitáb-i-Íqán: Refer to it, that you may be informed of the truth of the divine mysteries. Upon you be greetings and praise.

82

THE UNITY OF EXISTENCE

QUESTION: WHAT IS the nature of the "unity of exis- 1
tence" propounded by the Theosophists and the Sufis,
and what in reality do they intend by it?[161] Is this belief true
or not?

Answer: Know that the idea of the unity of existence 2
is ancient and is not restricted to the Theosophists and the
Sufis alone. Indeed, it was espoused by some of the Greek
philosophers, such as Aristotle, who said: "The uncompounded Reality is all things, but it is not any single one
of them."[162] "Uncompounded" stands here in contrast to
"composed"—that is to say, that solitary Reality, which is
sanctified and exalted above composition and division, has
resolved itself into countless forms. Thus, real Existence is all
things, but it is not any single one of them.

The proponents of the unity of existence hold that real 3
Existence is even as the sea, and that all created things are
like unto its waves. These waves, which signify the created
things, are the countless forms which that real Existence
assumes. Hence, that sanctified Reality is the pre-existent
sea, and the countless forms of created things are its originated waves.

4 Likewise, they compare this to the One and the infinite numbers, in that the former has manifested itself in the degrees of the latter, for numbers are the repetition of the One. Thus two is the repetition of one, and so on with the other numbers.

5 Among the proofs they adduce is this: All created things are the objects of the divine knowledge, and no knowledge can be realized without objects of knowledge, since knowledge pertains to something that exists, not to that which is non-existent. Indeed, how can utter non-existence attain specification and individuation in the mirror of knowledge? It follows that the realities of all created things, which are the objects of the knowledge of the Most High, had an intelligible existence, for they were the forms of the divine knowledge, and that they are pre-existent, for the divine knowledge is pre-existent. As long as the knowledge is pre-existent, so must be its objects. And the specifications and individuations of created things, which are the objects of the pre-existent knowledge of the divine Essence, are identical to the divine knowledge itself. The reason for this is that the reality, the knowledge, and the objects of the knowledge of the divine Being must be realized in a state of absolute unity. Otherwise, the divine Essence would become the seat of multiple phenomena, and a plurality of pre-existences would become necessary, which is absurd.

6 Thus, they reason, it is established that the objects of knowledge are identical with the knowledge itself, and that the knowledge is in turn identical with the Essence, which is to say that the knower, the knowledge, and the objects

of knowledge are one single reality. Any other conception would necessarily lead to a plurality of pre-existences and to an infinite regress, and indeed to countless pre-existences. And since the individuations and specifications of created things in the knowledge of God were identical to, and completely indistinguishable from, His Essence, true unity prevailed and all the objects of knowledge were comprised and incorporated, in an uncompounded and undivided manner, in the reality of the divine Essence. In other words they were, in an uncompounded and undivided manner, the objects of the knowledge of the Most High and identical with His Essence. And through the manifestational appearance of God, these individuations and specifications, which had an intelligible existence—that is, which were the forms of the divine knowledge—found actual existence in the external world, and thus that real Existence became resolved into countless forms. Such is the basis of their argument.

The Theosophists and the Sufis comprise two groups. 7 One group consists of the generality, who believe in the unity of existence out of sheer imitation and who have not grasped the true intent of the teachings of their renowned leaders. For the generality of the Sufis understand by "Existence" that common existence which is conceived by the mind and intellect of man, that is, which man can comprehend.

This common existence, however, is only one accident 8 among others that enter upon the realities of created things, while the essences of beings are the substance. This accidental existence, which is dependent upon things in the same way that the properties of things are dependent upon them, is but one accident among many.

9 Now, the substance is undoubtedly superior to the accident, for the substance is primary and the accident secondary; the substance subsists through itself while the accident subsists through something else—that is, it needs a substance through which it can subsist.

10 In this case, God would be secondary to and in need of His creation, and the creation could dispense entirely with Him.

11 To illustrate further, whenever individual elements combine in accordance with the universal divine order, a certain being comes into the world of existence. That is, when certain elements are combined, a vegetable existence is produced; when others are combined, an animal existence is produced; when yet others combine, other things come into being. In each case, the existence of things is a consequence of their realities. How then could such an existence, which is an accident among others and which requires a substance through which it can subsist, be essentially pre-existent and the Begetter of all things?

12 But the truly learned among the Theosophists and Sufis have concluded, after deep consideration of this matter, that there are two kinds of existence. One kind is this common existence which is conceived by the mind of man. This existence is originated and is an accident among others, whereas the realities of things are the substances. But what is meant by unity of existence is not this commonly perceived existence, but that real Existence which is sanctified and exalted

above all expression, an Existence through which all things are realized. This Existence is one; it is that One through which all things—such as matter, energy, and that common existence which is conceived by the human mind—have come to exist. This is the truth behind what the Theosophists and the Sufis believe.

In brief, the Prophets and the philosophers are in agreement on one point, namely, that the cause through which all things are realized is but one. The difference is that the Prophets teach that God's knowledge does not require the existence of created things, whereas the knowledge of the creatures requires the existence of objects of knowledge. If the divine knowledge stood in need of aught else, then it would be like the knowledge of the creatures and not that of God; for the Pre-existent is incommensurate with the originated and the originated is opposite to the Pre-existent. That which we affirm for creation to be among the requirements of origination we deny in God; for to be sanctified and exalted above all imperfections is one of the characteristics of the Necessary Being. 13

For instance, in the originated we see ignorance; in the Pre-existent we affirm knowledge. In the originated we see weakness; in the Pre-existent we affirm power. In the originated we see poverty; in the Pre-existent we affirm wealth. Hence the originated is the source of all imperfections, and the Pre-existent is the sum of all perfections. And since the knowledge of the originated is in need of objects of knowledge, the knowledge of the Pre-existent must be independent of their existence. It follows that the specifications and 14 individuations of created things, which are the objects of the divine knowledge, are not pre-existent. Moreover, the attributes of divine perfection are not so yielding to the exertions of the human mind as to enable us to determine whether the divine knowledge is in need of objects or not.

15   Briefly, that which was mentioned earlier is the foremost proof of the Sufis, and if we were to mention all of their arguments and respond to them, it would take a very long time. However, what was said represents the most decisive proof and the clearest argument that the learned among the Sufis and the Theosophists have advanced.

16   The real Existence through which all things are realized, that is, the reality of the divine Essence through which all things have come to exist, is acknowledged by all. The difference resides in the fact that the Sufis maintain that the realities of all things are the manifestation of the One, whereas the Prophets say that they emanate therefrom. And great indeed is the difference between manifestation and emanation. Appearance through manifestation means that a single thing becomes manifest in infinite forms. For example, when the seed, which is a single thing endowed with the perfections of the vegetable kingdom, manifests itself, it becomes resolved into the infinite forms of the branches, leaves, flowers, and fruit. This is called manifestational appearance, whereas in appearance through emanation the One remains transcendent in the heights of its sanctity, but the existence of the creatures is obtained from it through emanation, not manifestation. It can be compared to the sun: The rays emanate from it and shine forth upon

all things, but the sun remains transcendent in the heights of its sanctity. It does not descend; it does not resolve itself into the form of the rays; it does not appear in the identity of things through specification and individuation: The Pre-existent does not become the originated; absolute wealth does not fall captive to poverty; unqualified perfection is not transformed into utter imperfection.

In summary, the Sufis speak only of God and creation, [17] and believe that God has resolved Himself into, and manifested Himself through, the infinite forms of His creation, even as the sea which appears in the infinite forms of its waves. These originated and imperfect waves are identical to the pre-existent Sea, which is the sum of all the divine perfections. The Prophets, however, hold that there are the world of God, the world of the Kingdom, and the world of creation: three things. The first emanation is the outpouring grace of the Kingdom, which has emanated from God and has appeared in the realities of all things, even as the rays emanating from the sun are reflected in all things. And that grace—the rays—appears in infinite forms in the realities of all things, and is specified and individuated according to their capacity, receptivity, and essence. But the assertion of the Sufis would require that absolute wealth descend into poverty, that the Pre-existent be confined to originated forms, and that the very quintessence of power be reflected in the mirror of powerlessness and be subjected to the inherent limitations of the contingent world. And this is a self-evident error, for we observe that the reality of man, who is the noblest of all creatures, cannot descend to the reality of the animal; that the essence of the animal, which is endowed with the power of sensation, does not abase itself to the degree of the plant; and that the reality of the plant, which is the power of growth, does not degrade itself to the reality of the mineral.

18   In brief, superior realities do not descend or abase themselves to the degree of inferior realities. How, then, could the universal Reality of God, which transcends all descriptions and attributes, resolve itself, notwithstanding its absolute sanctity and holiness, into the forms and realities of the contingent world, which are the very source of imperfections? This is pure fantasy and untenable conjecture. On the contrary, that Essence of sanctity is the sum of all divine and lordly perfections, and all creatures receive illumination from His emanational appearance and partake of the lights of His celestial perfection and beauty, in the same way that all earthly creatures acquire the grace of light from the rays of the sun, without any descent or abasement of the latter into the recipient realities of these earthly beings.

19   After dinner, and considering the lateness of the hour, there is no time to explain further.

83

THE FOUR CRITERIA
OF COMPREHENSION

T HERE ARE ONLY four accepted criteria of compre- 1
hension, that is, four criteria whereby the realities of
things are understood.

The first criterion is that of the senses; that is, all that 2
the eye, the ear, the taste, the smell, and the touch perceive
is called "sensible". At present all the European philosophers hold this to be the most perfect criterion. They claim
that the greatest of all criteria is that of the senses, and they
regard it as sacrosanct. And yet the criterion of the senses is
defective, as it can err. For example, the greatest of the senses
is the power of vision. The vision, however, sees a mirage as
water and reckons images reflected in mirrors as real and
existing; it sees large bodies as small, perceives a whirling
point as a circle, imagines the earth to be stationary and the
sun to be in motion, and is subject to many other errors of a
similar nature. One cannot therefore rely implicitly upon it.

The second criterion is that of the intellect, which was 3
the principal criterion of comprehension for those pillars
of wisdom, the ancient philosophers. They deduced things
through the power of the mind and relied on rational arguments: All their arguments are based upon reason. But

despite this, they diverged greatly in their opinions. They would even change their own views: For twenty years they would deduce the existence of something through rational arguments, and then afterwards they would disprove the same, again through rational arguments. Even Plato at first proved through rational arguments the immobility of the earth and the movement of the sun, and then subsequently established, again through rational arguments, the centrality of the sun and the movement of the earth. Then the Ptolemaic theory became widespread, and Plato's theory was entirely forgotten until a modern astronomer revived it. Thus have the mathematicians disagreed among themselves, even though they all relied on rational arguments.

4   Likewise, at one time they would establish a thing by rational arguments and disprove it at another, again by rational arguments. So a philosopher would firmly uphold a view for a time and adduce a range of proofs and arguments to support it, and afterwards he would change his mind and contradict his former position by rational arguments.

5   It is therefore evident that the criterion of reason is imperfect, as proven by the disagreements existing between the ancient philosophers as well as by their want of consistency and their propensity to change their own views. For if the criterion of intellect were perfect, all should have been united in their thoughts and agreed in their opinions.

6   The third criterion is that of tradition, that is, the text of the Sacred Scriptures, when it is said, "God said thus in the Torah", or "God said thus in the Gospel." This criterion is not perfect either, because the traditions must be

understood by the mind. As the mind itself is liable to error, how can it be said that it will attain to perfect truth and not err in comprehending and inferring the meaning of the traditions? For it is subject to error and cannot lead to certitude. This is the criterion of the leaders of religion. What they comprehend from the text of the Book, however, is that which their minds can understand and not necessarily the truth of the matter; for the mind is like a balance, and the meanings contained in the texts are like the objects to be weighed. If the balance is untrue, how can the weight be ascertained?

Know, therefore, that what the people possess and believe to be true is liable to error. For if in proving or disproving a thing a proof drawn from the evidence of the senses is advanced, this criterion is clearly imperfect; if a rational proof is adduced, the same holds true; and likewise if a traditional proof is given. Thus it is clear that man does not possess any criterion of knowledge that can be relied upon. 7

But the grace of the Holy Spirit is the true criterion regarding which there is no doubt or uncertainty. That grace consists in the confirmations of the Holy Spirit which are vouchsafed to man and through which certitude is attained. 8

84

GOOD DEEDS AND THEIR
SPIRITUAL PREREQUISITES

1 QUESTION: THOSE WHO do good works, who are well-wishers of all mankind, who have a praiseworthy character, who show forth love and kindness to all people, who care for the poor, and who work for universal peace—what need do they have of the divine teachings, with which they believe they can well afford to dispense? What is the condition of such people?

2 Answer: Know that such ways, words, and deeds are to be lauded and approved, and they redound to the glory of the human world. But these actions alone are not sufficient: They are a body of the greatest beauty, but without a spirit. No, that which leads to everlasting life, eternal honour, universal enlightenment, and true success and salvation is, first and foremost, the knowledge of God. It is clear that this knowledge takes precedence over every other knowledge and constitutes the greatest virtue of the human world. For the understanding of the reality of things confers a material advantage in the realm of being and brings about the progress of outward civilization, but the knowledge of God is the cause of spiritual progress and attraction, true vision and insight, the exaltation of humanity, the appearance of divine

civilization, the rectification of morals, and the illumination of the conscience.

Second comes the love of God. The light of this love is 3 kindled, through the knowledge of God, in the lamp of the heart, and its spreading rays illumine the world and bestow upon man the life of the Kingdom. And in truth the fruit of human existence is the love of God, which is the spirit of life and grace everlasting. Were it not for the love of God, the contingent world would be plunged in darkness. Were it not for the love of God, the hearts of men would be bereft of life and deprived of the stirrings of conscience. Were it not for the love of God, the perfections of the human world would entirely vanish. Were it not for the love of God, no real connection could exist between human hearts. Were it not for the love of God, spiritual union would be lost. Were it not for the love of God, the light of the oneness of mankind would be extinguished. Were it not for the love of God, the East and the West would not embrace as two lovers. Were it not for the love of God, discord and division would not be transmuted into fellowship. Were it not for the love of God, estrangement would not give way to unity. Were it not for the love of God, the stranger would not become the friend. Indeed, love in the human world is a ray of the love of God and a reflection of the grace of His bounty.

It is clear that human realities differ one from another, 4 that opinions and perceptions vary, and that this divergence of thoughts, opinions, understandings, and sentiments among individuals is an essential requirement. For differences of degree in creation are among the essential requirements of existence, which is resolved into countless forms. We stand therefore in need of a universal power which can prevail over the thoughts, opinions, and sentiments of all, which can annul these divisions and bring all souls under the sway of the principle of the oneness of humanity. And it is clear and evident that the greatest power in the human world is the love of God. It gathers divers peoples under the shade of the tabernacle of oneness and fosters the greatest love and fellowship among hostile and contending peoples and nations.

5   Observe how numerous were the divers nations, races, clans, and tribes who, after the advent of Christ, gathered through the power of the love of God under the shadow of His Word. Consider how the differences and divisions of a thousand years were entirely abolished, how the delusion of the superiority of race and nation was dispelled, how the unity of souls and sentiments was attained, and how all became Christians in truth and in spirit.

6   The third virtue of humanity is goodly intention, which is the foundation of all good deeds. Some seekers after truth have held intention to be superior to action, for a goodly intention is absolute light and is entirely sanctified from the least trace of malice, scheming, or deception. Now, one can perform an action which appears to be righteous but which is in reality prompted by self-interest. For example, a butcher raises a sheep and guards its safety, but this good deed of the butcher is motivated by the hope of profit, and the end result of all this care will be the slaughter of the

poor sheep. How many are the goodly and righteous deeds that are in reality prompted by self-interest! But the pure intention is sanctified above such faults.

Briefly, good deeds become perfect and complete only 7 after the knowledge of God has been acquired, the love of God has been manifested, and spiritual attractions and goodly motives have been attained. Otherwise, though good deeds be praiseworthy, if they do not spring from the knowledge of God, from the love of God, and from a sincere intention, they will be imperfect. For example, human existence must encompass all perfections in order to be complete. The power of sight is highly prized and precious, but it must be aided by that of hearing; the hearing is highly prized, but it must be aided by the power of speech; the power of speech is highly prized, but it must be aided by that of reason; and so on with the other powers, organs, and members of man. When all these powers, senses, parts, and organs are combined together, perfection is attained.

In the world today we meet with souls who sincerely 8 desire the good of all people, who do all that lies in their power to assist the poor and succour the oppressed, and who are devoted to universal peace and well-being. Yet, however perfect they may be from this perspective, they remain deprived of the knowledge and the love of God and, as such, are imperfect.

Galen the physician wrote in his commentary on Plato's 9 treatise on the art of governance that religious beliefs exert a profound influence on true civilization, the proof being as follows: Most people cannot grasp a sequence of logical arguments, and stand therefore in need of symbolic allusions heralding the rewards and punishments of the next world. The sign of this is that we see today a people called Christians who believe in the rewards and punishments of the next world and who show forth goodly deeds that are like those of a true philosopher. Thus we all plainly see that they have no fear of death and that they are, by virtue of their ardent yearning for justice and equity, to be regarded as though they were true philosophers.[163]

10   Now observe closely how great the sincerity, the self-abnegation, the spiritual emotions, the pure intentions, and the good deeds of the Christian believers must have been for Galen—a philosopher and physician who was not himself a Christian—to attest to the morals and the perfections of these people and call them true philosophers. Such virtues and qualities cannot be attained through good deeds alone. If virtue only meant that some good be obtained and bestowed, then why do we not praise this burning lamp which lights the room, even though its light is without a doubt a good thing? The sun nurtures all earthly things and fosters their growth and development by its heat and light—what greater good is there than this? Nonetheless, since this good does not flow from goodly motives and from the love and knowledge of God, it does not impress in the least. But when someone offers a cup of water to another, he is shown appreciation and gratitude. An unthinking person might say, "This sun which gives light to the world and manifests this great bounty must surely be praised and glorified. For why should we praise a man for such a modest gift and not yield

thanks to the sun?" But if we were to gaze with the eye of truth, we would see that the modest gift bestowed by this person stems from the stirrings of conscience and is therefore praiseworthy, whereas the light and heat of the sun are not due to this and thus are not worthy of our praise and gratitude. In like manner, while those who perform good deeds are to be lauded, if these deeds do not flow from the knowledge and love of God they are assuredly imperfect.

Aside from this, if you consider the matter with fairness you will see that these good deeds of the non-believers also have their origin in the divine teachings. That is, the Prophets of old exhorted men to perform them, explained their advantages, and expounded their positive effects; these teachings then spread among mankind, successively reaching the non-believing souls and inclining their hearts towards these perfections; and when they found these actions to be laudable and to bring about joy and happiness among men, they too conformed to them. Thus these actions also arise from the divine teachings. But to see this, a measure of fair-mindedness is called for and not dispute and controversy.

Praise be to God, you have visited Persia and have witnessed the loving-kindness which, through the sanctified breezes of Bahá'u'lláh, Persians have come to show forth to all humanity. Formerly, if they chanced upon a follower of another religion, they would set upon him, display the utmost enmity, hatred, and malice, and even regard him as impure. They would burn the Gospel and the Torah and would wash their hands if they had been soiled by touching these Books. But now, most of them recite and interpret, as

351

required by the occasion, from the contents of these two Books in their assemblies and gatherings, and expound and elucidate their inner meanings and mysteries. They show kindness to their enemies and treat bloodthirsty wolves with tender care, as they would the gazelles of the meadows of God's love. You have seen their conduct and character, and you have heard of the morals which the Persians had in former times. Can this transformation of morals and this rectification of speech and conduct be brought about other than through the love of God? No, by God! If we undertook to spread such morals and manners merely by means of knowledge and learning, a thousand years would pass and still they would not have been achieved among the masses.

13   In this day, thanks to the love of God, this has been achieved with the greatest ease. Take heed, then, O ye of understanding heart!

NOTES

Foreword

1 See, for example, *Selections from the Writings of ʻAbduʼl-Bahá*, 30.2; *The Promulgation of Universal Peace: Talks Delivered by ʻAbduʼl-Bahá during His Visit to the United States and Canada in 1912*, trans. Howard Mac-Nutt (Wilmette, IL: Baháʼí Publishing Trust,2012), p. 427; *Paris Talks: Addresses Given by ʻAbduʼl-Bahá in 1911*, 2.1 and 28.6.

2 Chap. 46, par. 7.

3 Shoghi Effendi, *God Passes By* (Wilmette, IL: Baháʼí Publishing Trust, 1974, 2012 printing), p. 410.

4 From a letter dated 13 March 1923 written by Shoghi Effendi to the Baháʼís of Australasia.

5 From a letter dated 14 November 1940 written on behalf of Shoghi Effendi to an individual believer.

PART I

On the Influence of the Prophets in the Evolution of Humanity

1 Gen. 1:26.

2 Cf. John 6:42.

3 Cf. Jurjí Zaydán, *Umayyads and ʻAbbásids: Being the Fourth Part of Jurjí Zaydán's History of Islamic Civilization*, trans. D. S. Margoliouth (London: Darf Publishers, 1987), pp. 125–31.

4 ʻUmar.

5 Copernicus.

6 Qurʼán 36:38.

7 Qurʼán 36:40.

8   Galileo.

9   'Abdu'l-Bahá refers to the Báb by His title Ḥaḍrat-i-A'lá—His Holiness the Exalted One—but He will be designated here by the name under which He is known in the West.

10 'Abdu'l-Bahá refers to Bahá'u'lláh here by His title Jamál-i-Mubárak (the Blessed Beauty). He is also called Jamál-i-Qidám (the Ancient Beauty) and Qalam-i-A'lá (the Pen of the Most High), but He will be designated throughout as Bahá'u'lláh, the title by which He is known in the West.

11 Bahá'u'lláh was exiled first from Ṭihrán to Baghdád, then to Constantinople (Istanbul), then to Adrianople (Edirne), and was imprisoned in 'Akká, "the Most Great Prison", in 1868, in the precincts of which He passed away in 1892.

12 Two cities in Iraq which contain the tombs of the first and the third Imáms of the S͟híʻah denomination, respectively, and which are important centres of pilgrimage.

13 Bahá'u'lláh's first Tablet to Napoleon III was revealed in Adrianople (see *Epistle to the Son of the Wolf*, trans. Shoghi Effendi [Wilmette, IL: Bahá'í Publishing Trust, 1988, 2001 printing], p. 45), which Bahá'u'lláh called the "remote prison".

14 Cf. Súriy-i-Haykal (Súrih of the Temple), ¶138.

15 The son of the French consul in Syria who, according to Nabíl-i-A'ẓam, was a follower of Bahá'u'lláh; see H. M. Balyuzi, *Bahá'u'lláh: The King of Glory* (Oxford: George Ronald, 1980), p. 320.

16 Cf. Súriy-i-Haykal, ¶221.

17 "Yá Bahá'u'l-Abhá", an invocation of the Greatest Name of God (the All-Glorious or Most Glorious).

18 Bahá'u'lláh.

19 Cf. Kitáb-i-Íqán (The Book of Certitude), ¶213.

20 See Chapters 8–9 above.

21 See Dan. 9:24.

22 Cf. Num. 14:34; Ezek. 4:6.

23 That is, Muḥammad's wife and her cousin Varaqih-ibn-i-Nawfal.

24 As Muḥammad began His public ministry ten years before the Hijrah, this date corresponds to the year A.H. 1280, or A.D. 1863.

25 Rev. 11:3.
26 Qur'án 48:8.
27 Rev. 11:4.
28 Rev. 11:5.
29 Rev. 11:6.
30 Rev. 11:6.
31 Rev. 11:6.
32 Rev. 11:7.
33 Rev. 11:7.
34 Cf. Rev. 11:7.
35 Rev. 11:8.
36 Rev. 11:9.
37 Rev. 11:10.
38 Rev. 11:11.
39 Rev. 11:12.
40 The Báb and Quddús.
41 Rev. 11:12.
42 Rev. 11:13.
43 Rev. 11:13.
44 Rev. 11:14.
45 Ezek. 30:1–3.
46 Rev. 11:15.
47 Rev. 11:16–17.
48 "Regarding the four and twenty elders: The Master, in a Tablet, stated that they are the Báb, the 18 Letters of the Living and five others who would be known in the future." (From a letter dated 22 July 1943 written on behalf of Shoghi Effendi to an individual believer.) 'Abdu'l-Bahá in a Tablet identified one of the remaining five as Ḥájí Mírzá Muhammad-Taqí Afnán, Vakílu'd-Dawlih.
49 Rev. 11:18.
50 Rev. 11:18.
51 Rev. 11:18.
52 Rev. 11:18.
53 Rev. 11:19.
54 Rev. 11:19.

55 Rev. 11:19.

56 Rev. 11:19.

57 The translation of the paragraph to this point follows Shoghi Effendi's revision of this passage as quoted in *The World Order of Bahá'u'lláh: Selected Letters* (Wilmette, IL: Bahá'í Publishing Trust, 1991, 2012 printing), pp. 204–5, and *The Promised Day Is Come*, ¶297. It should be noted that the word *nahál*, which corresponds to "rod" in English and which has been rendered as such in paragraphs 1–2, has been rendered in this paragraph as "Branch". In both cases the reference is to Bahá'u'lláh.

58 Rev. 21:1–3.

59 Rev. 21:2.

60 Rev. 12:2.

61 Rev. 12:3–4.

62 Rev. 12:4.

63 Rev. 12:5.

64 Rev. 12:5.

65 Rev. 12:6.

66 Rev. 12:6.

67 Rev. 12:6.

68 The word *sa'ádat*, rendered here as "felicity", has further connotations of prosperity, joy, and well-being.

PART 2

Some Christian Subjects

69 Cf. Matt. 3:16–17; Mark 1:10–11; Luke 3:22.

70 Cf. Exod. 13:21–2.

71 Cf. John 10:38.

72 From Bahá'u'lláh's Tablet to Náṣiri'd-Dín Sháh, in Súriy-i-Haykal, ¶192.

73 Qur'án 19:17; cf. Luke 1:26–8.

74 Qur'án 36:36.

75 Cf. Qur'án 13:3.

76 John 1:12–13.

77 Gen. 2:7.

78 Cf. Matt. 3:11; Mark 1:8; Luke 3:16; John 1:33.

79 Cf. Acts 15:20.

80 'Abdu'l-Bahá refers here to the notions of heat and cold that played an important role in traditional Islamic medicine.

81 John 6:51.

82 Matt. 26:26.

83 Matt. 8:22; John 3:6.

84 Cf. Matt. 13:14–15; John 12:39–40.

85 Cf. Matt. 24:29–30.

86 See Kitáb-i-Íqán, ¶¶27–42 and 66–87.

87 Cf. John 3:13.

88 *Masíkh* (monster), a distortion of *Masíḥ* (Messiah).

89 Cf. 1 Thess. 5:2; 2 Pet. 3:10.

90 John 17:5.

91 Cf. John 6:50–1.

92 Cf. Gen. 2:16–17.

93 Cf. Gen. 3:5.

94 Cf. Gen. 3:11–15, 22.

95 Bahá'u'lláh.

96 Cf. John 6:51.

97 I.e., Jews and Christians.

98 Matt. 8:22.

99 Matt. 12:31–2.

100 Matt. 22:14.

101 Qur'án 2:105 and 3:74.

102 Matt. 22:14.

103 See, for example, Kitáb-i-Íqán, ¶¶156–79.

104 Cf. John 1:19–21.

105 That is, the individuality of John.

106 Cf. Matt. 23:34–6.

107 Matt. 16:18.

108 Peter's given name was Simon, but Christ called him Cephas, which corresponds to the Greek words *petros* or *petra*, meaning "rock".

109 Cf. Matt. 16:14–18.

PART 3

On the Powers and Conditions of the Manifestations of God

110 Elsewhere 'Abdu'l-Bahá's classification also includes the mineral spirit; see, for example, Chapter 64; *Selections from the Writings of 'Abdu'l-Bahá*, sec. 30; and *The Promulgation of Universal Peace: Talks Delivered by 'Abdu'l-Bahá during His Visit to the United States and Canada in 1912*, trans. Howard MacNutt (Wilmette, IL: Bahá'í Publishing Trust, 2012), pp. 95, 264–5, 336, 360, and 377–8.

111 From a Tradition attributed to Imám 'Alí.

112 Qur'án 6:103.

113 From a Tradition attributed to Imám 'Alí.

114 Qur'án 59:2.

115 Cf. John 14:11 and 17:21.

116 'Abdu'l-Bahá here anticipates a question about the beginning of Bahá'u'lláh's Revelation, which is taken up in greater detail in Chapters 16 and 39.

117 Cf. *Gleanings from the Writings of Bahá'u'lláh*, XLI; and *Súriy-i-Haykal*, ¶192.

118 John 1:1.

119 Matt. 6:9; Luke 11:2.

120 See, for example, Chapter 14.

121 John 1:1.

122 Cf. Exod. 20:4–5; Deut. 5:8–9.

123 Cf. Num. 13–14.

124 Qur'án 48:1–2.

125 Matt. 19:16–17.

126 Kitáb-i-Aqdas (The Most Holy Book), ¶47.

PART 4

On the Origin, Powers, and Conditions of Man

127 The word *naw'*, translated here and in following chapters as "species", has a range of meanings including kind, sort, and type. 'Abdu'l-Bahá is

not using the word in the modern biological sense but in the sense of changeless archetypal forms.

128 In a Tablet, Bahá'u'lláh attributes these words to Hermes.

129 See, for example, Chapters 2 and 80.

130 Qur'án 23:14 and Persian Hidden Word no. 9.

131 Gen. 1:26.

132 As will be seen in the next chapter, 'Abdu'l-Bahá uses the terms "appearance through emanation" and "procession through emanation" interchangeably.

133 See Chapter 80.

134 Cf. Gen. 2:7.

135 John 1:1.

136 John 1:1.

137 See, for example, John 14:10–11 and 17:21.

138 See Chapter 36.

139 See Gen. 9:22–7.

140 That is, that people cannot be held responsible for their own character.

141 Cf. *Gleanings from the Writings of Bahá'u'lláh*, XLI, and Súriy-i-Haykal, ¶192.

142 Cf. Rev. 22:13.

143 See Chapter 48.

144 Cf. John 3:5.

145 Cf. John 1:13.

146 Qur'án 23:14.

147 'Abdu'l-Bahá is here directly addressing Laura Clifford Barney, whose father had passed away in 1902.

148 Mírzá Yaḥyá, half-brother and avowed enemy of Bahá'u'lláh.

149 "The first duty prescribed by God for His servants is the recognition of Him Who is the Dayspring of His Revelation and the Fountain of His laws, Who representeth the Godhead in both the Kingdom of His Cause and the world of creation. Whoso achieveth this duty hath attained unto all good; and whoso is deprived thereof hath gone astray, though he be the author of every righteous deed." (Kitáb-i-Aqdas, ¶1.)

150 See Chapter 84 for a fuller discussion of this subject.

151　Rom. 9:21.

152　See Chapters 32, 62, and 63.

PART 5

Miscellaneous Subjects

153　Cf. Matt. 5:39.

154　A Bahá'í sitting at table.

155　Matt. 8:22.

156　Cf. Aristotle, *Physics* 194b16–195a1.

157　The Tree of Zaqqúm, mentioned in Qur'án 17:60, 37:62–6, 44:43–6, and 56:52–3.

158　Cf. Qur'án 37:180.

159　Qur'án 59:2.

160　See Chapter 33 for a fuller discussion of this subject.

161　While, as 'Abdu'l-Bahá explains, the idea is of ancient origin, its history in Islamic thought begins with Ibnu'l-'Arabí (1165–1240). "Ibnu'l-'Arabí is a thoroughgoing monist, and the name given to his doctrine (*vaḥdatu'l-vujúd*, the unity of existence) justly describes it. He holds that all things pre-exist as ideas in the knowledge of God, whence they emanate and whither they ultimately return." R. A. Nicholson, "Mysticism", *The Legacy of Islam*, ed. Sir Thomas Arnold and Alfred Guillaume (Oxford University Press, 1931), p. 224.

162　Cf. Plotinus, *Ennead* 5.2.1: "The One is all things and not a single one of them . . ." (Armstrong's trans.); and Plato, *Parmenides* 160b2–3: "Thus, if there is a One, the One is both all things and nothing whatsoever, alike with reference to itself and to the Others" (Cornford's trans.). In the tradition of the Islamic philosophers, certain of the writings of Plotinus are attributed to Aristotle.

163　See Ibn Abí Uṣaybi'ih, *'Uyúnu'l-Anbá' fí Ṭabaqáti'l-Aṭibbá'* (Cairo, 1882), 1:76–7.

INDEX

References to the text of *Some Answered
Questions* are by chapter and paragraph
numbers; references to the Foreword and
Author's Preface are by roman numeral
page numbers.

Aaron, God's rebuke to, 44.4, 44.8–10
'Abdu'l-Bahá, xi–xii, xiii, xiv–xv, xvi,
   xix, xx
Abel, 64.4
Abraham, 4, 30.10, 18.2
   descendants of, 4.4, 57.6
   as Educator, 4.4, 4.6
   exile to the Holy Land, 4.2–5
   proofs of station as Manifestation,
     4.1
   religion of, 11.7, 43.5
   sign of, 14.13
Abú Sufyán, 13.6
Adam, 11.7
   cycle beginning with, 41.5
   descendants of, 30.8, 30.11
   lacked parents, 18.2–5
   man's material nature inherited
     from, 29.2, 29.4, 29.7–8
   sin of, 29.9, 30
Adrianople, 4.5, 9.4n11, 9.5, 9.13,
   9.16n13
Afnán, Hájí Mírzá Muḥammad-Taqí,
   Vakílu'd-Dawlih, 11.36n48

Africa, cannibalism among tribes of,
   3.3, 29.5, 77.13
'Akká, 4.5, 9.4, 9.5, 9.13–16, 10.2,
   48.6–7
'Alí, Imám, 11.12–23, 11.26–30,
   37.2n111, 37.8n113. *See also* Imáms
Alpha and Omega (Revelation of
   John), 58.5, 80.7
Alteration. *See* Change(s)
Amity. *See* Fellowship; Unity
Amnesty. *See* Forgiveness
Ancient Beauty. *See* Bahá'u'lláh
Angels, 11.1, 11.3, 11.35
Anger, 11.45, 57.10
Animal kingdom, 15.3–6, 32.2, 46.6,
   49.3, 73.6, 78.3, 82.17
   as captives of nature, 48.9–10
   degrees and stations in, 32.6, 62.1
   distinguishing man from, xiv–xv,
     3.3–4, 3.6, 29.5–6, 47.10–11, 48,
     49.4, 55.5
   existence in, 17.4, 49.3, 57.4, 82.11
   inability to comprehend, 59.6
   need for training, 3.1, 3.3, 57.8
   perfections of, 64.1, 70.5
   senses of, 48.2, 48.4, 48.5–7, 55.4,
     58.2
   spirit of, 36.2, 36.3, 48.11, 55.5, 55.4
Anthropomorphists, 37.5
Antioch, Peter's tomb in, 34.4
Apostle of God. *See* Muḥammad

361

Muḥammad (*continued*)
  tales about, 7.1–2, 7.10
  treatment of Christians by, 7.9
Muḥammad-Taqí Afnán, Ḥájí Mírzá
  (Vakílu'd-Dawlih), 11.36n48
Murder, laws against, 76.3
Muslims. *See also* Arab tribes, Muḥam-
  mad's education of; Islam;
  Muḥammad
  Bahá'u'lláh's teaching of, 9.6
  calendar of, 10.20, 13.13
  God's rebukes to, 44.11
  persecution of, 7.2, 7.7
Mutavakkil, 77.9
Mysteries. *See also* Discoveries
  divine, 42.3, 55.5, 81.15
  found in man, 64.4

Najaf, Iraq, 9.6
Najrán, 7.9
Napoleon, Bahá'u'lláh's epistle to, 9.16
Náṣiri'd-Dín Sháh, Bahá'u'lláh's epistle
  to, 9.17, 9.22, 16.8
Nature, 1. *See also* Animal kingdom;
  Human kingdom; Mineral
  kingdom; Vegetable kingdom
  attributes of, 16.3, 19.6
  innate, 57.4, 57.9–12
  law of, 78.2
  man's dominance over, 1.4, 48.9–10
  perfections in, 15.8
Naw' (species), 46.1n127
Necessary relationships, 40.8–9
Noah, 11.7, 30.10, 57.7
Non-existence, 2.4, 60.5, 63.1, 79.2. *See
  also* Existence
  absolute, 47.3, 53.7
  evil as, 74.3–4, 74.6–7
  relative nature of, 80.5–7
Nuṣayrís, beliefs of, 81.13

Olive trees (Revelation of John), 11.13
One, the, 82.2n162, 82.4

Oneness. *See* God, oneness of; Unity
Oppression, 76.6, 77.10, 78.4
Order
  in contingent world, 2.5
  natural, 1, 22.1–2, 47.5–6, 51.3, 51.5,
    52.5, 81.10
  social, 3.6, 3.9
  universal, 47.9, 82.11
Original sin, 29.9, 30. *See also* Sin(s)
Originality, 47.10–11, 49.2–8, 50
Origination, 17.7, 38.5–6, 53.5, 80,
  82.12–14
Orthodox Christians, baptismal rite,
  20.5
Ottoman Empire, moon as emblem
  of, 13.4

Palestine, 12.8
Papacy, 34, 43.12
Paradise, 11.35, 42.5, 60.2, 60.3, 61.3. *See
  also* Heaven
  Adam and Eve expelled from, 30.4,
    30.6
Parents, 57.5, 62.6. *See also* Families
Paul (Apostle), 20.2, 29.8
Peace, 11.37, 78.4
  brought by Bahá'u'lláh, 12.4, 12.7
  brought by Christ, 3.13–14, 12.3
Pen of the Most High. *See* Bahá'u'lláh
Pentecost. *See* Holy Spirit, descent of
Perception, 56.1, 61.3, 71.7, 74.1–2
Perfection(s). *See also* God, perfections of;
  Man, perfections of
  acquisition of, 32.5, 47.9, 52.2–3,
    81.4, 81.11
  of Bahá'u'lláh, 9.5
  of Christ, 21.2, 21.4, 21.10, 29.12,
    31.2, 37.13, 54.5
  of creation, 15.2, 62.1
  degrees of, 64.2, 64.5, 66.4
  divine, 3.7, 18.2, 18.6, 30.7, 31.3, 36.7,
    39.1, 59.8, 64.5
  human, 32.4, 46.2–3, 46.6, 47.9–11

Index

as sign of God, 37.13, 38.5–6

in sleep, 61.2–3

space and time traversed by, 67.2, 67.5

understanding modes of, 61.1

Spirit of faith, 36.6, 55.2, 55.5. *See also* Faith and faithfulness

Spirit of God. *See* Jesus Christ, spirit of

Spiritual disclosures, 71

Splendour, heavenly, as station of Manifestations, 38.1, 38.4, 38.8

Springtime
material, 14.2, 14.6, 16.9, 36.7, 42.4, 67.4

spiritual, 14.7–8, 14.11, 36.8–9, 42.5, 43.5

Stars, 1.2, 23.5, 26.1, 26.5, 37.12, 69

Statues, worship of, 43.8, 43.9, 43.11

Steadfastness, 67.7

Strikes, 78

Substance, 82.8–12

Sudan, people of, 3.3

Suffering, 75

Sufis, 82.1–7, 82.12, 82.15, 82.16, 82.17

Summer, 14.3, 14.8–9, 42.4

Sun, 13.4, 35.6, 36.3, 63.3, 84.10
cycles of, 14.12–13, 14.15, 42.4

earth nurtured by, 53.2

as emblem of Persia, 13.4

existence of, 26.5, 46.5

light of, 28.2, 37.12, 39.3, 39.6, 42.2, 53.2–3, 84.10

Manifestations compared to, 42.5, 43.3

mirror's relationship to, 24.2, 25.4–5, 27.4–6, 36.7, 37.5, 39.4, 54.5–6, 55.5, 61.6, 67.5, 81.11

perfect organization of, 1.2, 18.2

prophethood compared to, 38.7

rays of, 31.2, 36.7, 45.2, 49.5, 50.2–3, 52.3, 52.5–6, 55.6, 80.4, 82.16–18

reality of, 59.4, 59.8

as source of life, 42.2, 53.2

Tablet of the Testament. *See* Bahá'u'lláh, Writings of, Book of the Covenant

Taste, sense of, 56.1, 56.4, 83.2
in animals, 48.5, 73.6

Teachings, divine
of Bahá'u'lláh, 9.13

of Christ, 21.4, 21.7

spread of, 13.2, 42.5

true happiness found in, 15.8, 84.11

unchanging nature of, 11.42–43

Telegraph, 1.4, 17.5, 48.4. *See also* Inventions

Temple (Jerusalem), 11.3–8, 11.11, 11.42

Ten Commandments, 43.9

Tests. *See* Martyrdoms; Torment

Theft, laws against, 11.10, 76.3

Theosophists, 81.9, 82.1–7, 82.12, 82.15

Things
discoveries of, 58.4

excellence or baseness of, 76.2–3

existence of, 80.3, 80.7

imperfection of, 38.6

knowledge of, 45.2, 59.3–4, 82.5–6

non-existent, 60.5

progress of all, 63

realities of, 3.10, 20.2, 22.1, 35.4, 40.8, 71.6, 84.2

Thought(s), 20.7, 56.2, 56.3, 56.4. *See also* Mind, human
Manifestations' enlightenment of, 42.3, 42.5

Ṭihrán, Bahá'u'lláh's exile from, 9.5

Time, 39.7, 47, 67.1–2. *See also* Preexistence

Torah, 54.1, 83.6, 84.12. *See also under* Bible, verses from
advent of Twin Manifestations foretold in, 10.16–22

commandments and laws in, 11.12, 20.5, 20.8, 43.9, 76.2

day stands for year in, 10.12, 10.16

Index